SCIENCE ENCYCLOPEDIAS

THE HUMAN BODY

ENCYCLOPEDIA

BY LINDA CERNAK

Abdo Reference

An Imprint of Abdo Publishing
abdobooks.com

TABLE OF CONTENTS

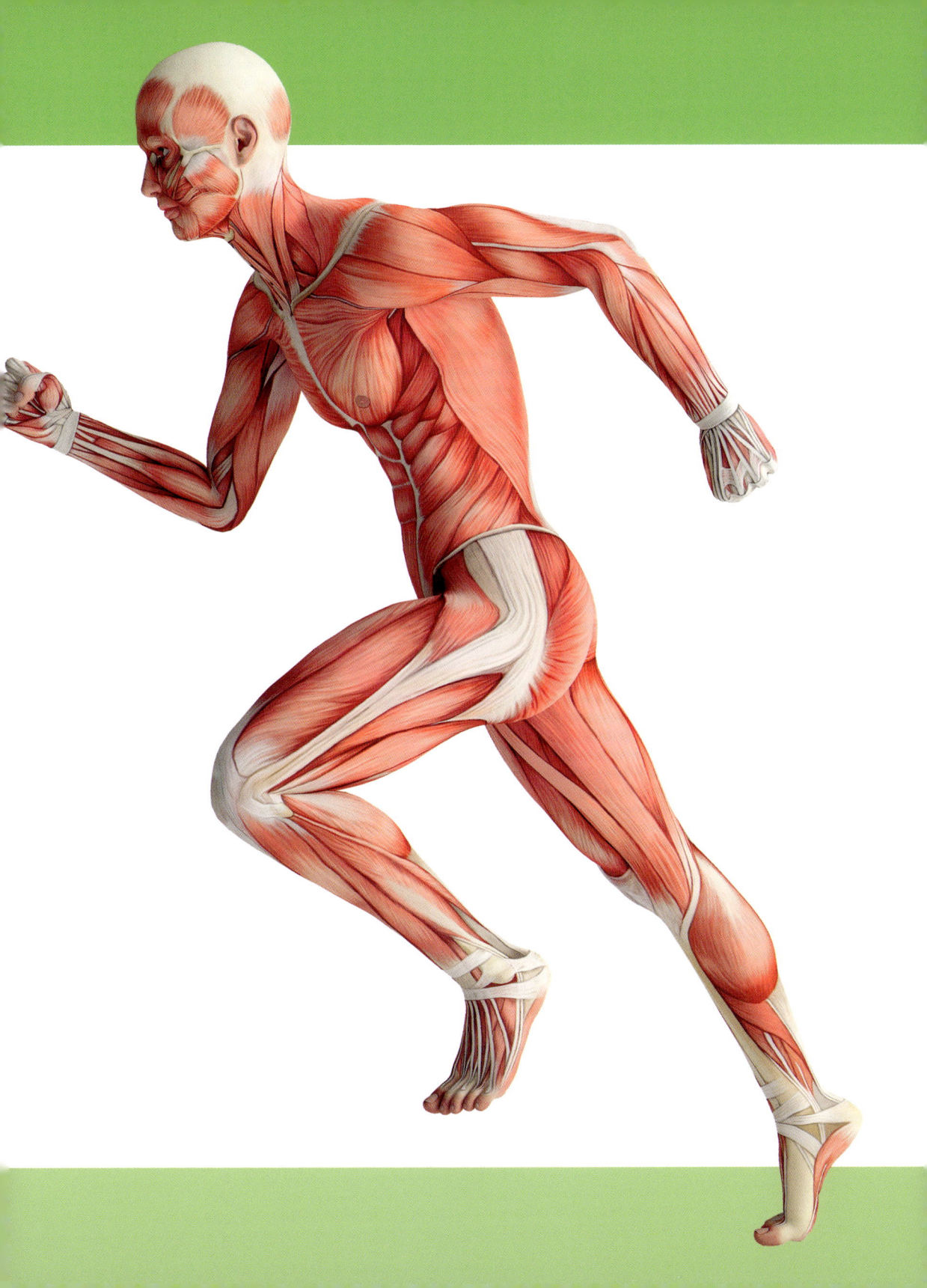

BODY BASICS

The human body is made up of many important systems that help it function. These include the circulatory, digestive, endocrine, immune, muscular, nervous, reproductive, respiratory, and skeletal systems. These groupings all have their own important organ systems. They can be broken down into smaller units such as cells, tissues, and organs.

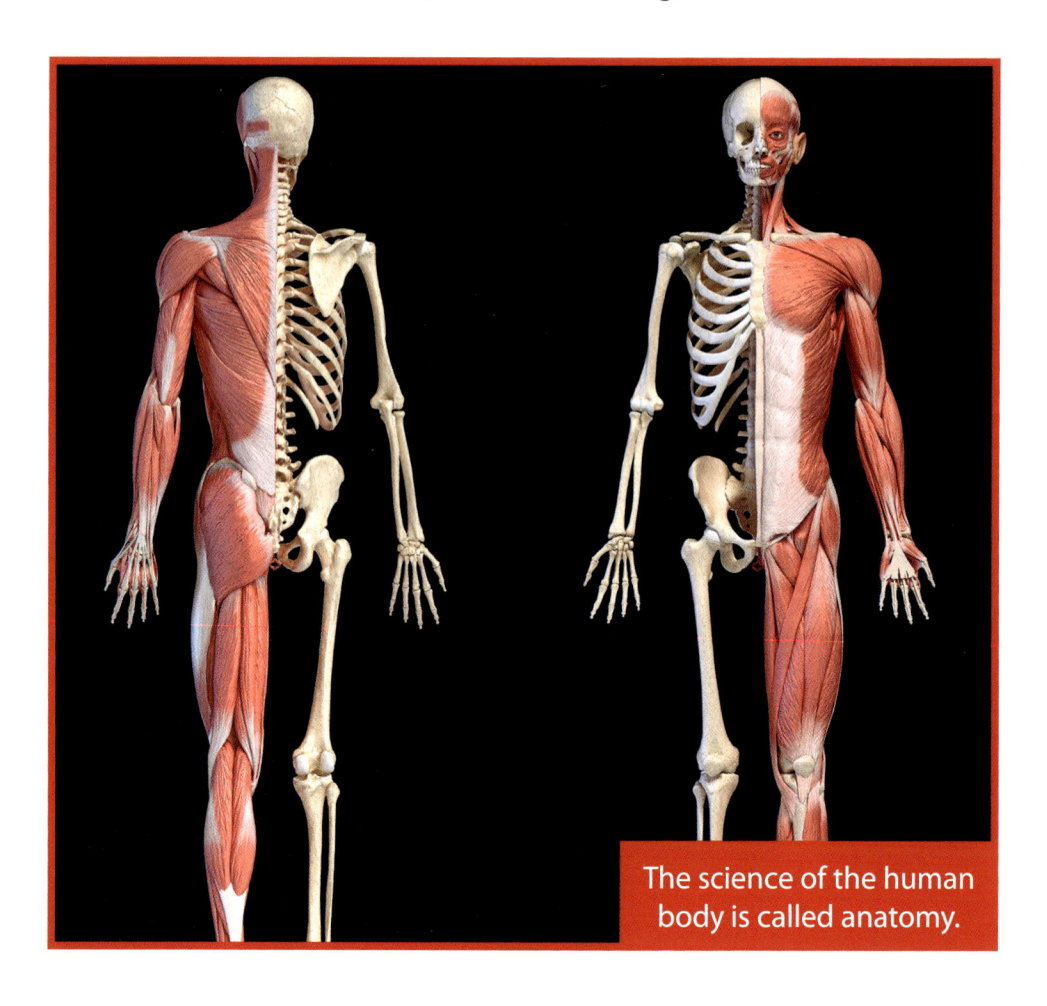

The science of the human body is called anatomy.

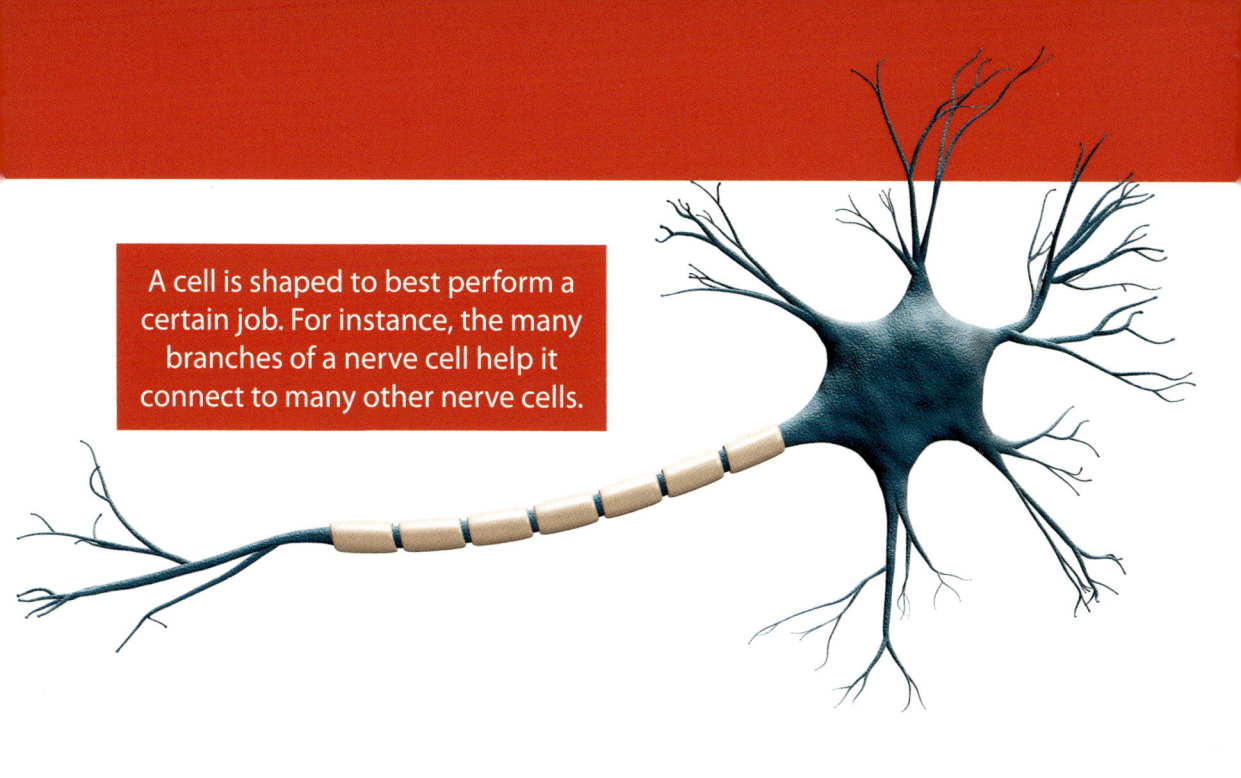

A cell is shaped to best perform a certain job. For instance, the many branches of a nerve cell help it connect to many other nerve cells.

Cells are the smallest units of life. They can only be seen with the help of a microscope. The human body has trillions of cells. They come in many shapes. The shape of the cell helps it do its job. For example, nerve cells allow body parts to communicate. Nerve cells are long and thin. They have many branches that allow them to connect to other nerve cells. Red blood cells are shaped like discs. They are flexible and able to squeeze through thin blood vessels. There are many other types of cells. Each has a specific job.

A group of similar cells forms tissue. The cells work together. Tissues can be seen without a microscope. There are four types of tissue in the human body. Epithelial tissue forms skin. It also lines organs and other structures in the body. Muscle tissue forms muscle. It helps the body move. Nerve tissue is made of nerve cells. It allows different parts of the body to communicate. Messages can be carried along nerve tissue. Connective tissue is the fourth type. It connects tissues together. This gives the body support.

A group of tissues working together forms an organ. Organs may be made up of several types of tissue. The heart is an organ. Muscle tissue allows the heart to contract. Nerve tissue sends signals to the heart. Connective tissue provides structure. The heart is just one organ in the human body. Other organs include the brain, the lungs, and the stomach.

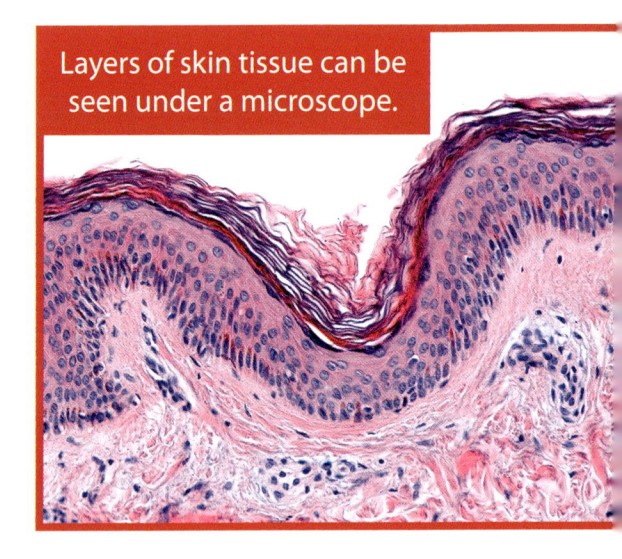

Layers of skin tissue can be seen under a microscope.

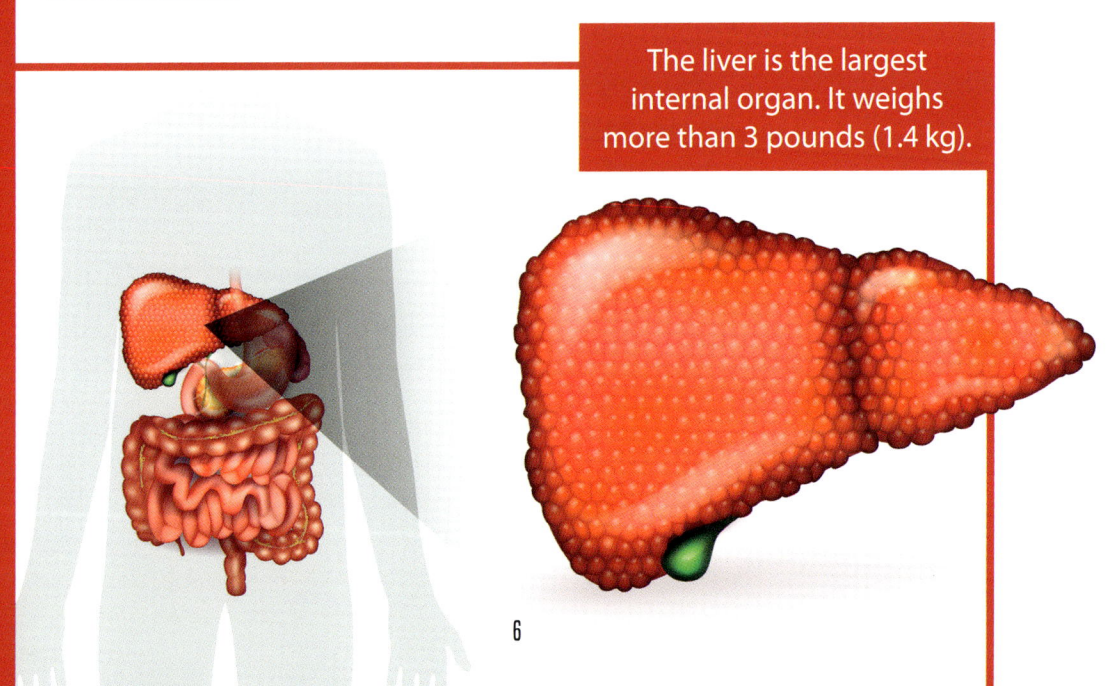

The liver is the largest internal organ. It weighs more than 3 pounds (1.4 kg).

Organs have specific jobs. They make sure the body receives nutrients. They get rid of waste. Organs help people see, hear, and taste. They digest food. They keep the body healthy.

Organs often work together. They can be grouped into organ systems. The digestive system includes all the organs that help digest food. The nervous system includes the brain, spinal cord, and nerves. Together they send messages throughout the body. An organ system may also work together with a different organ system. For example, the circulatory system and respiratory system both help deliver oxygen to the body. Organ systems form the basis of the human body. Understanding these systems and how they function together is important to knowing how the body works.

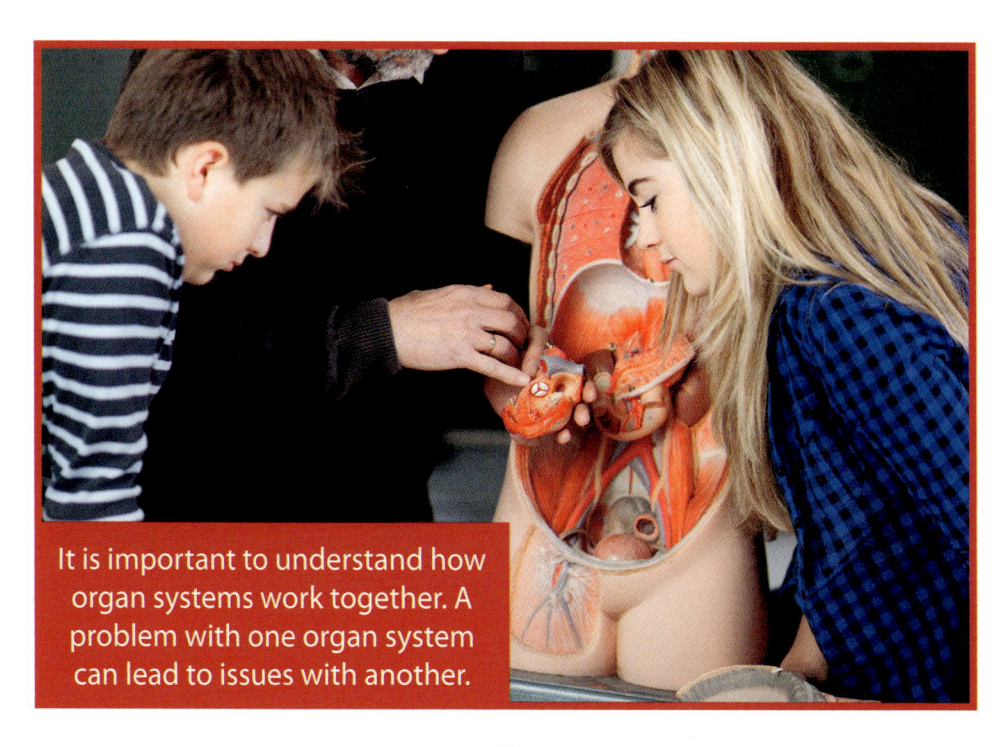

It is important to understand how organ systems work together. A problem with one organ system can lead to issues with another.

THE CIRCULATORY SYSTEM

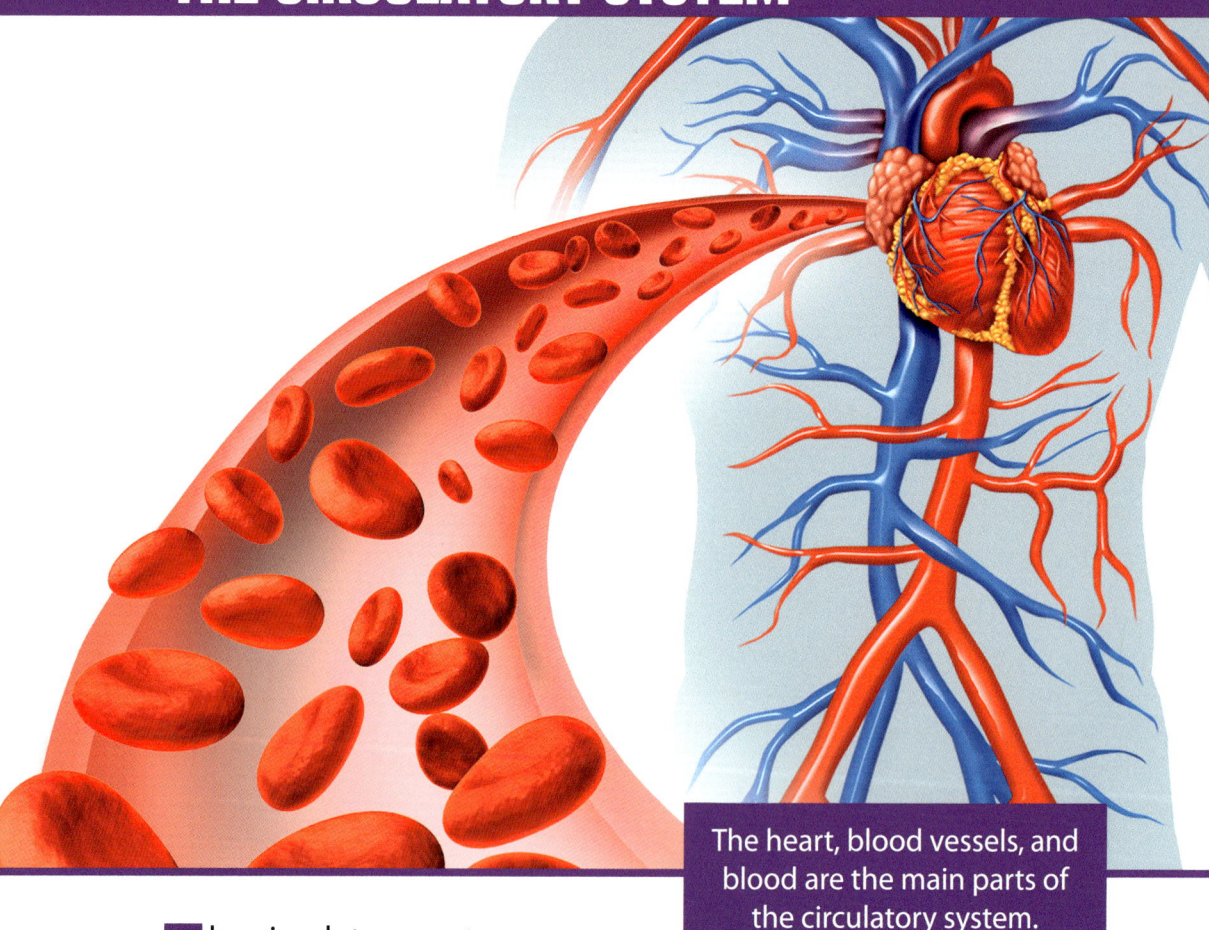

The heart, blood vessels, and blood are the main parts of the circulatory system.

The circulatory system pumps blood throughout the body, which is necessary for all bodily functions. It carries oxygen from the lungs to cells throughout the body. The cells need oxygen to work properly. The circulatory system also transports nutrients to the body's cells. Nutrients help the body grow. They keep the body healthy. The circulatory system also helps the body get rid of carbon dioxide. Carbon dioxide is a waste product. It builds up as the body uses oxygen and sugars for energy. High levels of carbon dioxide are harmful to the body.

Blood, blood vessels, and the heart make up the circulatory system. Blood carries oxygen and nutrients throughout the body. It picks up carbon dioxide from cells. Blood vessels are tubes that run through all parts of the body. They allow blood to travel to distant cells. The heart pumps blood through blood vessels.

WHAT'S IN BLOOD?

Transporting oxygen throughout the body is a very important task, but blood has other roles too. It helps people regulate body temperature. Blood also contains cells that protect people from infections.

The amount of blood in the human body depends on a person's weight. A newborn baby has about 1 cup (0.2 L) of blood.

The circulatory system carries oxygen to all parts of the body.

An adult who weighs 150 pounds (68 kg) has about 1.5 gallons (5.7 L) of blood. Blood makes up approximately 10 percent of an adult's weight.

New red and white blood cells are constantly being made in the centers of some bones.

Blood is made up of four main parts. Most of the blood is made of plasma. This liquid makes up 55 percent of a person's blood. The remaining 45 percent of blood includes red blood cells, white blood cells, and platelets. These parts are solid.

Platelets are much smaller than red blood cells and white blood cells.

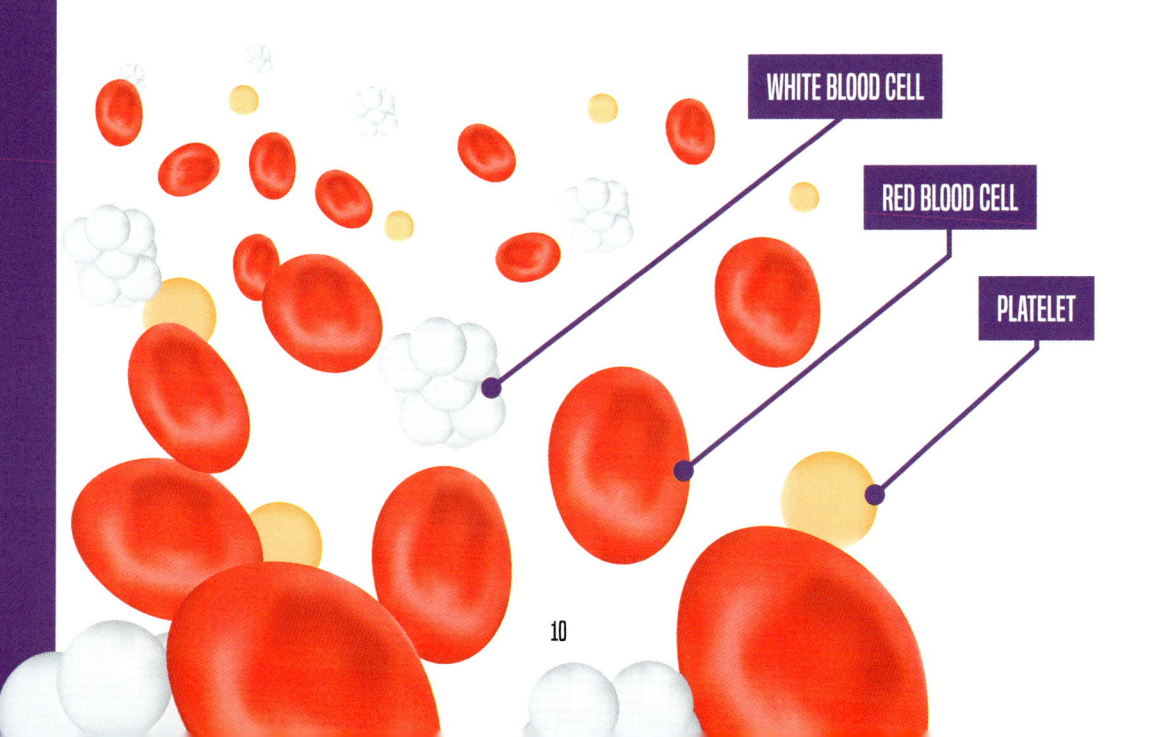

WHITE BLOOD CELL

RED BLOOD CELL

PLATELET

Plasma is the fluid, or liquid, part of blood. It is a light yellow color. About 90 percent of plasma is water. Without plasma, blood cells and platelets could not flow throughout the body. Plasma is responsible for delivering nutrients to the body. These nutrients include salts, proteins, and sugars. Plasma also carries waste products to the kidneys to be removed. It delivers chemical messengers called hormones. Hormones help regulate bodily processes such as growth.

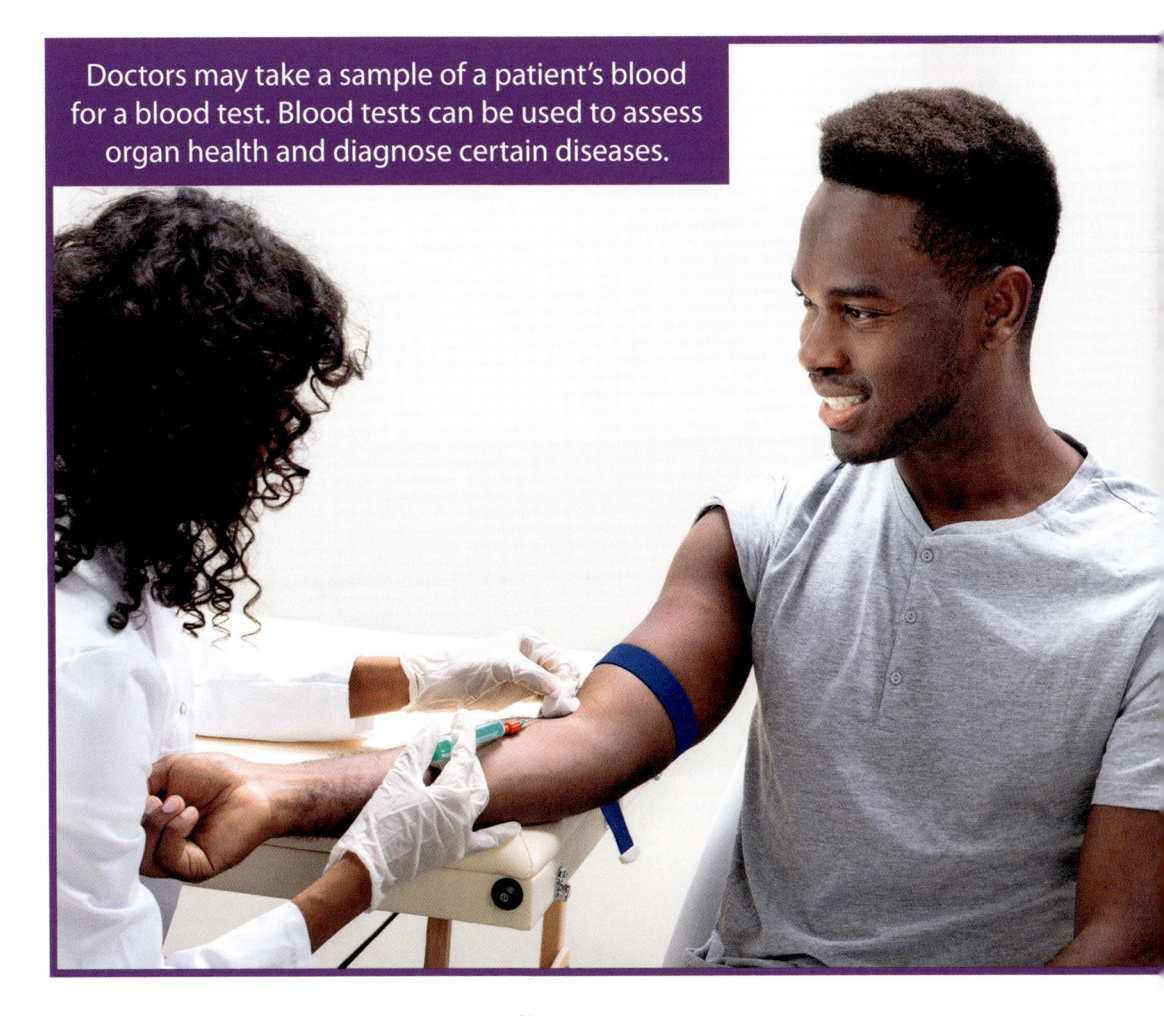

Doctors may take a sample of a patient's blood for a blood test. Blood tests can be used to assess organ health and diagnose certain diseases.

Red blood cells have a special protein called hemoglobin. This protein gives red blood cells their color. It also allows red blood cells to carry oxygen. Red blood cells pick up oxygen from the lungs. They carry the oxygen throughout the bloodstream. They deliver oxygen to cells throughout the body. Once red blood cells reach tissues of the body, gas exchange occurs. The cells use oxygen to produce energy. All cells need oxygen to function. When oxygen is used, carbon dioxide forms as a waste product. The red blood cells pick up the carbon dioxide. They travel back to the lungs, where carbon dioxide is exhaled.

Sickle cell anemia is a disease that causes red blood cells to become misshapen. The hooked shape causes problems with blood flow.

Red blood cells are flexible. They can squeeze through small blood vessels to deliver oxygen. But this can damage the blood cells. The body constantly grows new red blood cells to replace the old ones.

White blood cells protect the body from infection and disease. Germs such as bacteria and viruses can make people sick. White blood cells attack germs. They travel through the bloodstream. This allows the cells to quickly reach the area where the germs are. Some white blood cells can pass through the walls of blood vessels. This way, they can get into the tissues affected by germs.

Platelets are cell fragments. They help form blood clots. When a person gets a cut, bleeding may occur. Platelets rush to the site of the cut. They clump together and release a chemical that allows clots to form. It also helps the cut heal. The clot seals the cut and stops the bleeding. The clot hardens. It provides a foundation for new tissue to grow. Cells grow underneath the clot. After the wound has healed, the clot will fall off by itself.

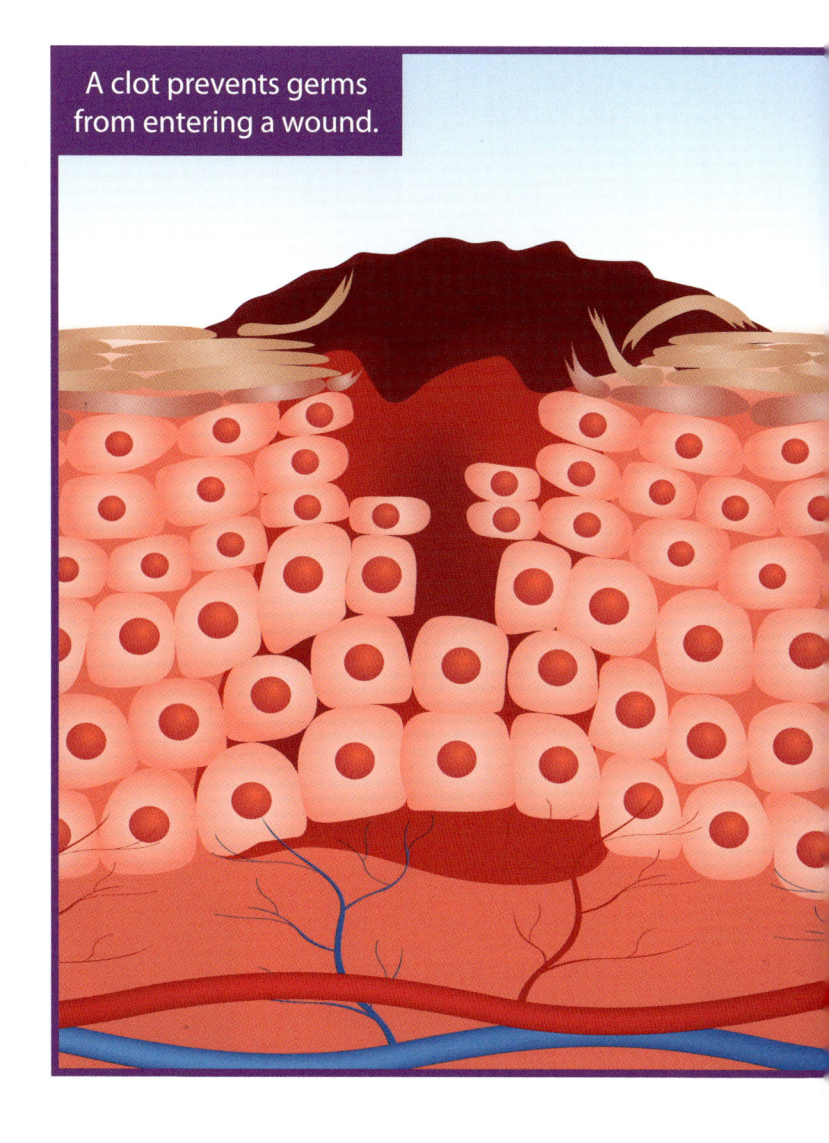

A clot prevents germs from entering a wound.

Bandages and antibiotics help wounds recover. They prevent harmful bacteria from entering an open cut.

Platelets are an important part of blood. Someone who does not have enough platelets cannot form clots. He or she may lose extreme amounts of blood. Having too many platelets can cause other issues. Clots may form in the bloodstream. They can block blood flow. They may cause heart attacks or strokes. Strokes occur when blood flow to the brain is blocked. The brain is unable to receive oxygen and nutrients.

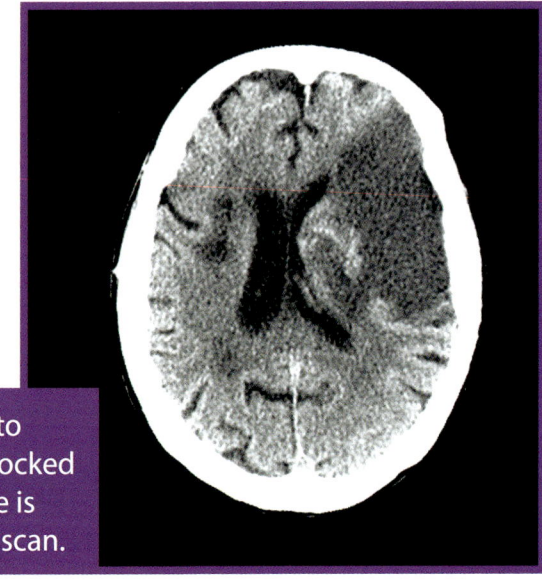

A brain scan can be used to determine the location of a blocked vessel in the brain. Damage is visible in the top right of this scan.

BLOOD VESSELS

Blood vessels circulate blood throughout the body. They come in different sizes. Large blood vessels connect the heart to other major organs. Blood vessels become smaller as they branch out. This allows blood to reach the tips of the fingers and toes.

The body has three different kinds of blood vessels. They are arteries, veins, and capillaries. Arteries are the blood vessels that carry blood away from the heart. Most arteries carry blood that is rich in oxygen. They help deliver oxygen and nutrients to the body. Arteries have thick, muscular walls.

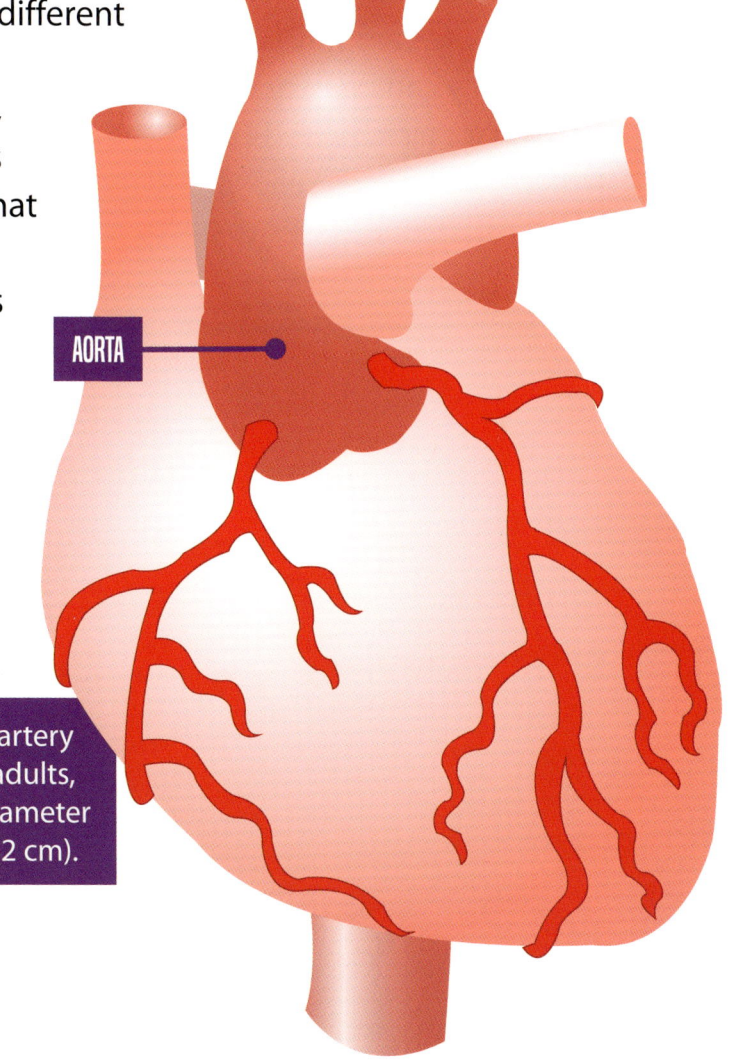

AORTA

The aorta is the largest artery in the body. In healthy adults, this blood vessel has a diameter larger than 0.75 inches (2 cm).

Veins carry blood toward the heart. Most veins carry blood that has high amounts of carbon dioxide. The heart collects this blood and sends it to the lungs. There, carbon dioxide is extracted from the blood and is exhaled as a person breathes. Many veins have valves inside them. The valves stop blood from flowing backward. The walls of veins are thinner than the walls of arteries.

Capillaries are tiny blood vessels. They connect arteries and veins. They can be very narrow. Some capillaries are just wide enough for a single red blood cell to pass through them. This way, capillaries can reach between cells. Capillaries have thin walls. This allows gases to easily pass through these vessels.

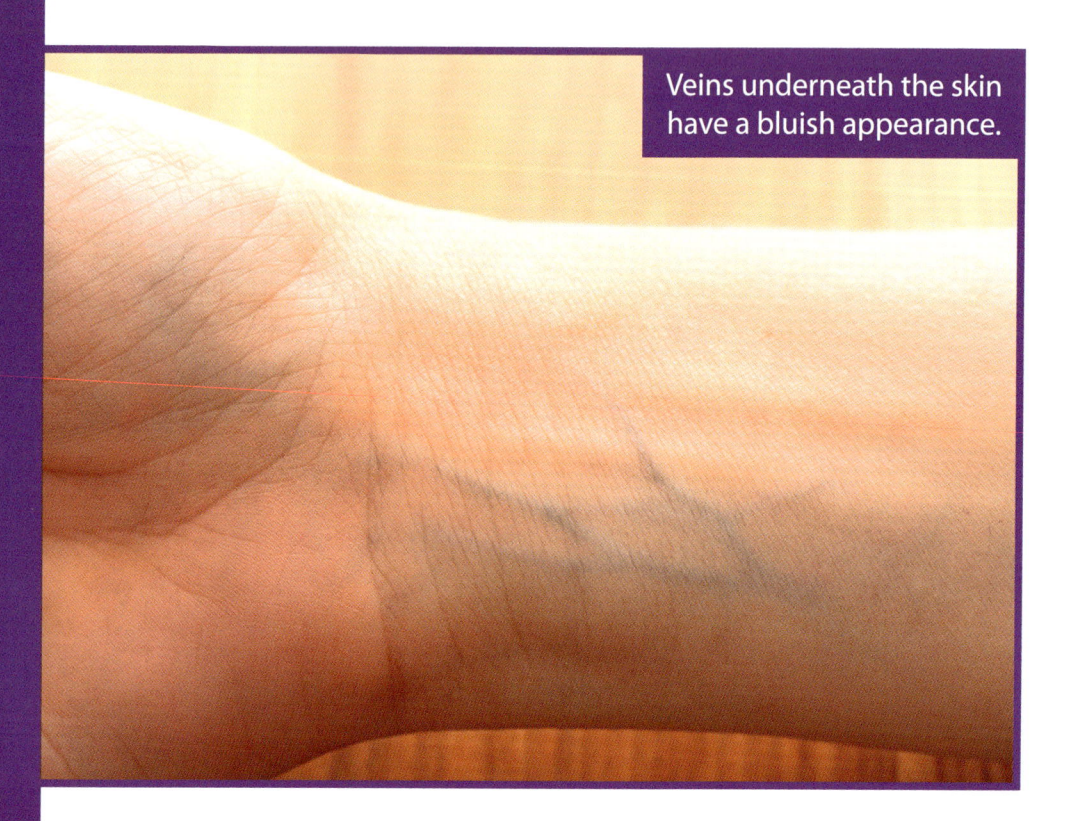

Veins underneath the skin have a bluish appearance.

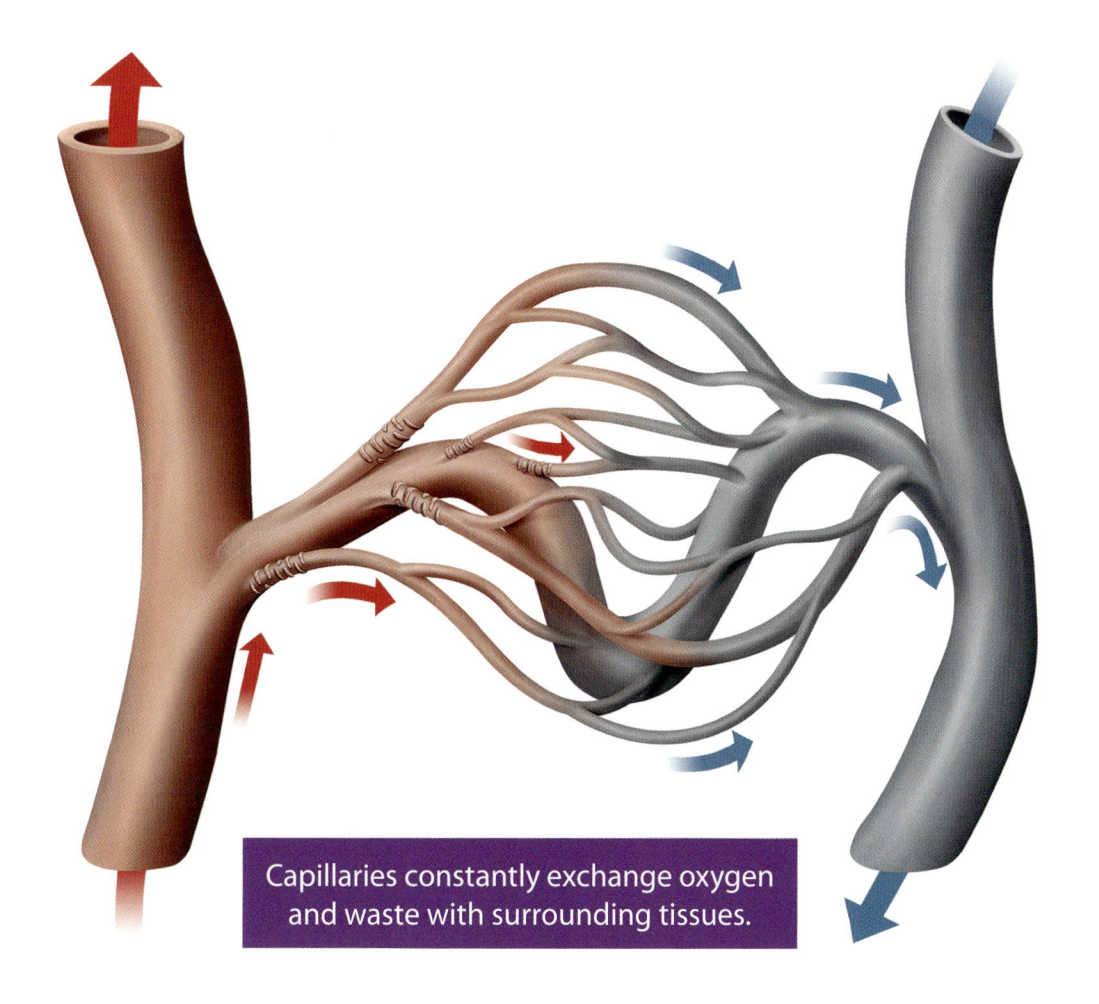

Capillaries constantly exchange oxygen and waste with surrounding tissues.

Oxygen passes out of capillaries into cells of the body. Carbon dioxide enters into the capillaries.

Red blood cells travel through the arteries. They carry oxygen. The red blood cells enter capillaries. This is where gas exchange occurs. Red blood cells deliver oxygen to other cells in the

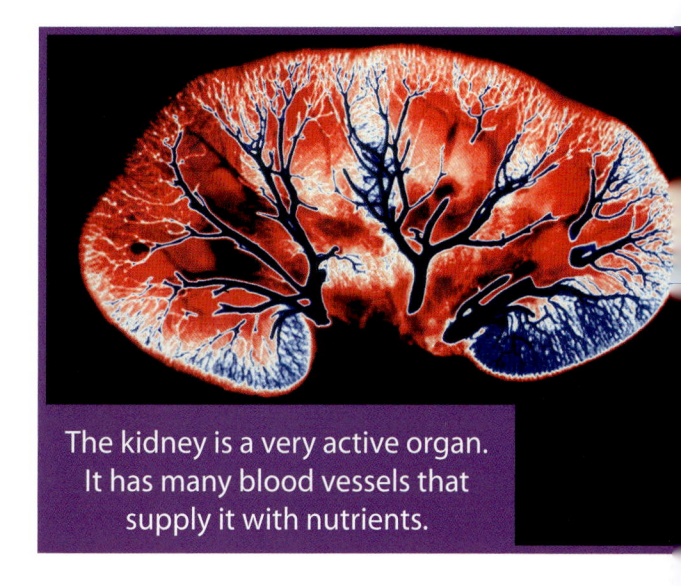

The kidney is a very active organ. It has many blood vessels that supply it with nutrients.

body. They also pick up carbon dioxide in the capillaries. After passing through the capillaries, blood enters the veins. Veins carry the blood toward the heart.

The average adult has 100,000 miles (161,000 km) of blood vessels.

Fatty deposits called plaque can build up in blood vessels over time. Plaque narrows blood vessels. This makes it difficult for blood to flow. Parts of the body may not get enough oxygen. In severe cases, blood flow may be completely blocked. This can result in a heart attack or a stroke.

THE HEART

The heart is the main organ of the circulatory system. It is a muscle. It beats about 100,000 times each day. It pumps blood to all parts of the body. The heart squeezes, or contracts. This movement pushes blood forward. It causes blood to flow through blood vessels. The heart also pushes

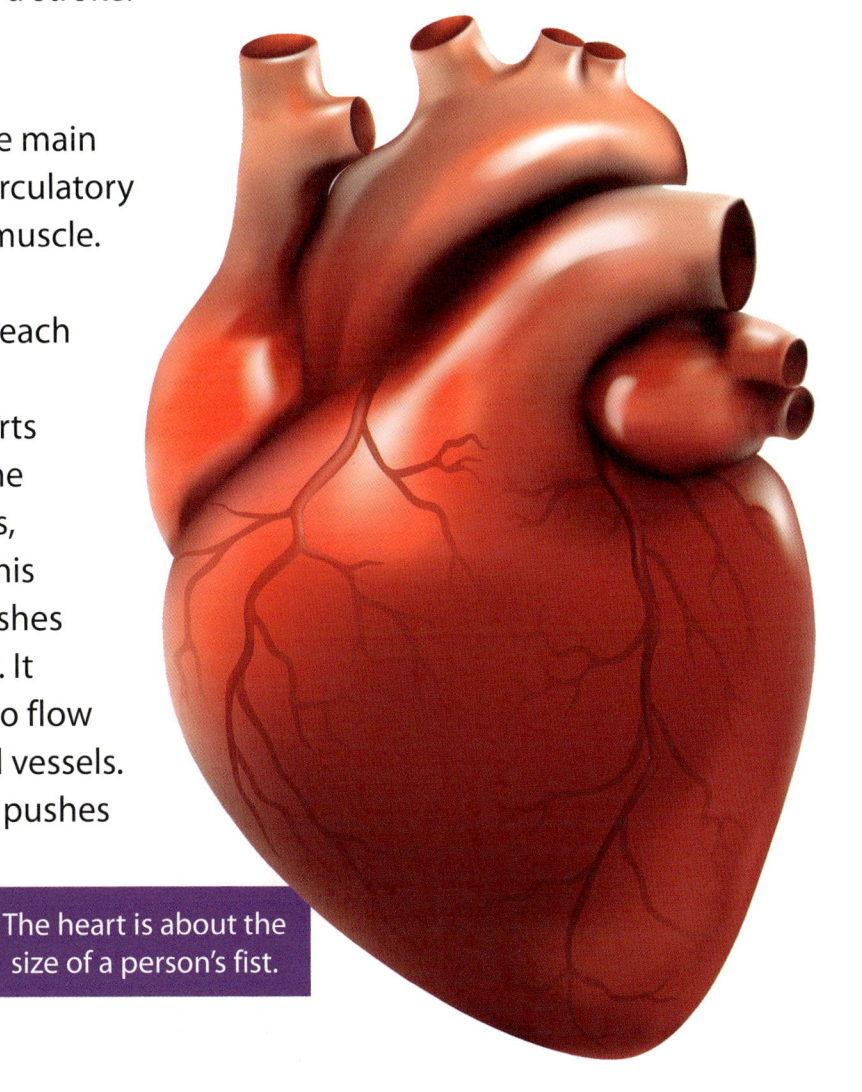

The heart is about the size of a person's fist.

blood toward the lungs. Red blood cells pick up oxygen at the lungs.

Heart rate varies depending on a person's age and activity level. Young children and teens tend to have a higher resting

heart rate than adults. Children between the ages of six and 15 having a resting heart rate of about 70 to 100 beats per minute. The heart beats more rapidly during exercise. This allows oxygen to be delivered quickly to the rest of the body.

Doctors can use a stethoscope to listen to a patient's heartbeat.

The heart is divided into four chambers. The upper chambers are the right and left atria. The lower chambers are the right and left ventricles. Valves and tissue separate the chambers. The valves prevent blood from flowing backward.

BLOOD FLOW THROUGH THE HEART

Two large veins carry blood into the right side of the heart. They are the superior and inferior vena cavas. The blood in these veins has high amounts of carbon dioxide. When the heart contracts, blood in the right side of the heart flows into the pulmonary artery. This is the only artery in the

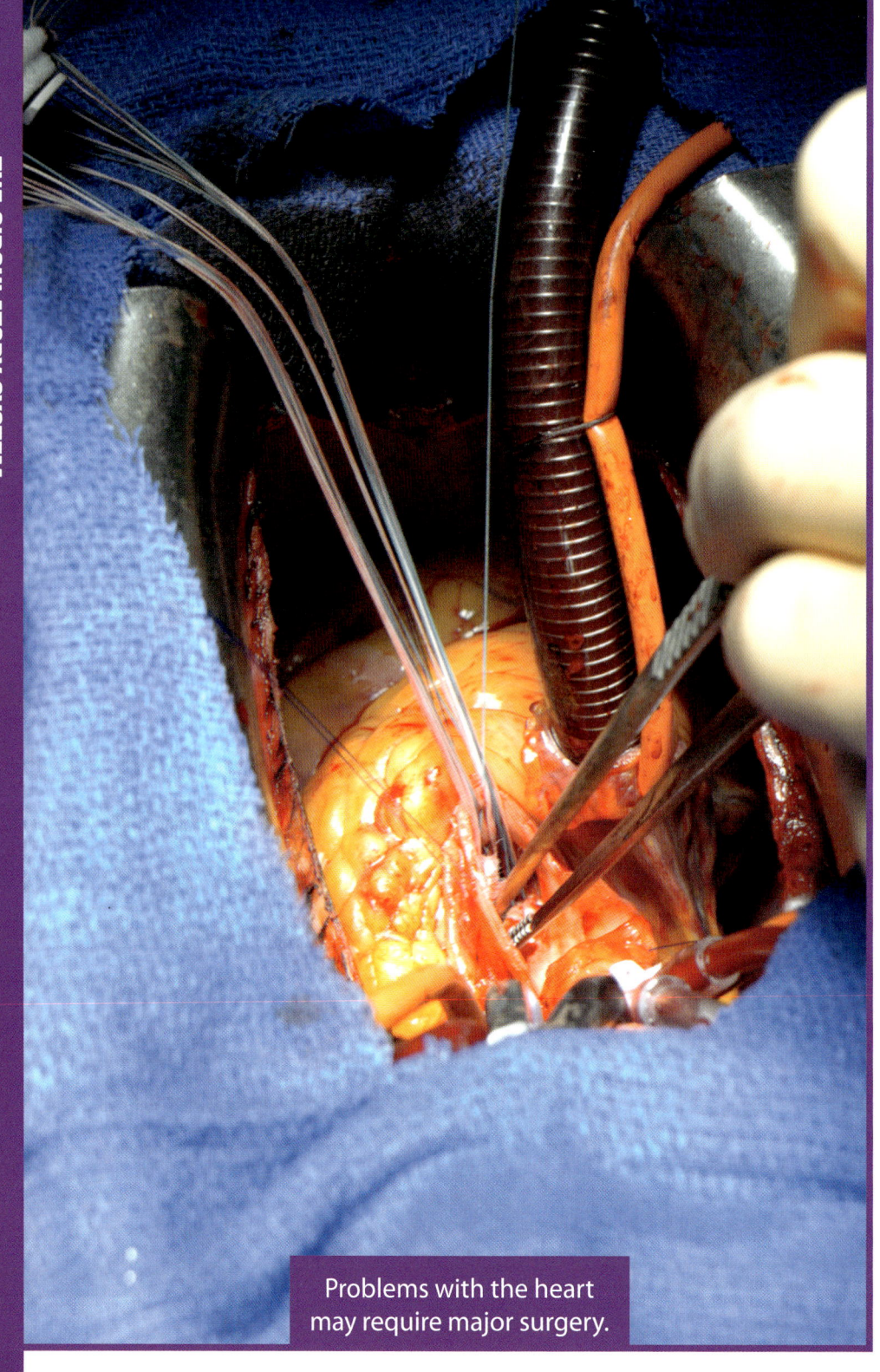

Problems with the heart
may require major surgery.

body that carries blood that is low in oxygen. It connects the heart to the lungs.

Blood enters small capillaries in the lungs. This is where gas exchange occurs. Like capillaries in the rest of the body, these blood vessels have thin walls. Gases can easily pass through these vessels. Carbon dioxide passes out of the capillaries and into the lungs. At the same time, oxygen in the lungs passes into the capillaries.

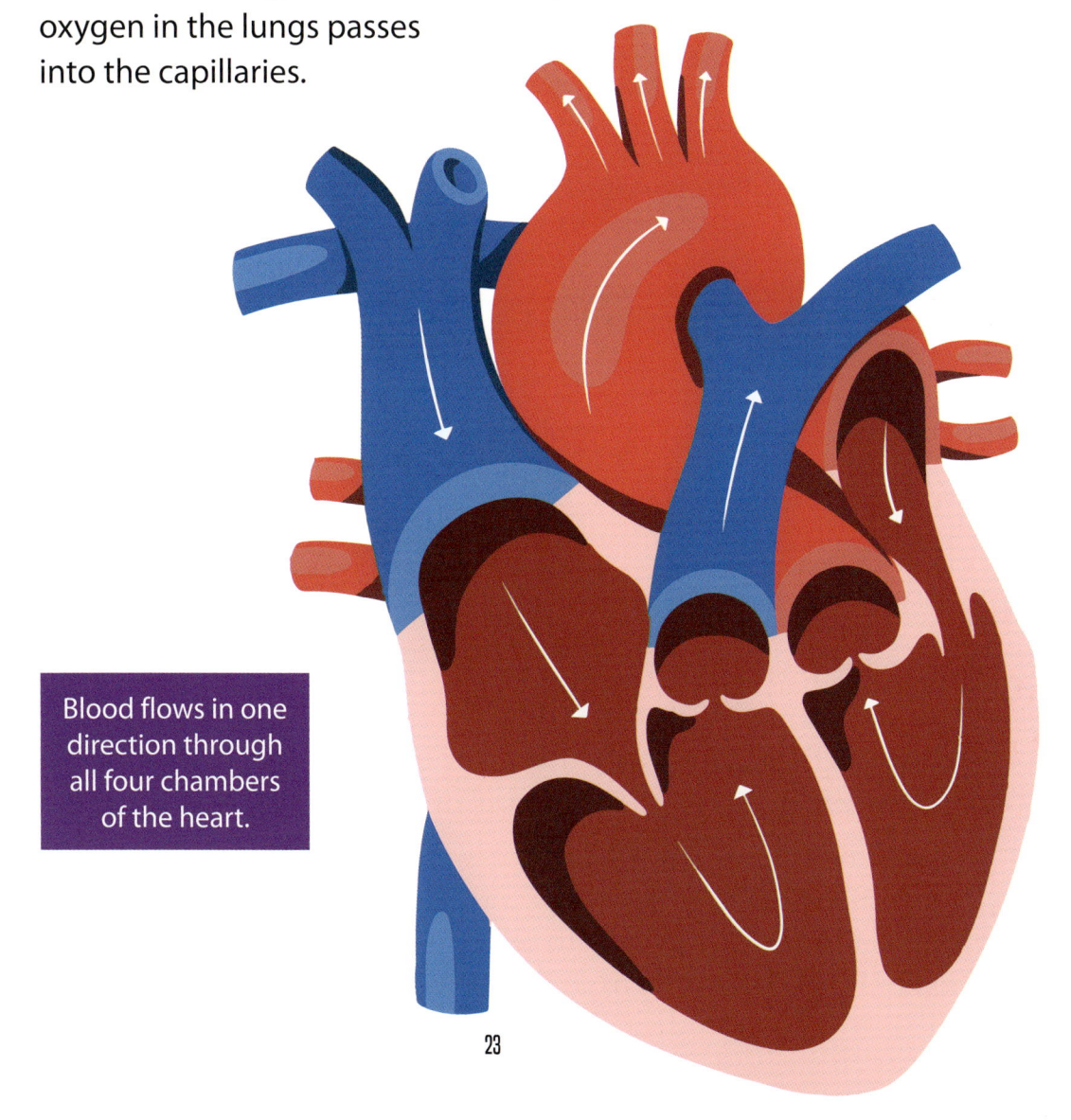

Blood flows in one direction through all four chambers of the heart.

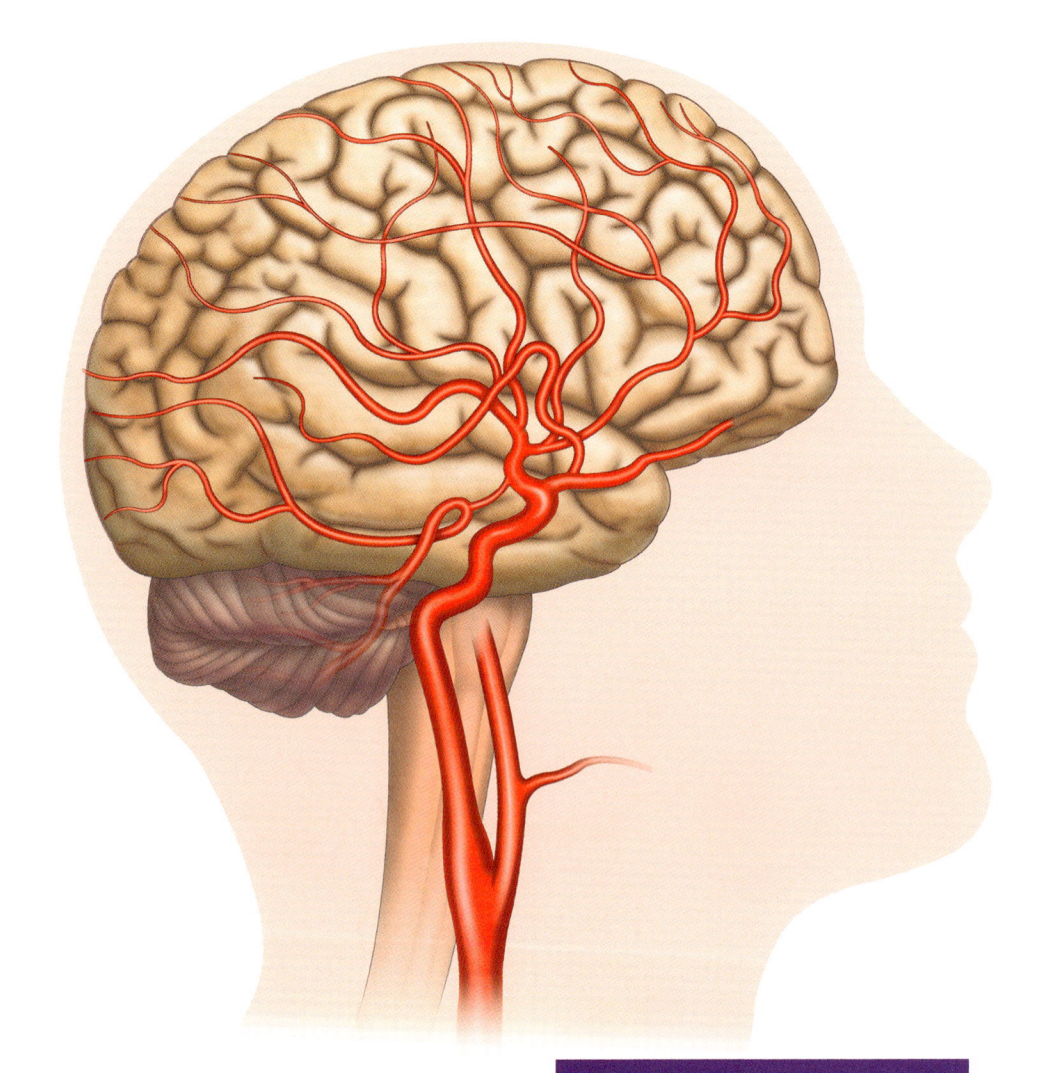

The brain needs a large amount of blood and oxygen to function properly.

Capillaries in the lungs widen into the pulmonary veins. The pulmonary veins are the only veins in the human body that carry oxygen-rich blood. They connect the lungs to the left side of the heart. When the heart contracts, blood from the left side of the heart enters the aorta. The aorta is the body's largest artery. Major arteries branch out from the aorta. They lead to different body organs. They help supply the body with oxygen and nutrients.

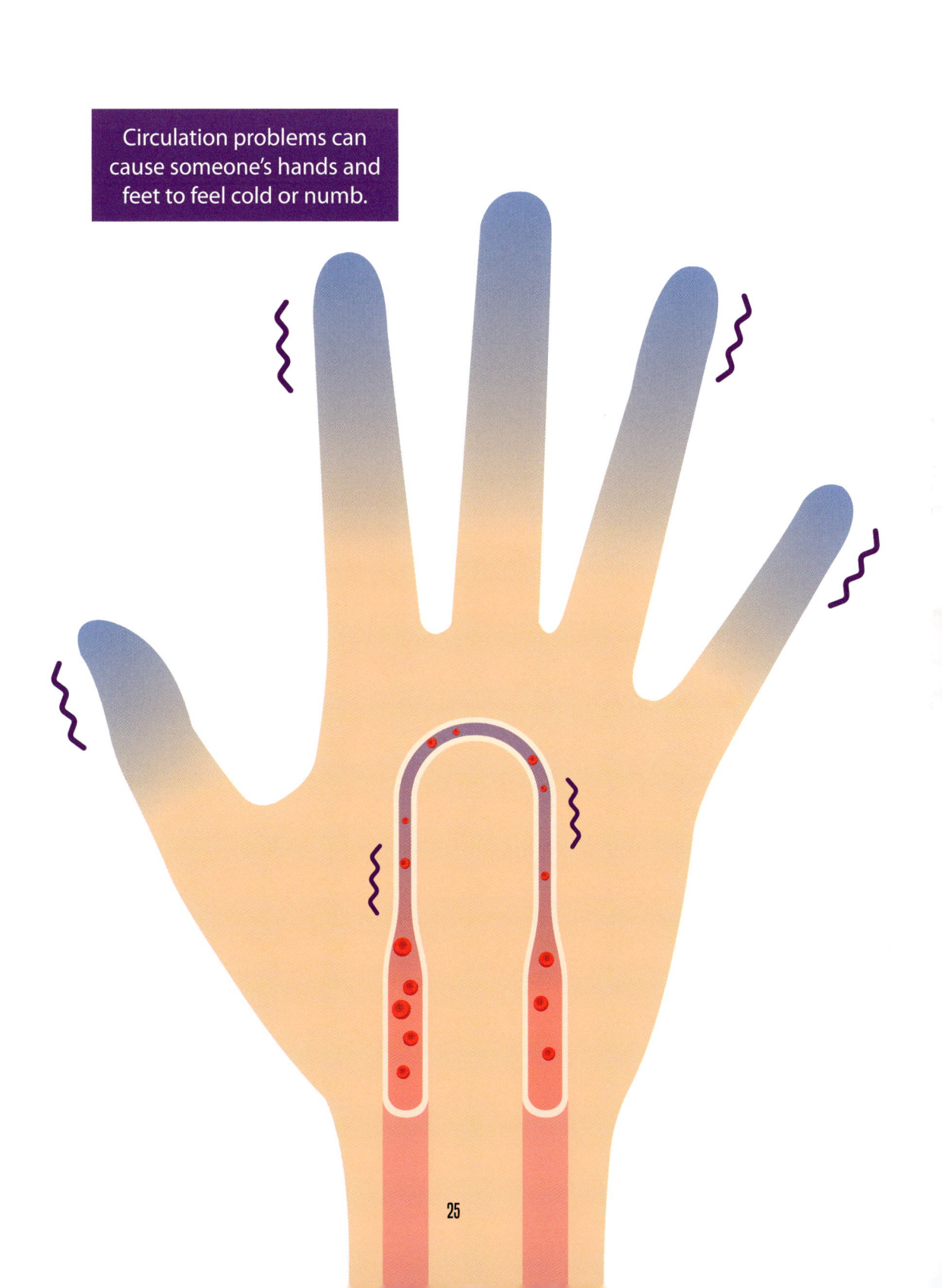

Circulation problems can cause someone's hands and feet to feel cold or numb.

THE DIGESTIVE SYSTEM

The digestive system includes all the organs that help digest food. It breaks food down into nutrients that the body uses for energy. Nutrients are the basic parts that make up food. They include proteins, fats, carbohydrates, minerals, and vitamins. The body needs a balance of these nutrients to stay healthy. These nutrients allow the body to grow and repair itself. Cells in the digestive system absorb nutrients. They also absorb water that the body needs.

Many of the main organs in the digestive system are located in the abdomen.

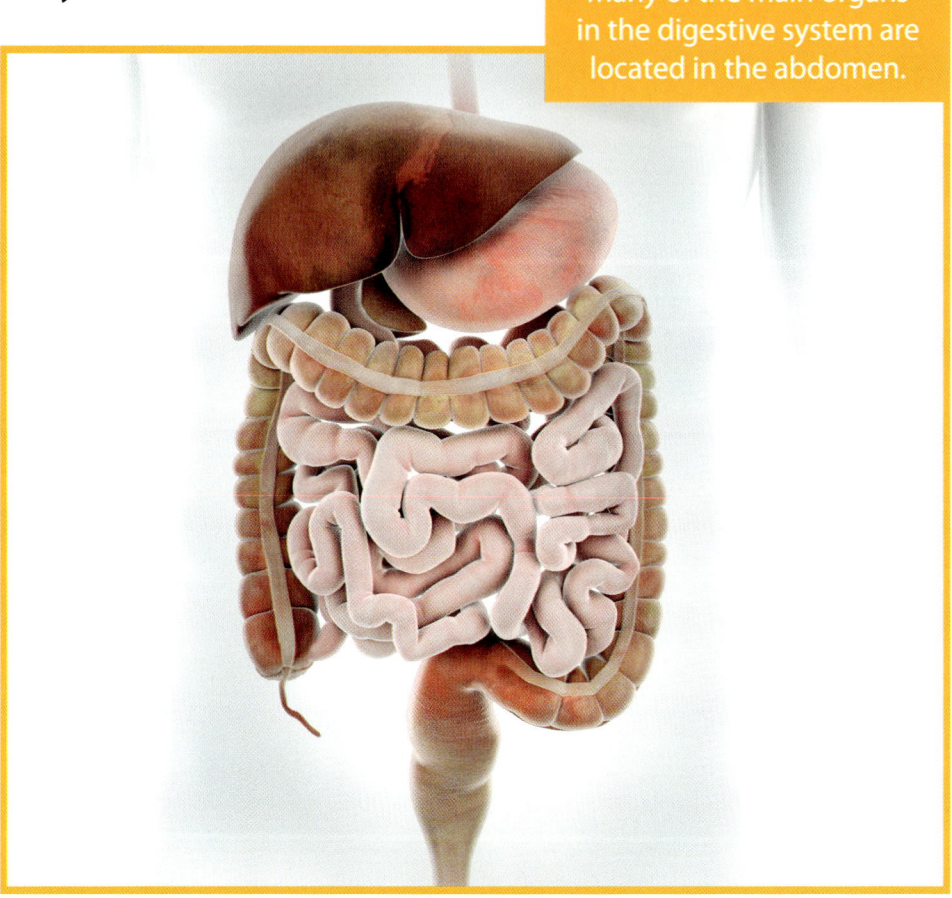

Eating a well-balanced meal helps a person get all the nutrients he or she needs.

Food follows a path through the organs of the digestive system. This path is called the digestive tract. It starts in the mouth. Food then travels down a tube called the esophagus and enters the stomach. The small and large intestines are the next organs in the digestive tract. Each organ has a special role in digestion.

The digestive system also includes several organs that are not part of the digestive tract. The liver, pancreas, and gallbladder release liquids and enzymes into the digestive tract. In this way, they help break down food.

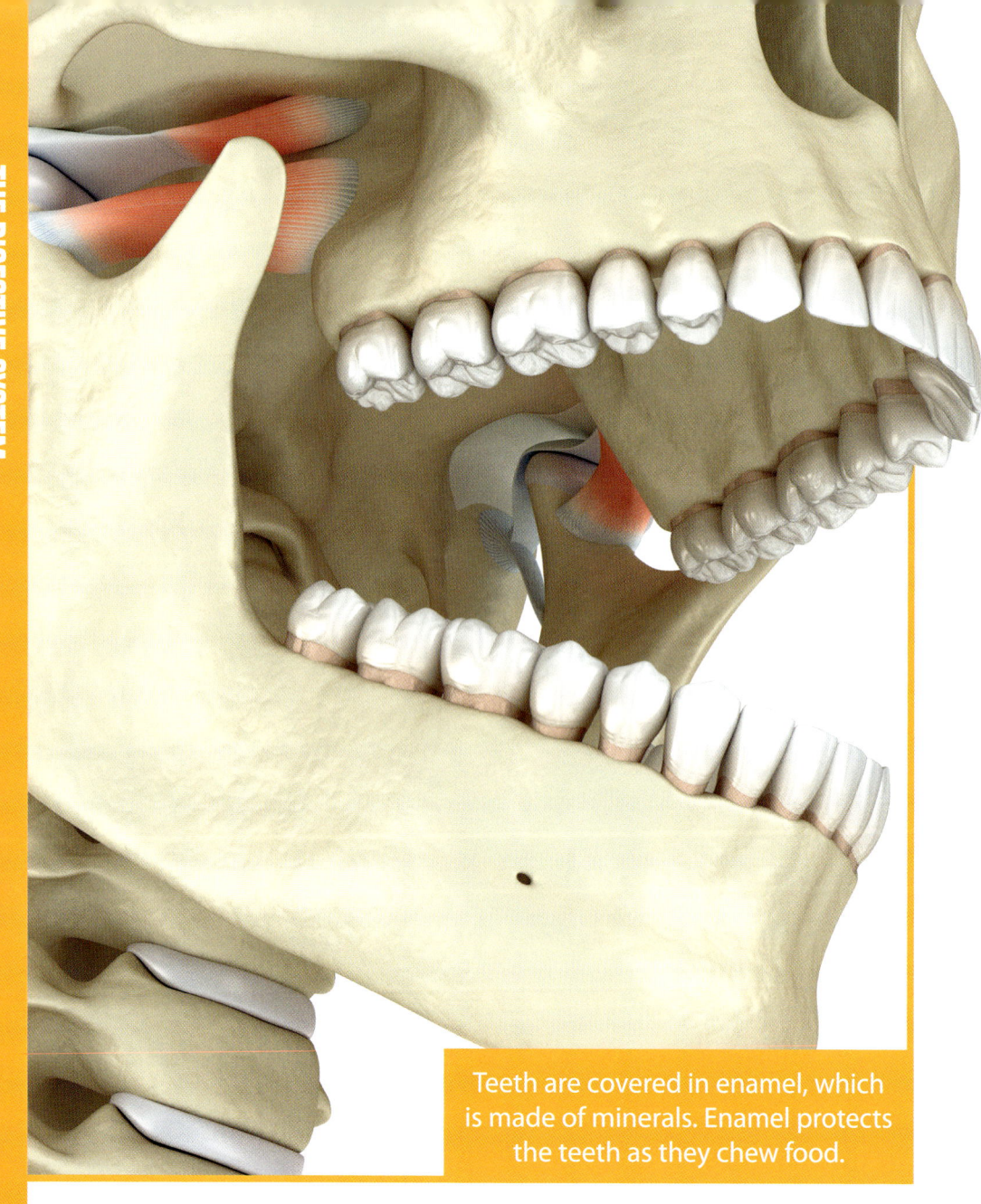

Teeth are covered in enamel, which is made of minerals. Enamel protects the teeth as they chew food.

CHEWING AND SWALLOWING

Digestion begins in the mouth. Chewing tears food into small pieces. Small pieces of food are easier to swallow and digest. But chewing does not break food down into nutrients.

Saliva also helps break down food. This liquid makes food soft and moist. Soft food is easier to chew and break apart. Saliva is released by salivary glands in the mouth. These glands produce saliva even before a person begins eating. The scent of food can cause salivary glands to become active. More saliva is released as food is chewed. Saliva is made mostly of water. It also contains enzymes that help break down food into nutrients. The enzymes digest starches found in food. The starches break apart into sugars that can be absorbed for energy.

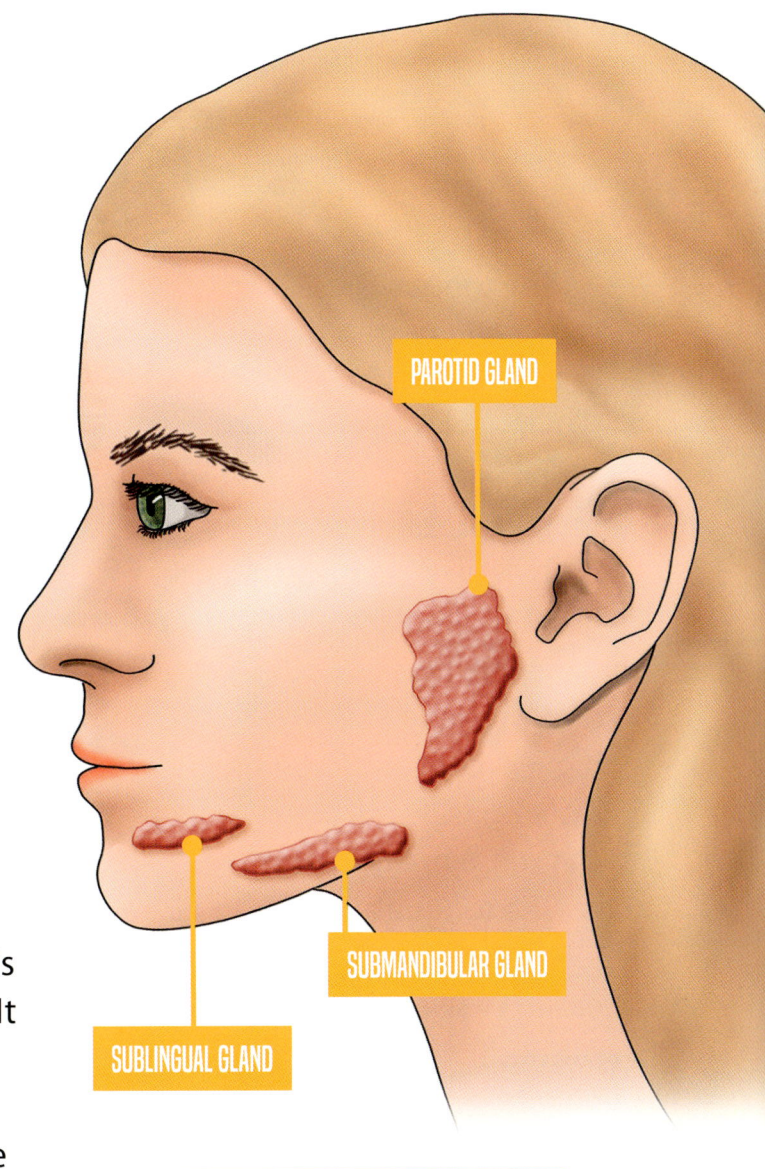

PAROTID GLAND

SUBMANDIBULAR GLAND

SUBLINGUAL GLAND

People have three pairs of salivary glands that are all connected to the mouth.

Some areas of the tongue are more sensitive to certain tastes. But all taste buds can pick up each taste.

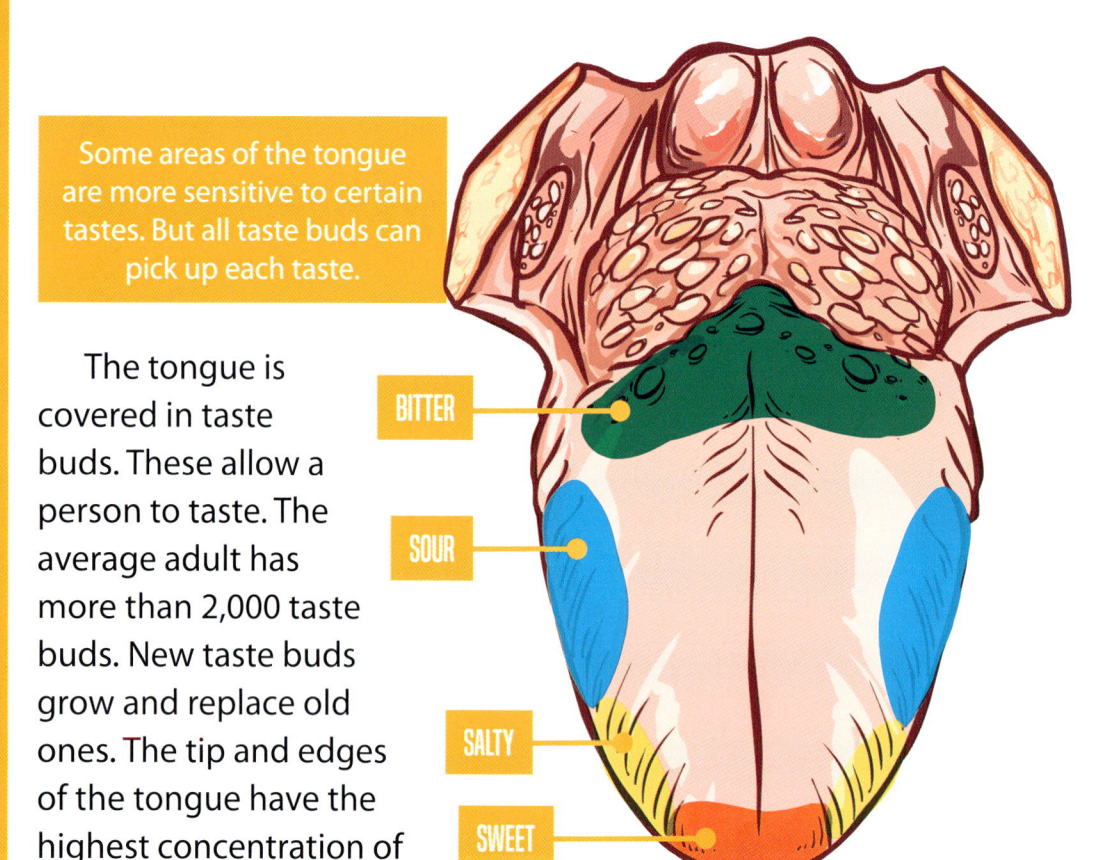

BITTER

SOUR

SALTY

SWEET

The tongue is covered in taste buds. These allow a person to taste. The average adult has more than 2,000 taste buds. New taste buds grow and replace old ones. The tip and edges of the tongue have the highest concentration of taste buds. These areas can sense many flavors.

The tongue also aids in digestion. It is a muscle that pushes food around the mouth. It helps shape the food so that it is easier to swallow. When a person is done chewing, the tongue pushes the food to the back of the mouth. The lump of food is now called a bolus.

The bolus enters the throat after a person swallows. The throat is divided into two sections. They are the esophagus and the windpipe. A flap called the epiglottis covers the windpipe. It prevents food from going down this pipe. If food does enter the windpipe, a person will choke. The bolus passes through the esophagus.

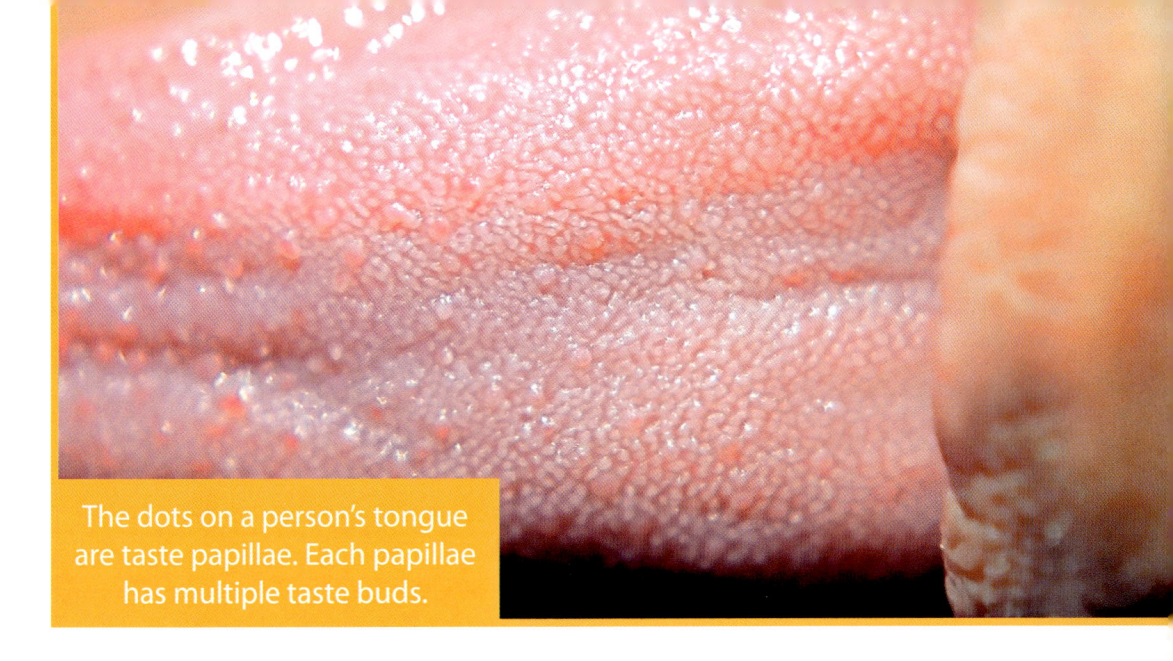

The dots on a person's tongue are taste papillae. Each papillae has multiple taste buds.

Muscles in the esophagus help move the bolus toward the stomach. They contract in a wave-like pattern called peristalsis. This movement pushes the bolus forward along the digestive tract. A muscle at the bottom of the esophagus blocks the entrance to the stomach. It prevents stomach contents from flowing back into the esophagus. If stomach contents do move backward

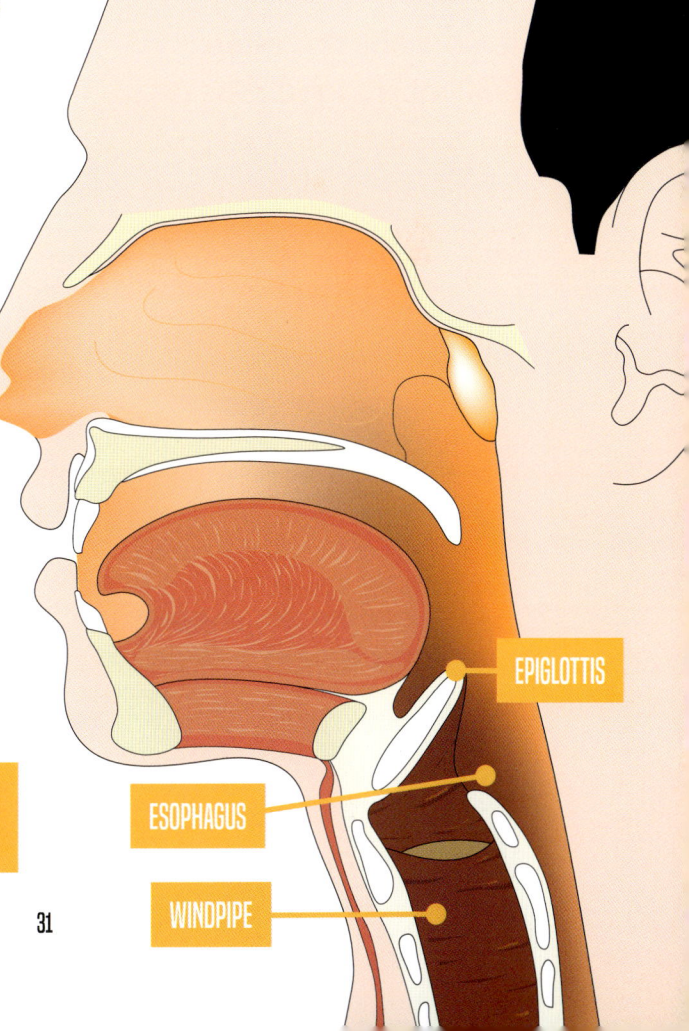

EPIGLOTTIS

ESOPHAGUS

WINDPIPE

The epiglottis folds over the windpipe as a person swallows.

into the esophagus, it creates a burning feeling. This is called heartburn. The muscle relaxes when the bolus reaches it. A valve opens up, allowing the bolus to pass through.

THE STOMACH AND INTESTINES

The stomach is a sack-like organ. It is located on the left side of the upper body. It stretches as it fills with food. When empty, the adult stomach has a volume of about 2.5 fluid ounces (75 mL). It can expand to hold about 1 quart (950 mL) of food. One of the reasons people feel full is because their stomachs are stretched out.

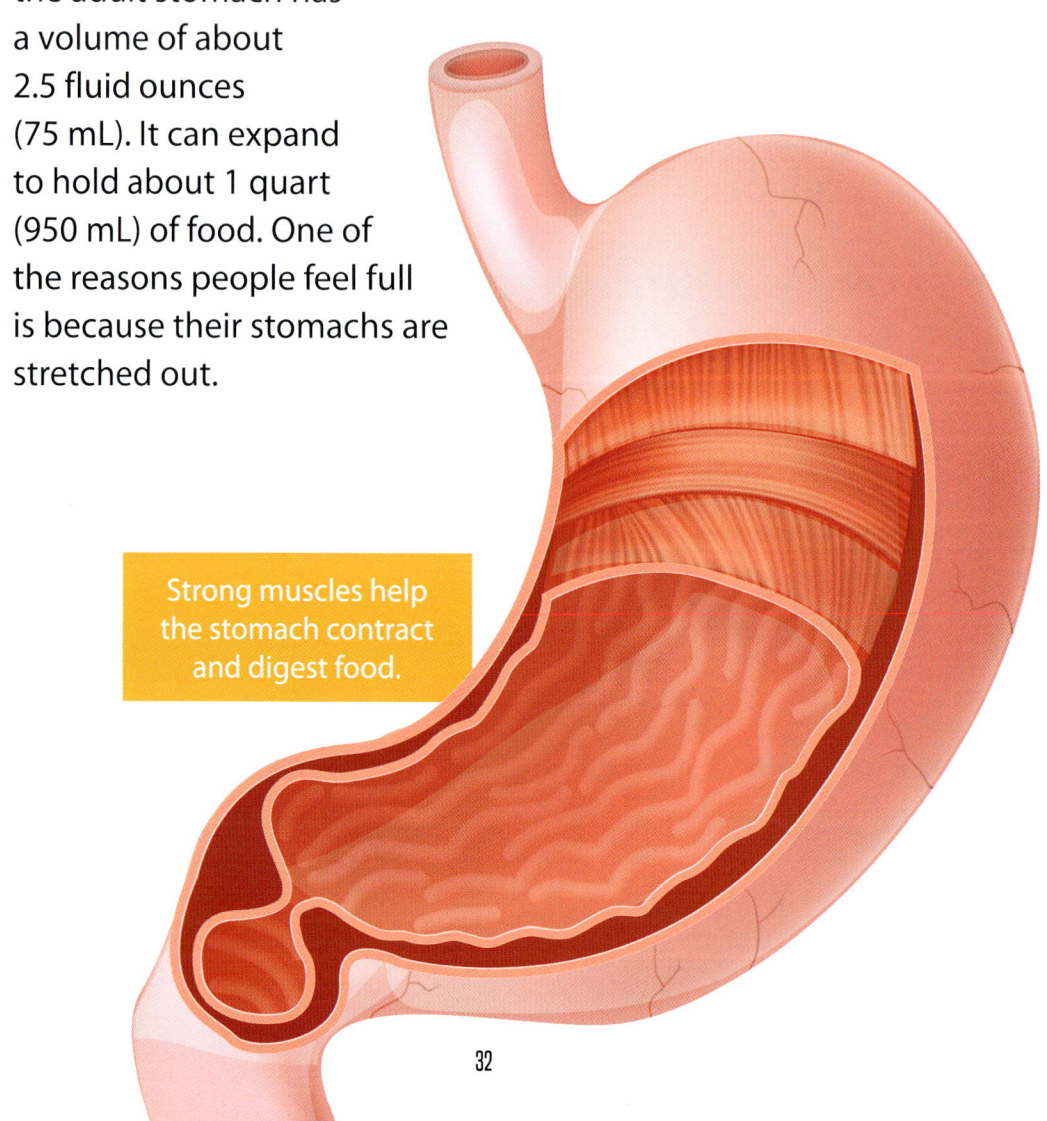

Strong muscles help the stomach contract and digest food.

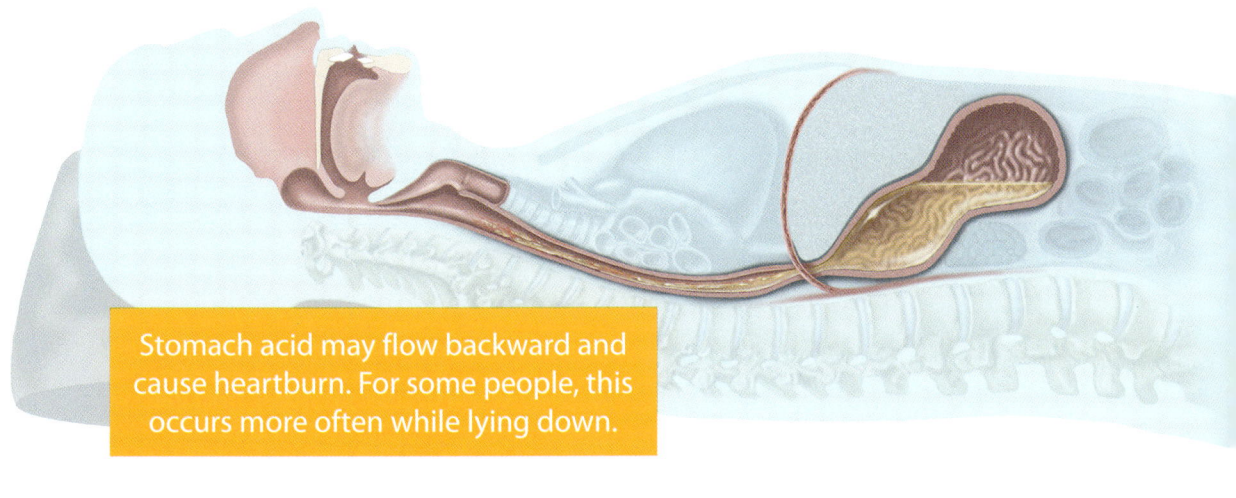

Stomach acid may flow backward and cause heartburn. For some people, this occurs more often while lying down.

The stomach has digestive juices. These juices are very acidic. They digest tough materials such as meat and plants. The digestive juices also contain enzymes. These enzymes break down food into nutrients that the body can use. Carbohydrates are broken down into sugars. Enzymes transform proteins into smaller parts called amino acids. The stomach is the first organ in the digestive system that breaks protein into usable parts.

The acids and digestive juices in the stomach are strong enough

Stomach contents are expelled when a person vomits. Vomiting is one way the body gets rid of harmful substances.

to break down tissue. So, the stomach is lined with mucus. The mucus protects the stomach from digesting itself. The stomach is also lined with epithelial cells. They offer additional protection from stomach acids. These cells are constantly being replaced. The stomach loses and regrows approximately 500,000 epithelial cells each minute. The entire stomach lining is replaced about every three days.

The stomach is made out of strong muscles. It contracts and churns food. It mixes food around. This movement breaks food down into smaller pieces. It also helps cover food in the digestive juices.

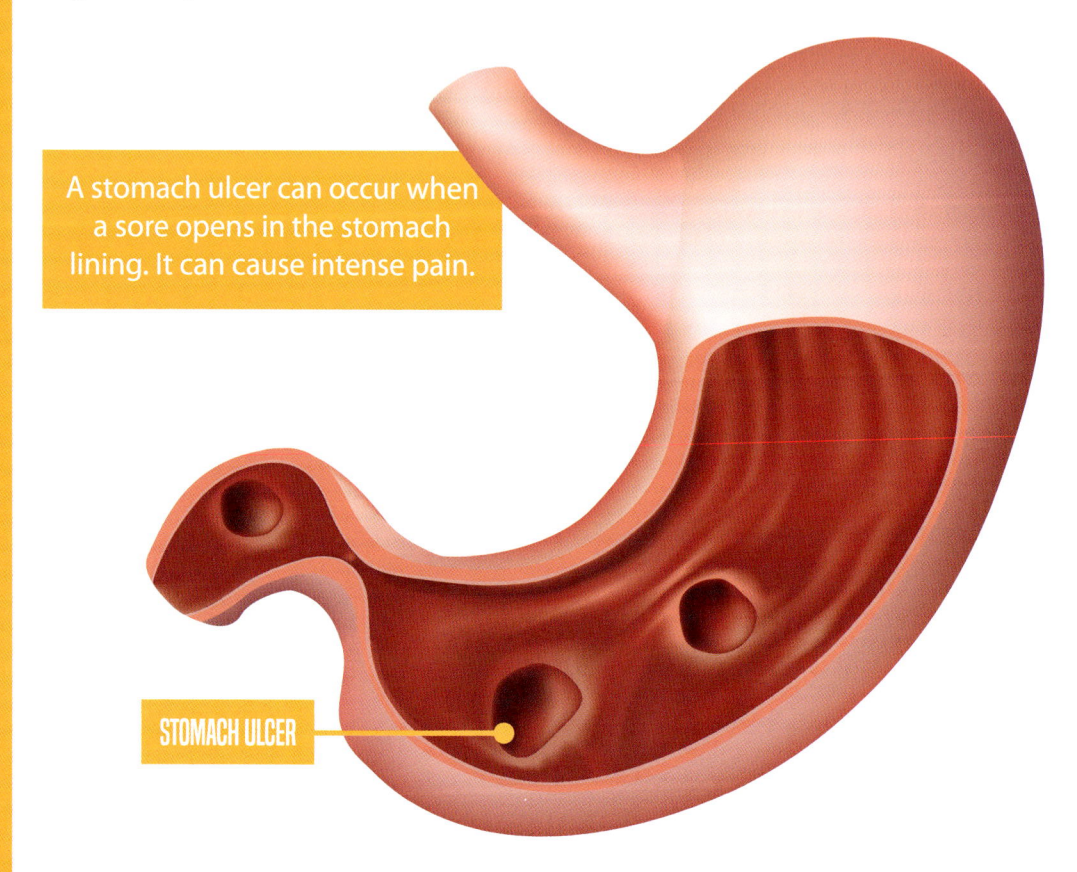

A stomach ulcer can occur when a sore opens in the stomach lining. It can cause intense pain.

STOMACH ULCER

Foods that are high in fat and protein, like fried foods and meat, take the longest to digest.

Food is digested in the stomach for a couple of hours. The length of time it takes to digest food depends on the type of food that was eaten. The size of the meal also influences digestion time. The food eventually becomes a thick paste called chyme. A muscle relaxes at the base of the stomach. It creates an opening into the small intestine. The chyme continues along the digestive tract.

DUODENUM

The small intestines can be divided into three sections. They are the duodenum, jejunum, and ileum.

ILEUM

JEJUNUM

The small intestine is the longest organ in the digestive system. It stretches for about 20 feet (6 m). The length helps the small intestine absorb as many nutrients as possible. It is called the small intestine because it is narrow. It is about 1 inch (2.5 cm) wide.

Chyme travels through the small intestine by peristalsis. Digestion continues in the first part of the small intestine. Bile—which helps break down fats and some vitamins—and enzymes split chyme down into even smaller parts. These digestive materials were created in other digestive organs, such as the liver and pancreas.

The primary role for the rest of the small intestine is to absorb nutrients. The small intestine is covered in finger-like projections called villi, which create folds and ridges. Villi increase the surface area of the small intestine. A large surface area means the small intestine is able to absorb many nutrients.

The small intestine absorbs more than 95 percent of the sugars and amino acids that the body needs. It also absorbs fats, vitamins, salts, and water. Villi connect to the bloodstream.

The absorbed nutrients enter the bloodstream and are delivered throughout the body.

The small intestine connects to the large intestine. The large intestine is only about 5 feet (1.5 m) long. But it is much

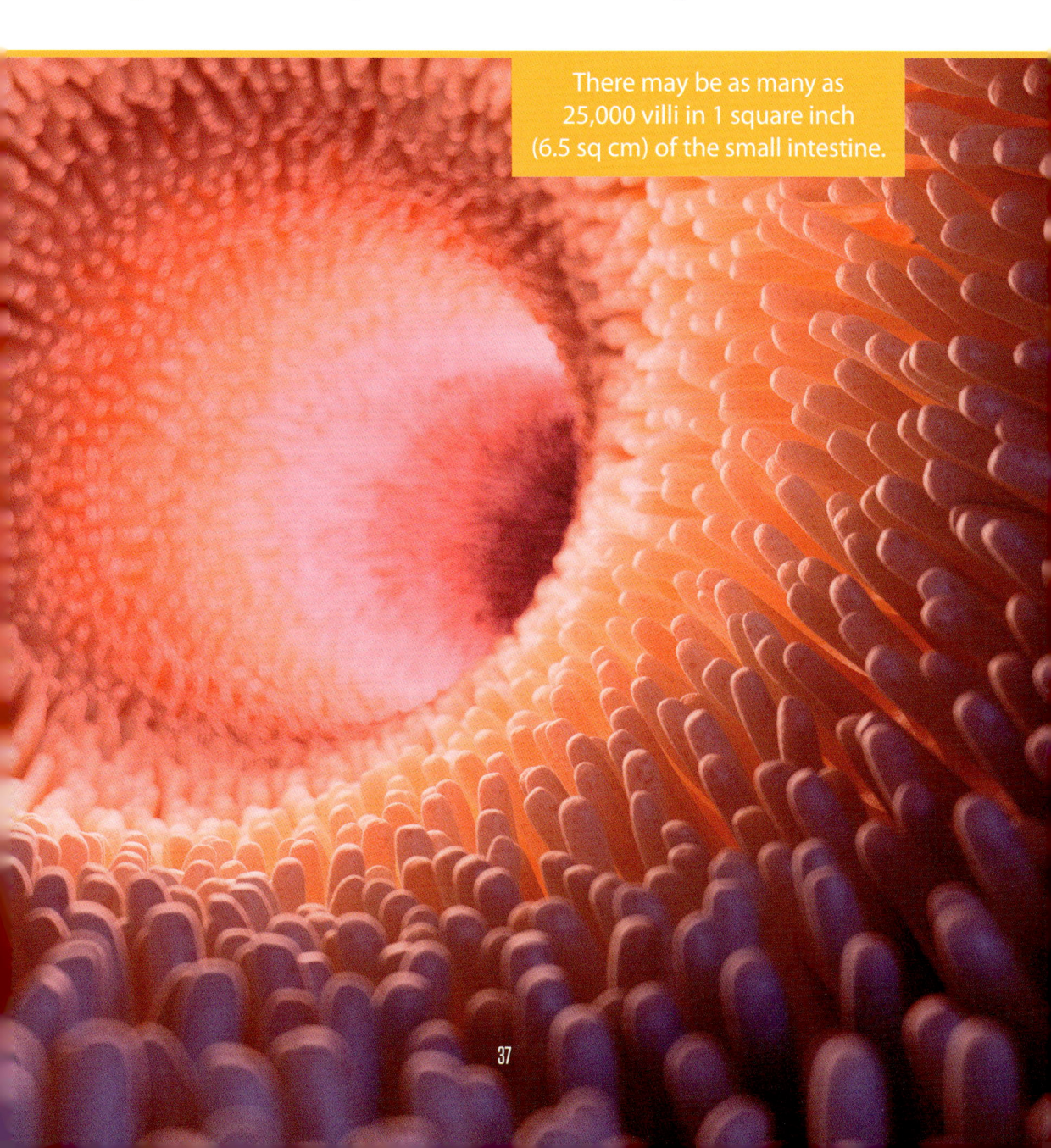

There may be as many as 25,000 villi in 1 square inch (6.5 sq cm) of the small intestine.

wider than the small intestine. It has a width of about 3 inches (7.6 cm). The large intestine is also called the colon.

By the time food reaches the large intestine, most of the nutrients have already been absorbed. Much of what enters the large intestine is waste. The large intestine absorbs any remaining water. It is lined with mucus that allows waste to move through the intestine. It can take 24 hours for waste to

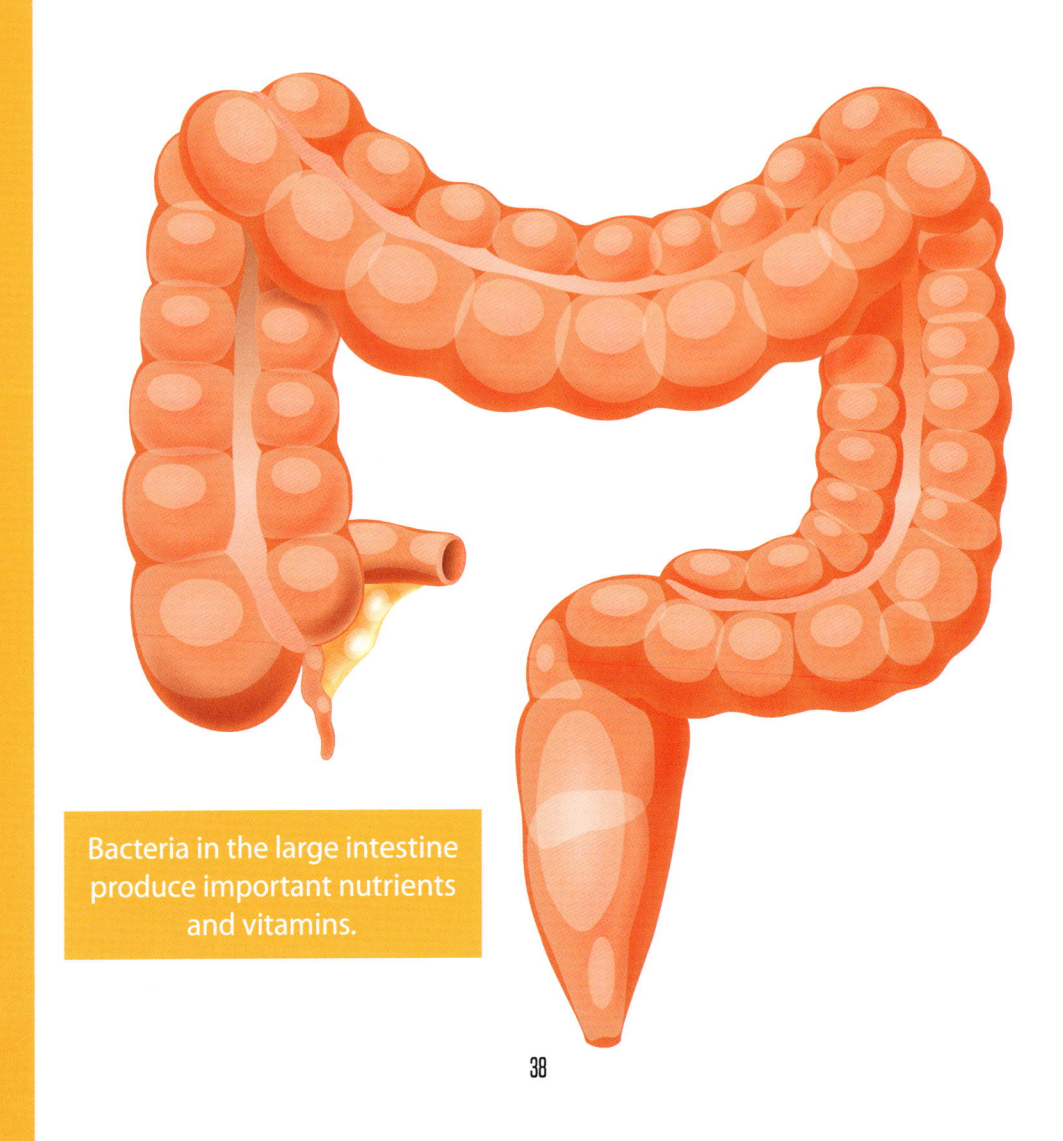

Bacteria in the large intestine produce important nutrients and vitamins.

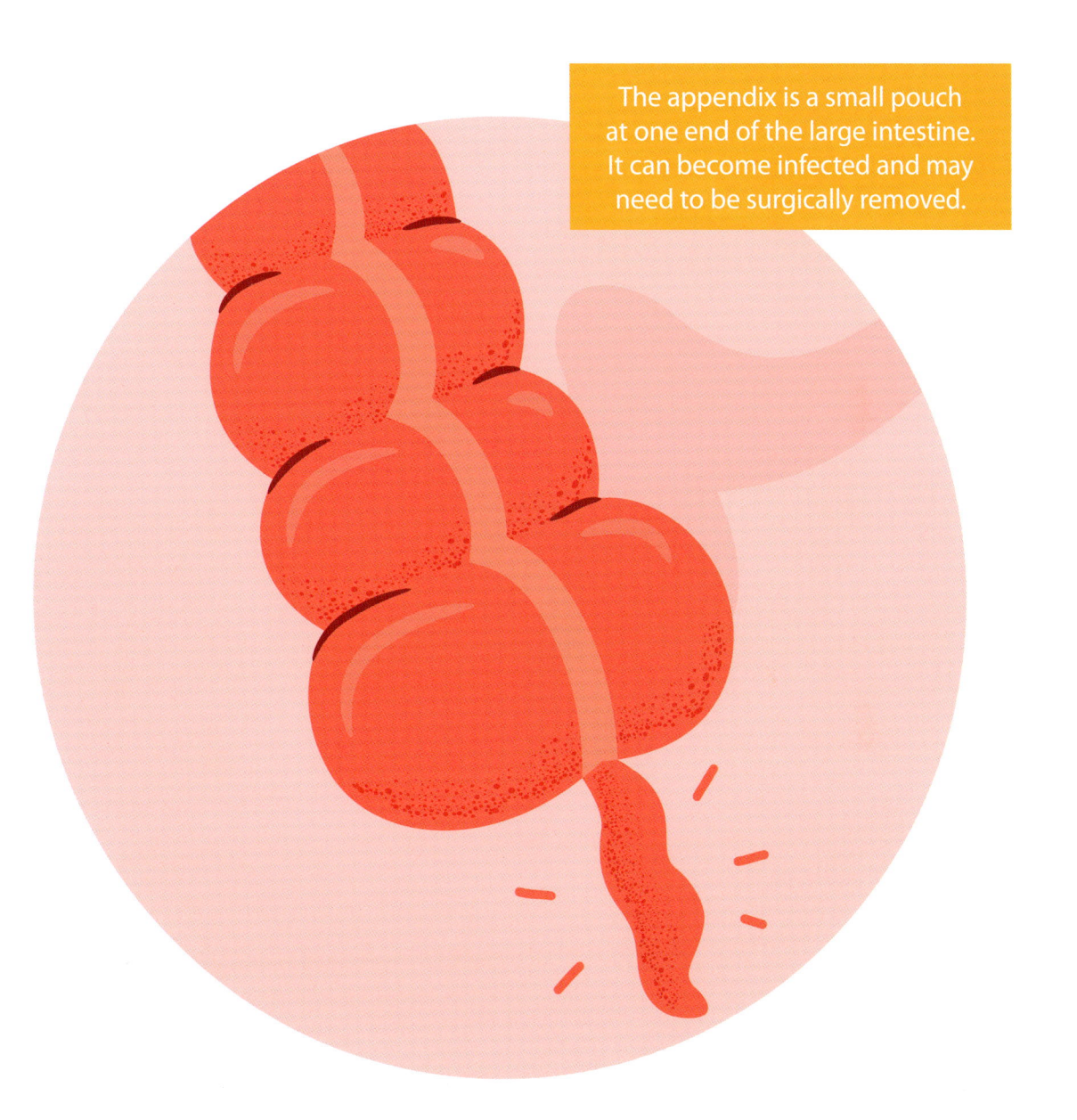

The appendix is a small pouch at one end of the large intestine. It can become infected and may need to be surgically removed.

pass through the large intestine. During this time, the waste is shaped into a stool. This is eventually excreted through the anus as feces.

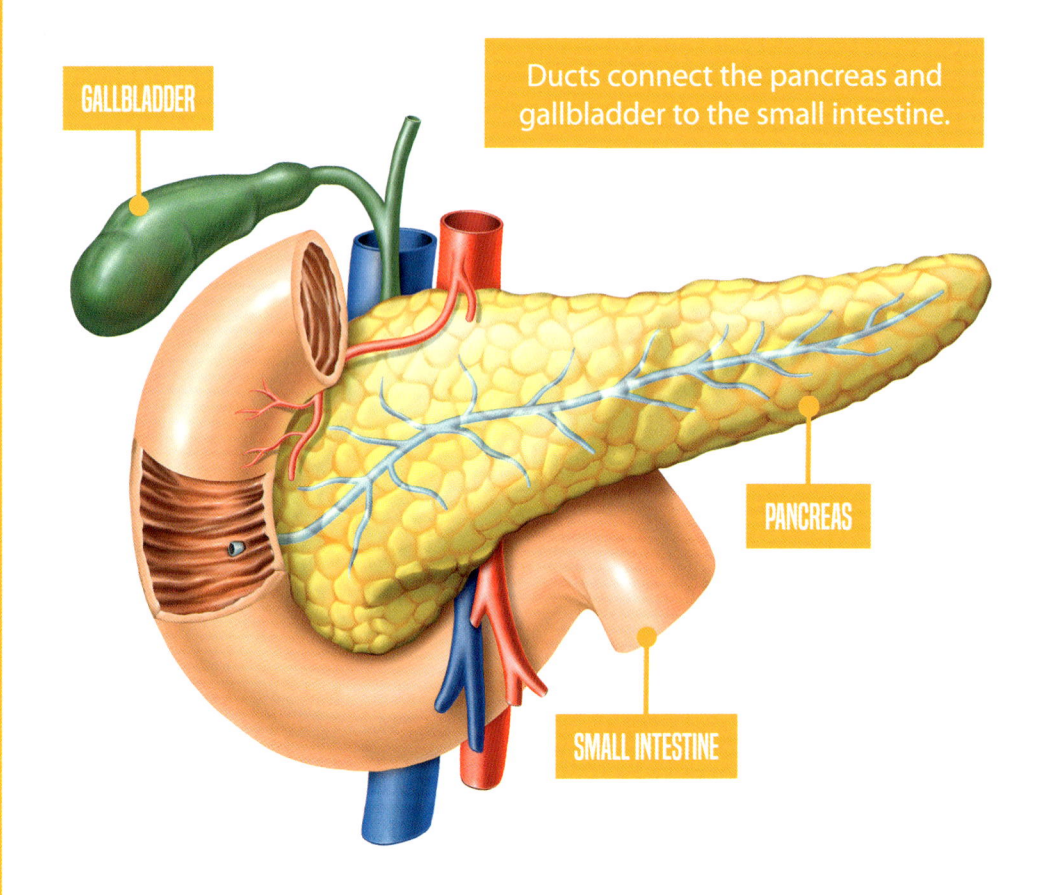

GALLBLADDER

Ducts connect the pancreas and gallbladder to the small intestine.

PANCREAS

SMALL INTESTINE

OTHER DIGESTIVE ORGANS

The digestive system includes the pancreas, liver, and gallbladder. These organs are not part of the digestive tract. They produce juices and enzymes that help break down food into nutrients.

The pancreas creates digestive juices that are filled with enzymes. These fluids are released into the upper part of the small intestine. The pancreas creates about 8 fluid ounces (235 mL) of digestive juices every day. The enzymes in the digestive juices break food down into nutrients.

The pancreas produces enzymes that break down starches and sugars.

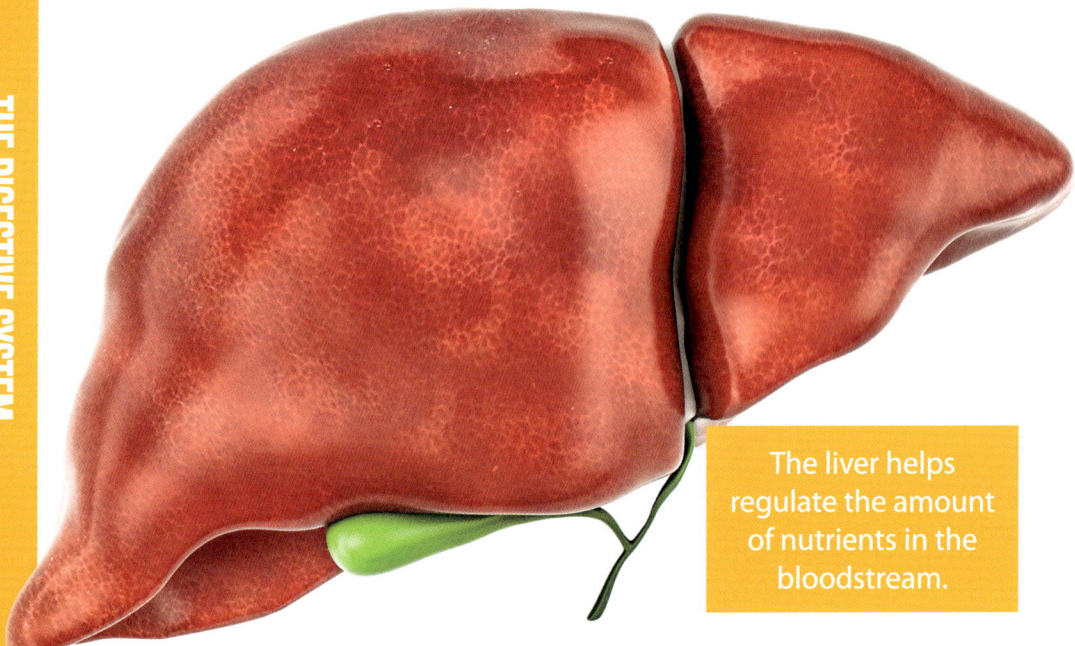

The liver helps regulate the amount of nutrients in the bloodstream.

The liver produces bile and releases it into the small intestine. Some bile is also released by and stored in the gallbladder. In addition, the liver plays an important role in removing waste products. It can break down toxic materials

Problems with the digestive system can cause stomach pain, nausea, and other symptoms.

Gallstones can be larger than a dime.

such as drugs and alcohol. This reduces the effect that these materials have on the body. The liver keeps the body healthy by removing toxins.

The gallbladder stores some of the bile the liver produces. The bile becomes more concentrated. It is more effective at breaking down tough fats. The gallbladder releases this bile into the small intestine.

Some people experience gallstones. This is when the bile in the gallbladder becomes hard and rock-like. Gallstones can be very painful. They may block the flow of bile. People may have their gallbladders removed. A person can live without a gallbladder. In those cases, bile flows directly from the liver into the small intestine.

THE ENDOCRINE SYSTEM

The endocrine system includes organs called glands. These glands are located throughout the body. Major glands include the pituitary gland and the hypothalamus. They are both located in the brain. The pineal gland is also in the brain. Other major endocrine glands include the thyroid and parathyroid glands. These are located near the throat. Adrenal glands are on top of the kidneys. The pancreas is near the liver. The testes are an important endocrine organ in males. The ovaries are a major organ in females.

Major endocrine glands are located throughout the body. A male is born with testes. A female has ovaries and a uterus.

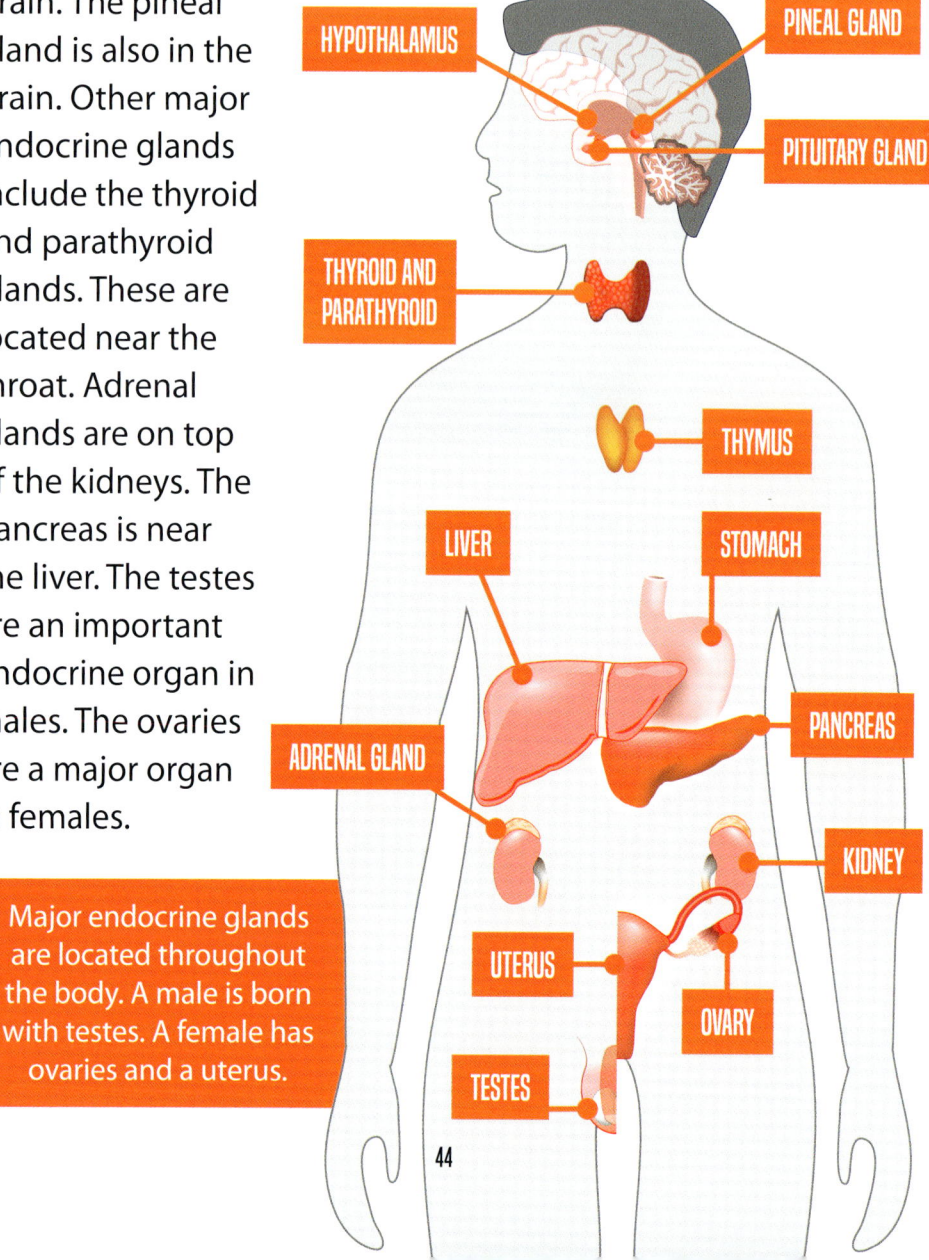

HYPOTHALAMUS

PINEAL GLAND

PITUITARY GLAND

THYROID AND PARATHYROID

THYMUS

LIVER

STOMACH

PANCREAS

ADRENAL GLAND

KIDNEY

UTERUS

OVARY

TESTES

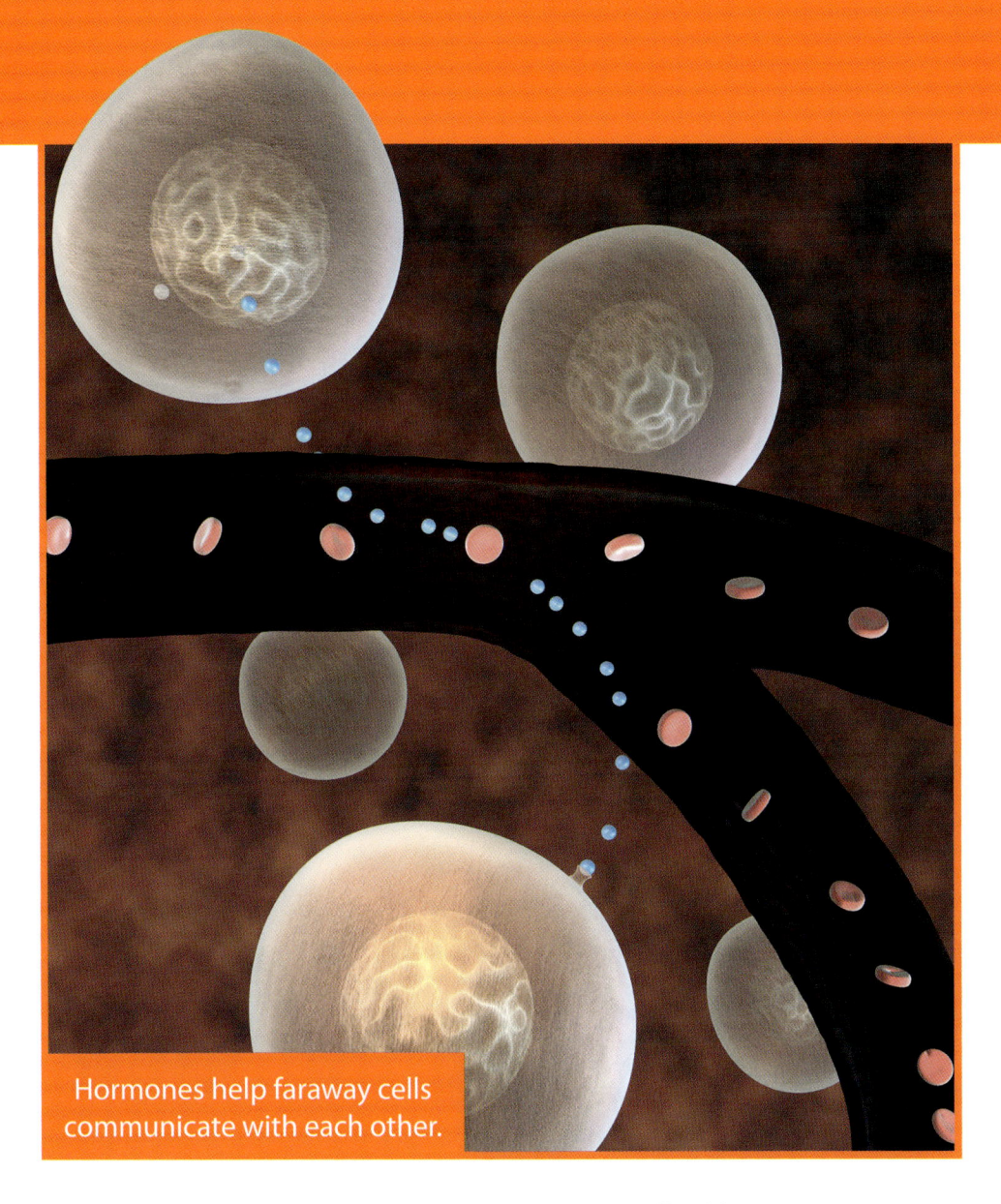

Hormones help faraway cells communicate with each other.

Glands release chemical messengers called hormones. Hormones regulate many bodily processes. They affect when a person is hungry or thirsty. They regulate a person's sleep cycle. Hormones also play roles in growth and development. They influence mood. They affect blood pressure, heart rate, body temperature, and much more.

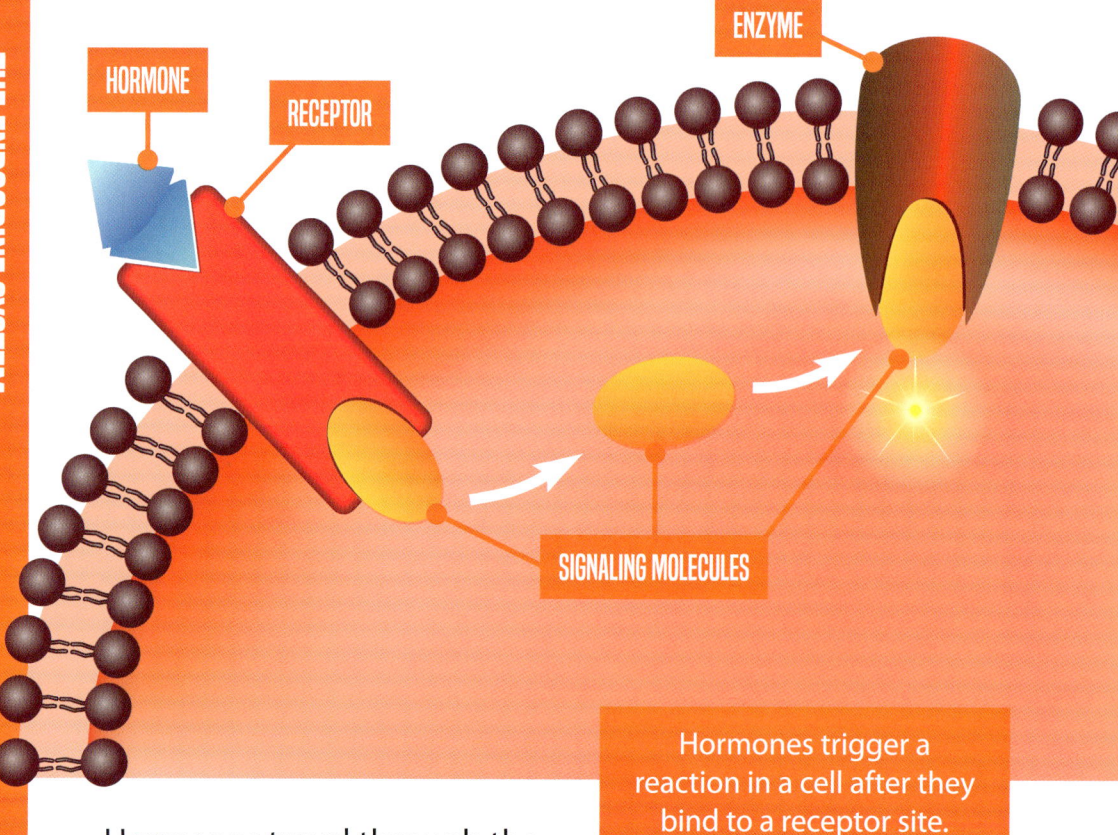

HORMONE

RECEPTOR

ENZYME

SIGNALING MOLECULES

Hormones trigger a reaction in a cell after they bind to a receptor site.

Hormones travel through the bloodstream. They regulate the processes of organs. They can travel to all parts of the body. But they only target specific cells. Hormones bind to receptor sites on cells. Different hormones have different shapes. Receptor sites also come in different shapes. A hormone will fit into only one type of receptor site. They fit together like a key in a lock. Once the hormone binds to a receptor site, it triggers a change in the cell's activity.

The endocrine system maintains a balance of hormones. This balance is called homeostasis. Too much or too little of a hormone can cause health issues. When there is too much of a certain hormone, the endocrine system slows down the production of that hormone. When there is too little of a certain hormone, the endocrine system signals to increase the production of that hormone.

Doctors may prescribe medication to someone who has an imbalance of hormones.

GLANDS IN THE BRAIN

The hypothalamus links the nervous system with the endocrine system. This gland is located near the bottom of the brain. It releases several hormones that regulate the activity of other endocrine glands. Many of the hormones it produces react with the pituitary gland. Together the hypothalamus and pituitary gland play important roles in maintaining homeostasis. The hypothalamus also helps regulate sleep, appetite, and body temperature.

HYPOTHALAMUS

The hypothalamus is located above the pituitary gland.

PITUITARY GLAND

The pituitary gland is attached to the hypothalamus. It produces many types of hormones. One example is the growth hormone. This hormone helps keep muscles and bones healthy.

The pituitary gland produces hormones that affect the activity levels of other endocrine glands. For this reason, the pituitary gland is considered to be the master gland of the endocrine system. For example, the pituitary gland produces thyroid-stimulating hormone (TSH). High amounts of TSH increase activity in the thyroid gland, which helps control things like how a person uses energy.

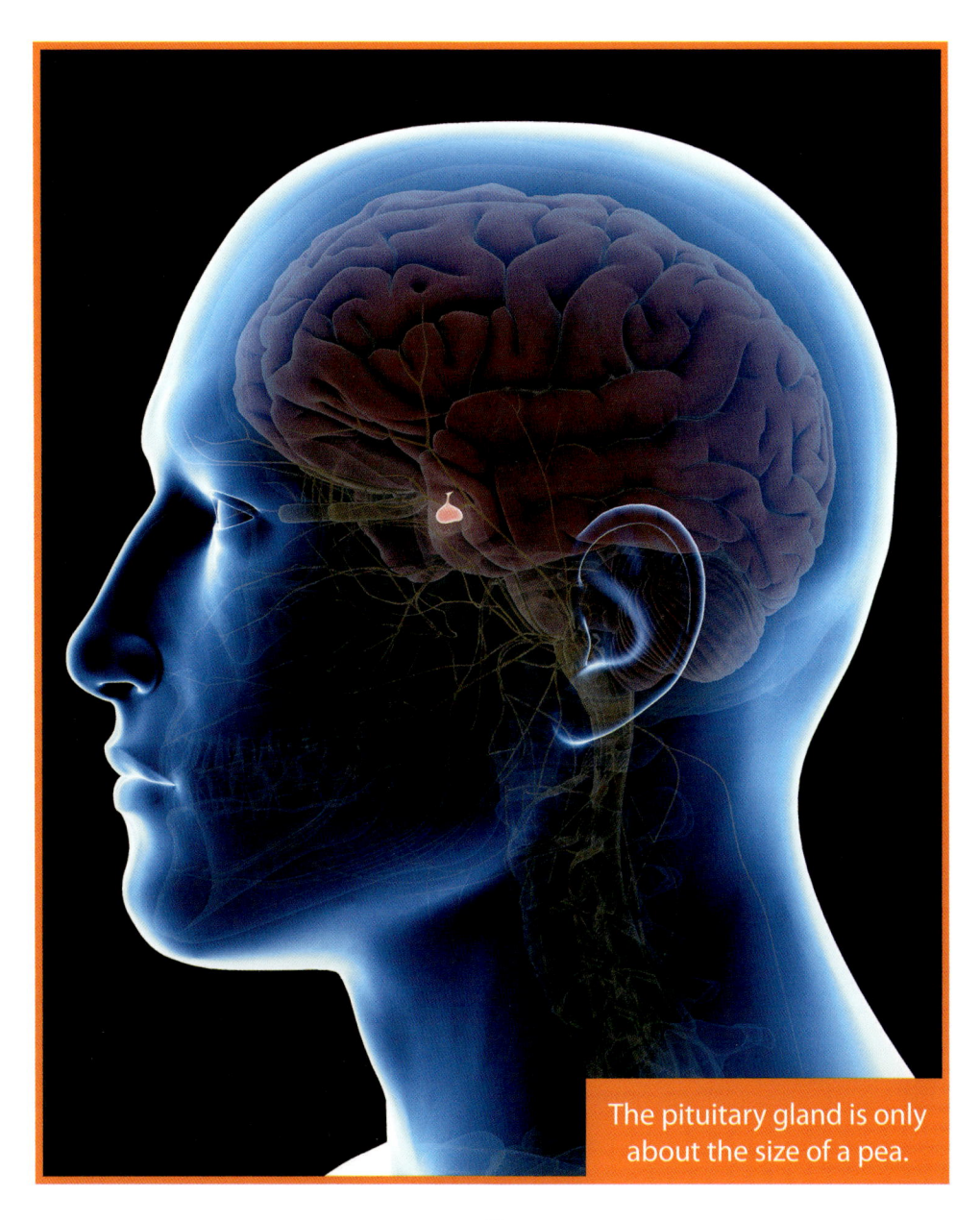

The pituitary gland is only about the size of a pea.

Because the pituitary gland releases many types of hormones, problems with this gland can result in many symptoms. It may release too much or too little of certain hormones. People who produce too little growth hormone may not grow quickly. Their muscles are weak. High levels of growth hormone can lead to problems with bone health and movement. There are many other symptoms that may indicate a problem with the pituitary gland. People may constantly feel tired. They may have trouble regulating body temperature. They may experience extreme thirst. Problems with the pituitary gland can be severe. But people can take medication to help regulate their hormones.

A low amount of growth hormone causes some forms of dwarfism. People with dwarfism are much shorter than average.

Constantly feeling cold and weak can be a sign of a pituitary gland issue.

The pituitary gland uses feedback loops to keep hormone levels balanced. This is similar to how a thermostat keeps a constant temperature in a home. The heater turns on when the temperature falls below the set point. After the correct temperature has been reached, the heater turns off. Similarly, the pituitary gland releases TSH when thyroid hormone levels are low. TSH causes the thyroid gland to produce its own hormones. When thyroid hormone levels become high, the pituitary gland stops releasing TSH.

The pineal gland is also located in the brain. It is near the center of the brain. The pineal gland produces the hormone melatonin. This hormone is important in regulating sleep. It makes a person feel sleepy. The pineal gland secretes more melatonin after the sun goes down. It signals to the body that it is time to sleep.

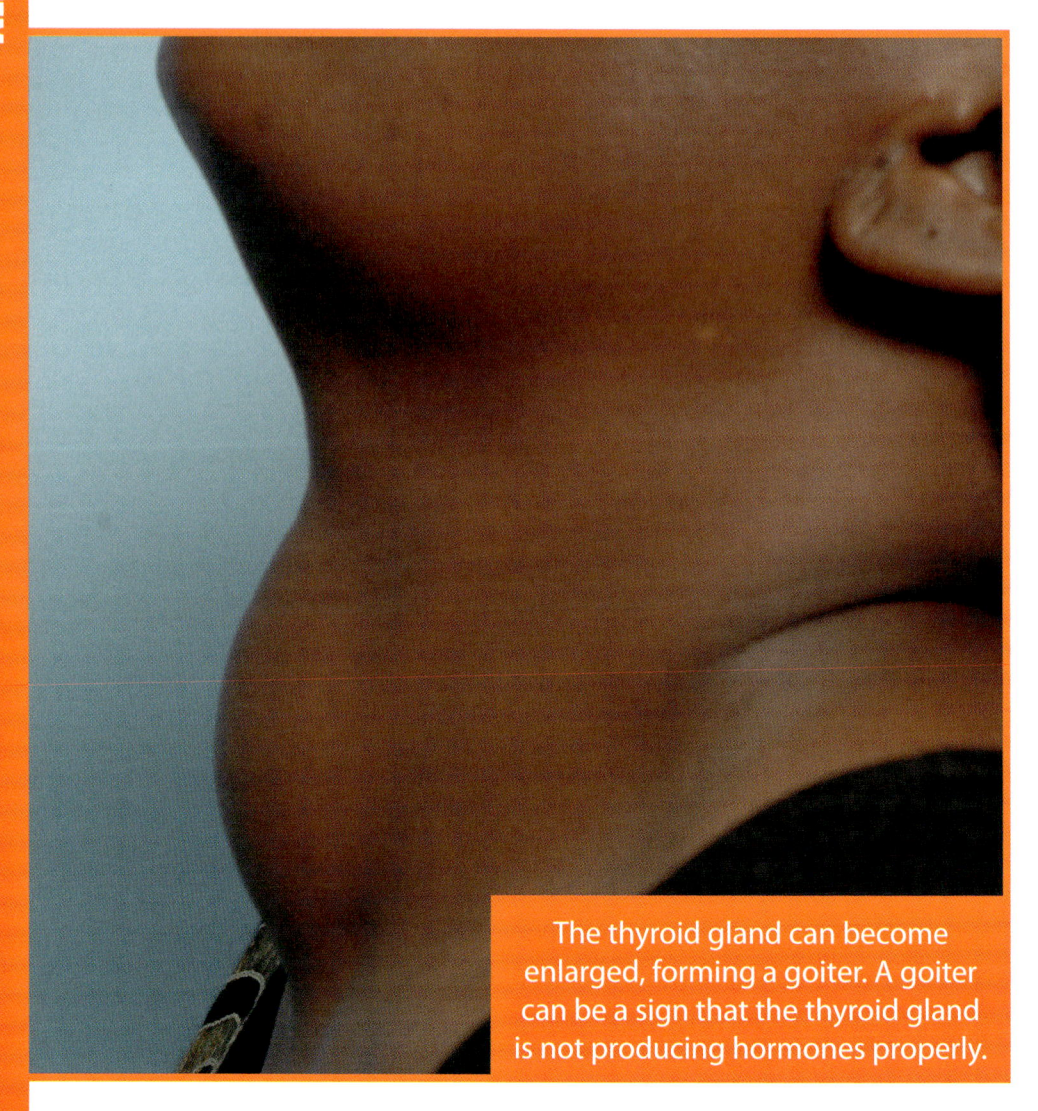

The thyroid gland can become enlarged, forming a goiter. A goiter can be a sign that the thyroid gland is not producing hormones properly.

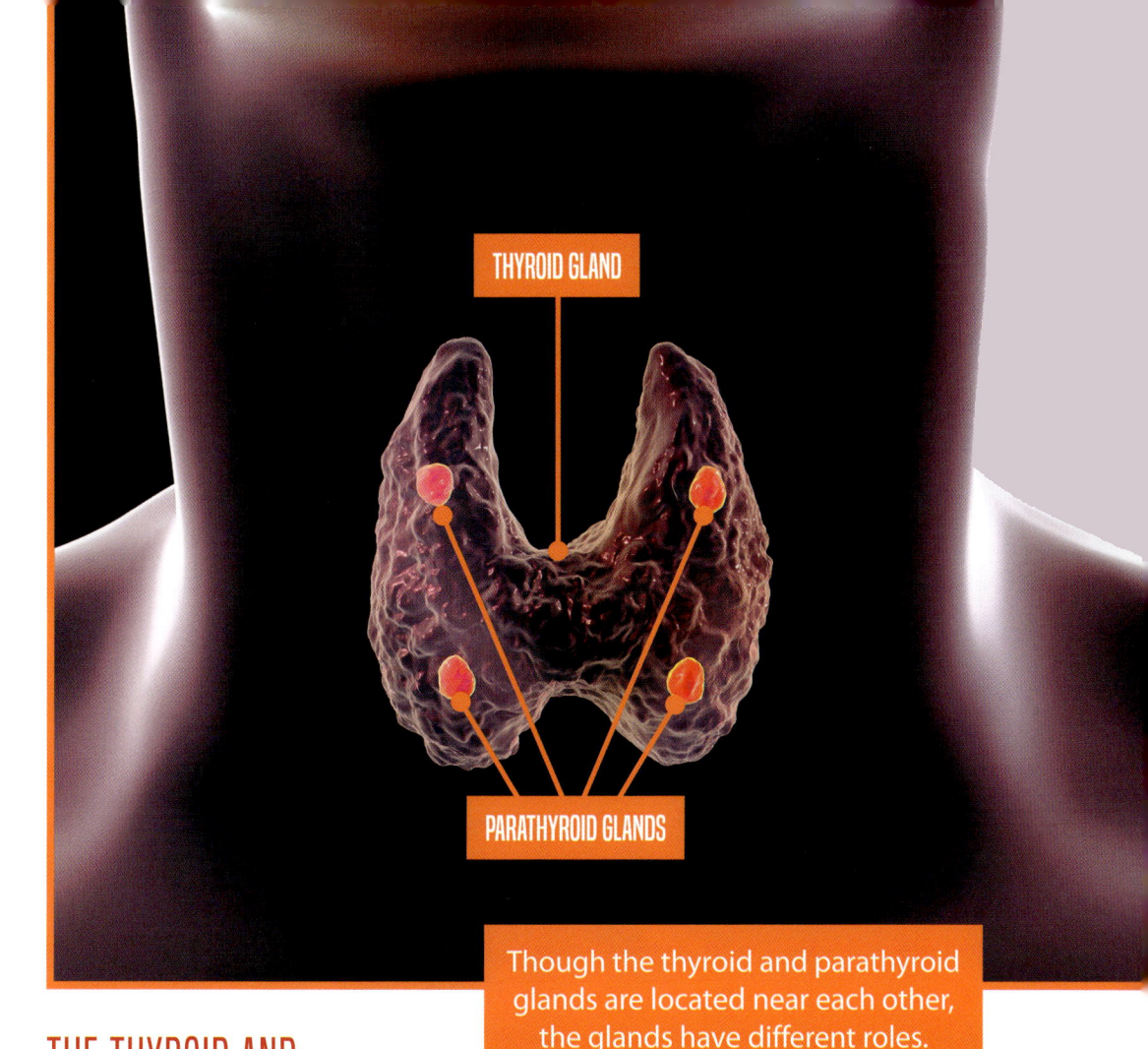

THYROID GLAND

PARATHYROID GLANDS

Though the thyroid and parathyroid glands are located near each other, the glands have different roles.

THE THYROID AND PARATHYROID GLANDS

The thyroid and parathyroid glands are located at the base of the neck. The thyroid gland is about 2 inches (5 cm) long. It is shaped like a butterfly. This gland regulates metabolism, which is how the body turns food into energy. The thyroid gland releases two hormones that influence metabolism. They are T3 and T4. They affect weight gain and weight loss. They also affect body temperature and heart rate.

Producing too much or too little T3 and T4 can cause health problems. People who produce too much of these hormones use energy too quickly. They may have a fast heart rate. They may lose extreme amounts of weight. People who do not produce enough thyroid hormones have a slow metabolism. They may gain weight and get cold easily.

The parathyroid glands are found behind the thyroid gland. There are four of them, each about the size of a grain of rice. These glands release parathyroid hormone. This hormone controls calcium levels in the bloodstream. Parathyroid hormone also affects how much calcium is absorbed by the intestines. Calcium is an important mineral. Without calcium, bones become brittle and weak. Nerves and the heart

High levels of parathyroid hormone can cause someone to feel extremely thirsty.

Headaches and memory loss can be signs of low levels of parathyroid hormone. But problems with the parathyroid glands are rare.

also need calcium to function. Bones become weak if the parathyroid glands are overactive. High levels of parathyroid hormone cause bones to release calcium into the bloodstream. Weak bones are at risk for fractures.

THE ADRENAL GLANDS

The adrenal glands are at the top of both kidneys. They are shaped like triangles. The adrenal glands are made up of two parts. The adrenal cortex is the outer layer. The adrenal medulla is the inner layer. These layers produce different hormones. They regulate different bodily processes.

The adrenal cortex releases several hormones. One is cortisol. The body produces cortisol when it is under stress. But cortisol has many functions. It regulates how much sugar is in the blood. It also plays a role in metabolism and water balance. The adrenal cortex also produces aldosterone. This hormone helps regulate blood pressure. In addition, the adrenal cortex produces some types of steroid hormones. These hormones can be building blocks for other hormones.

The adrenal medulla produces two main hormones. They are epinephrine and norepinephrine. These hormones are released in times of stress. They trigger the fight-or-flight response. They prepare the body to react quickly. The hormones cause an increase in heart rate. This delivers more oxygen to the muscles and brain. Epinephrine and norepinephrine also cause the body to increase its metabolism. This creates extra energy. The hormones improve a person's focus. They help a person face danger.

In addition to producing hormones, the kidneys regulate the amount of water, salts, and minerals in the body.

THE PANCREAS

The pancreas sits next to the stomach. It is about 6 inches (15 cm) long. It produces enzymes that help with digestion. But it is also a part of the endocrine system.

The pancreas plays an important role in maintaining blood sugar. When carbohydrates are digested, they break down into a simple sugar called glucose. Glucose enters the bloodstream. When there is a lot of glucose in the blood, the pancreas releases the hormone insulin. Insulin lowers the amount of glucose in a person's blood by helping to store glucose in the liver, muscles, and fat. The glucose can later be used for energy. The pancreas also produces

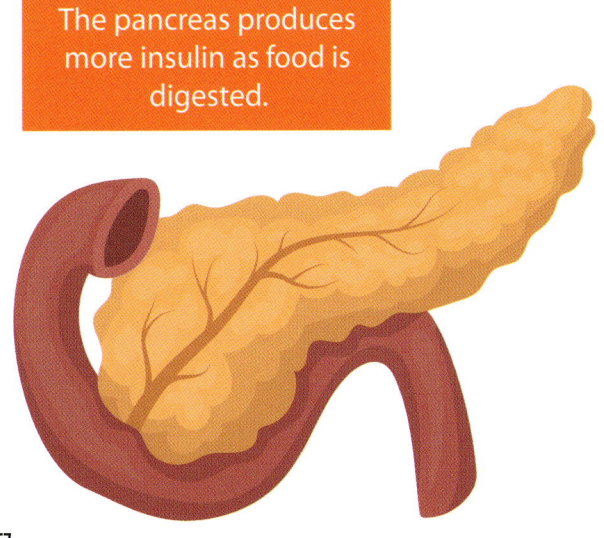

The pancreas produces more insulin as food is digested.

57

A glucometer can be used to measure blood sugar levels.

another hormone called glucagon. This hormone has the opposite effect of insulin. Glucagon signals for the stored glucose to be released into the bloodstream. Low blood sugar levels trigger glucagon release. Together glucagon and insulin help balance a person's blood sugar levels.

It is important to keep blood sugar levels balanced. Too much or too little blood sugar can be life-threatening. People who have low blood sugar may be tired and shaky. They may be confused. They may faint. Eating or drinking something rich in sugars can help increase blood sugar. Having high blood sugar levels can cause other problems. People with high blood sugar may experience headaches. They may feel nauseous. In severe cases, high blood sugar can cause a coma. High blood sugar is usually a sign that the pancreas is not producing enough insulin.

Type 2 diabetes is a disease that affects how a person's body responds to insulin. Exercise can help prevent this form of diabetes.

THE OVARIES AND TESTES

The ovaries and testes are also called the gonads. They are parts of the reproductive system. But they also release hormones that are important in the body's development. The gonads begin to release sex hormones during puberty.

The ovaries are female sex organs. They are shaped like ovals. Females have two ovaries. There is one on either side of the lower torso. The ovaries release two kinds of sex hormones. They are estrogen and progesterone. Males produce these hormones in lesser amounts.

Estrogen helps with the development of breasts during puberty. It also causes a female's hips to become wider.

A pregnancy test measures the amount of a hormone called human chorionic gonadotropin.

Males typically have higher levels of testosterone than females, which allows males to build muscle quickly.

In addition, this hormone has a role in regulating the menstrual cycle. This is the monthly cycle in which a female's body releases an egg. Hormones prepare the body for pregnancy. If a female becomes pregnant, estrogen helps the body prepare for giving birth. Progesterone is also released as part of the menstrual cycle. It helps the body prepare to have a child. It readies parts of the reproductive system for pregnancy.

The testes are the male sex organs. They are located in the scrotum. The testes release testosterone. Female ovaries also produce testosterone in small amounts. Testosterone causes physical changes to the male body during puberty. It causes males to grow facial hair. It triggers a growth spurt. Testosterone also helps make sure that male sex organs develop properly. After puberty, testosterone maintains healthy muscles and bones.

THE IMMUNE SYSTEM

The immune system is the body's defense system. It keeps people healthy. The immune system includes lymph nodes, white blood cells, and antibodies. Together they prevent infections and stop people from getting sick. The immune system fights against germs such as bacteria and viruses. These tiny particles can cause illnesses such as the flu, chicken pox, a lung infection called pneumonia, and much more. Germs that cause diseases are called pathogens.

People are born with protection against germs. This includes the skin and other epithelial lining. They form a physical barrier against germs. The germs cannot enter the body.

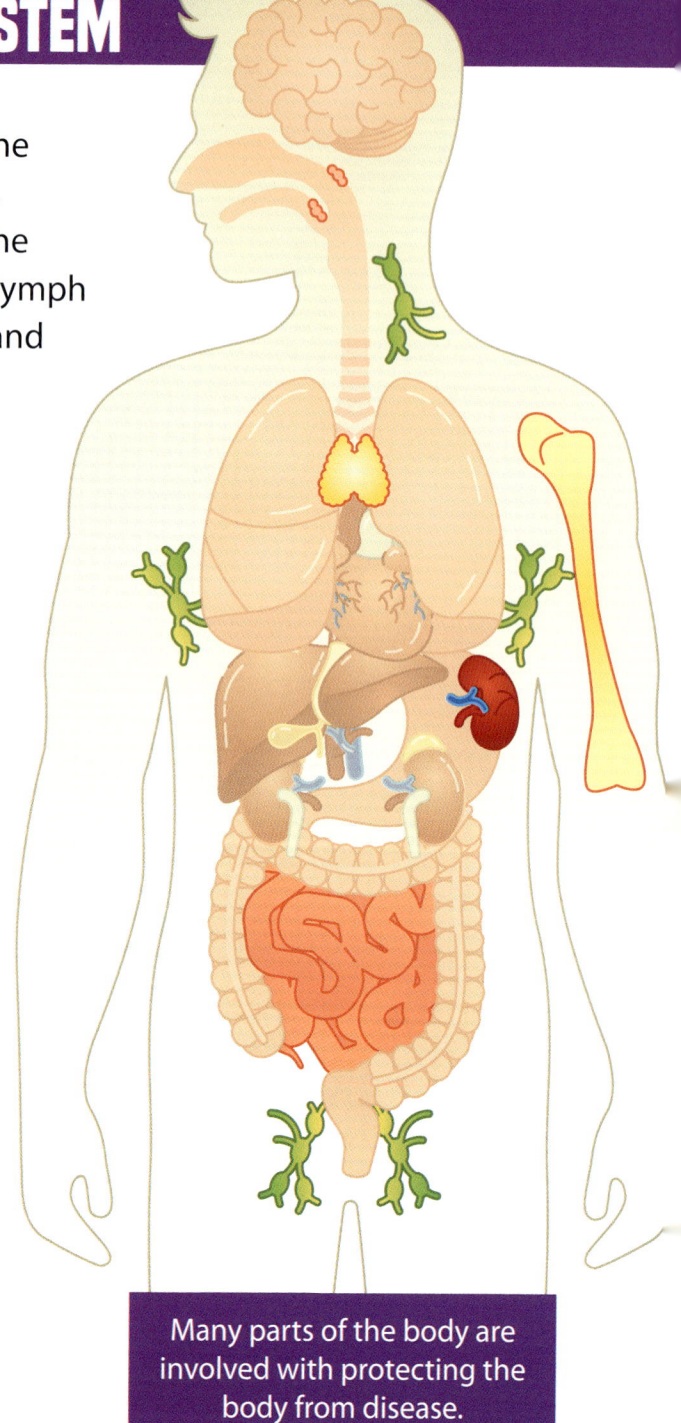

Many parts of the body are involved with protecting the body from disease.

Openings such as the nose and airways have mucus. They also have small hairs called cilia. Mucus and cilia offer protection against invaders. Mucus is sticky. It can trap bacteria and viruses before they get deep into the body. Mucus can also stop dust, pollen, and other small particles. Cilia move mucus and trapped particles. Mucus is removed from the body by coughing or blowing one's nose. It may also be swallowed.

People produce more mucus when they are sick. This helps rid the body of germs.

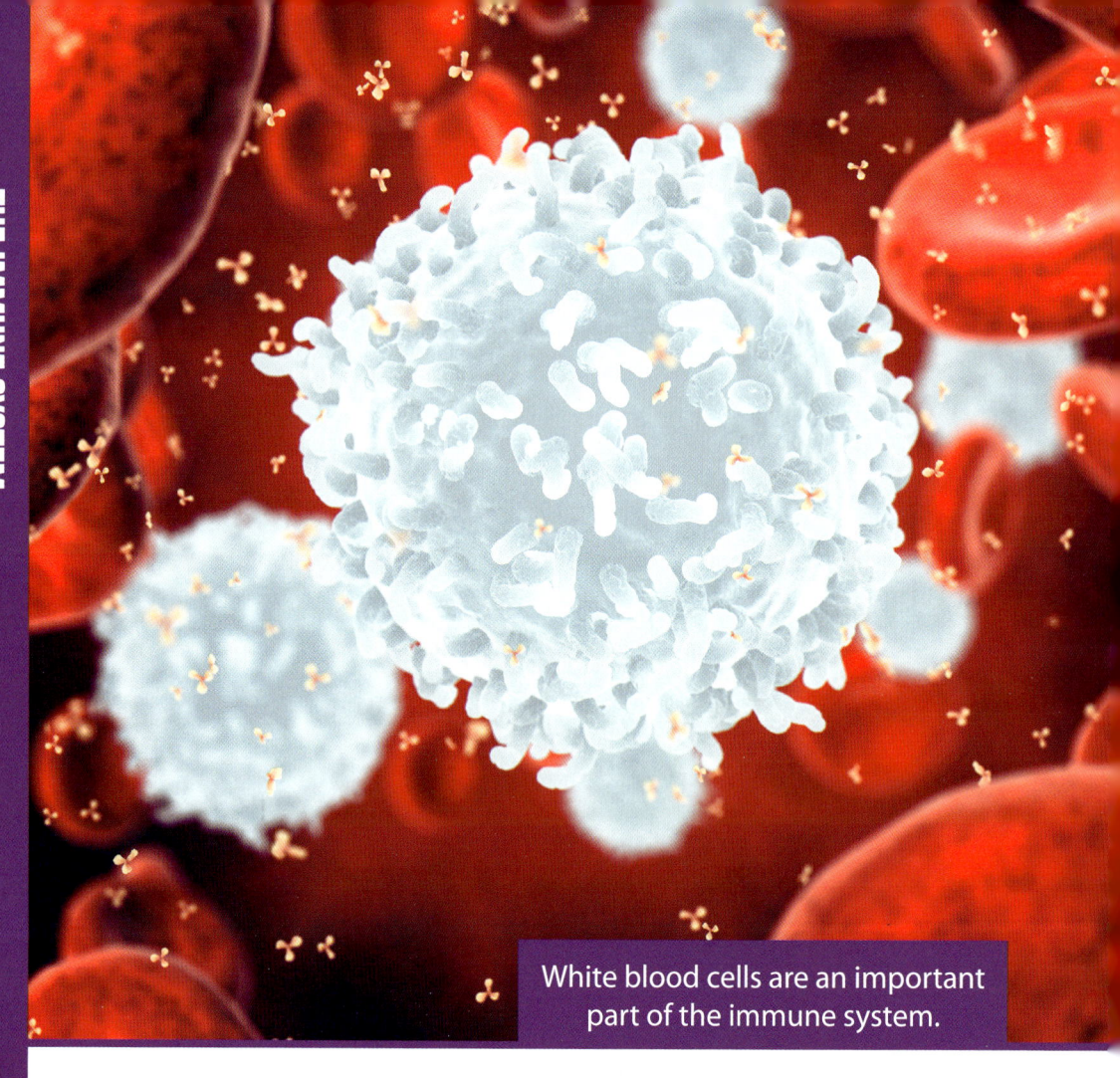

White blood cells are an important part of the immune system.

Other parts of the immune system develop with age. This is how some white blood cells work. They learn to recognize bacteria and viruses. The next time the bacterium or virus enters the body, the immune system is better prepared to fight it. This is why vaccines are effective. Vaccines are types of medicines that boost the immune system. Scientists create a vaccine that looks a bacterium or virus. The vaccine is injected into the body through a shot. It triggers the immune system. If a person is later infected with the real bacterium or virus, the immune system already knows how to fight back.

When the immune system is at work, people begin to experience symptoms of illness. For example, a runny nose is a sign that someone has a cold. The immune system triggers the nose to produce more mucus, which helps prevent more pathogens from entering through the nose. A runny nose means that the immune system is working.

Some vaccines inject a portion of a pathogen's genetic information in order to help a person fight the pathogen in the future.

LYMPH NODES AND ORGANS

Lymph nodes are bean-shaped glands. There are about 600 lymph nodes located throughout the human body. Some are small, only a few cells in size. Others are organized into large organs, such as the spleen. Large lymph nodes are also located in the neck and chest.

Lymph is part of the immune system. It is a fluid that is similar to blood plasma. Lymph gathers pathogens and damaged cells from tissues throughout the body. It flows into lymph nodes, which filter the lymph. Lymph nodes also store white blood cells. The white blood cells are released when a pathogen is detected in the body.

Lymph nodes trap pathogens before they can spread to other parts of the body. They may become swollen when a person is sick. For example, a person with strep throat may notice the lymph nodes in his or her throat are swollen. These lymph nodes are the tonsils. They become swollen because they are infected with bacteria that cause strep throat.

Lymph nodes trap and destroy pathogens. The destroyed pathogens enter the bloodstream, where they are eventually removed from the body.

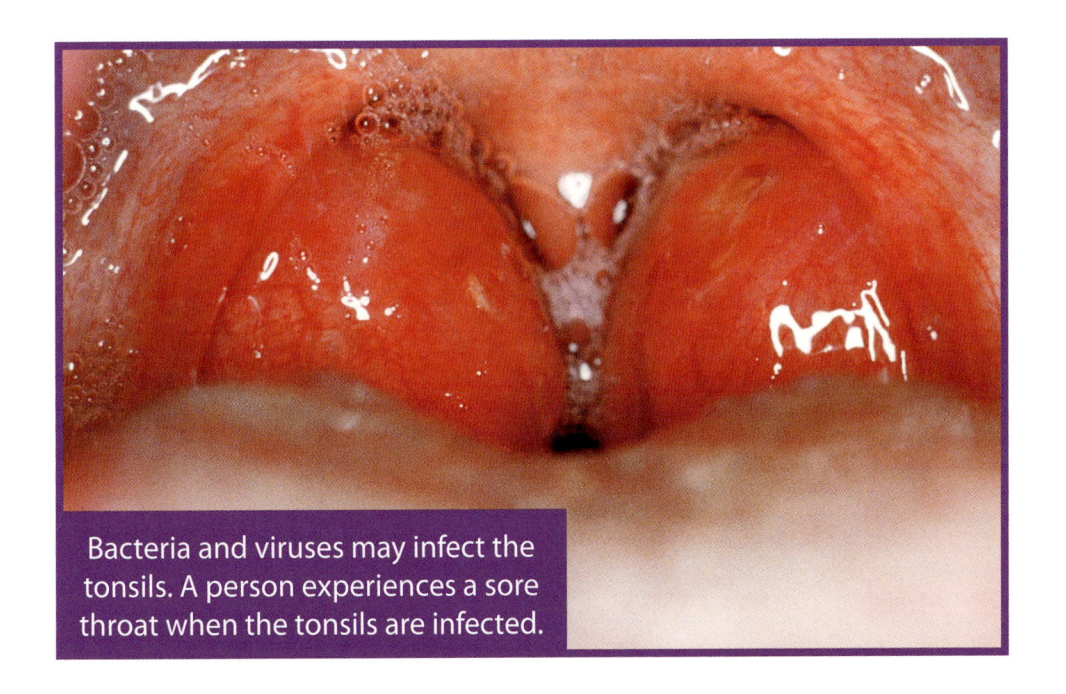

Bacteria and viruses may infect the tonsils. A person experiences a sore throat when the tonsils are infected.

The spleen is the largest organ in the immune system. The average adult has a spleen that is about 5 inches (13 cm) long. It weighs about 6 ounces (170 g). It sits just above the stomach. Like lymph nodes, the spleen filters lymph. It traps and destroys pathogens. It produces and stores white blood cells that protect against infection.

The spleen destroys old and damaged red blood cells.

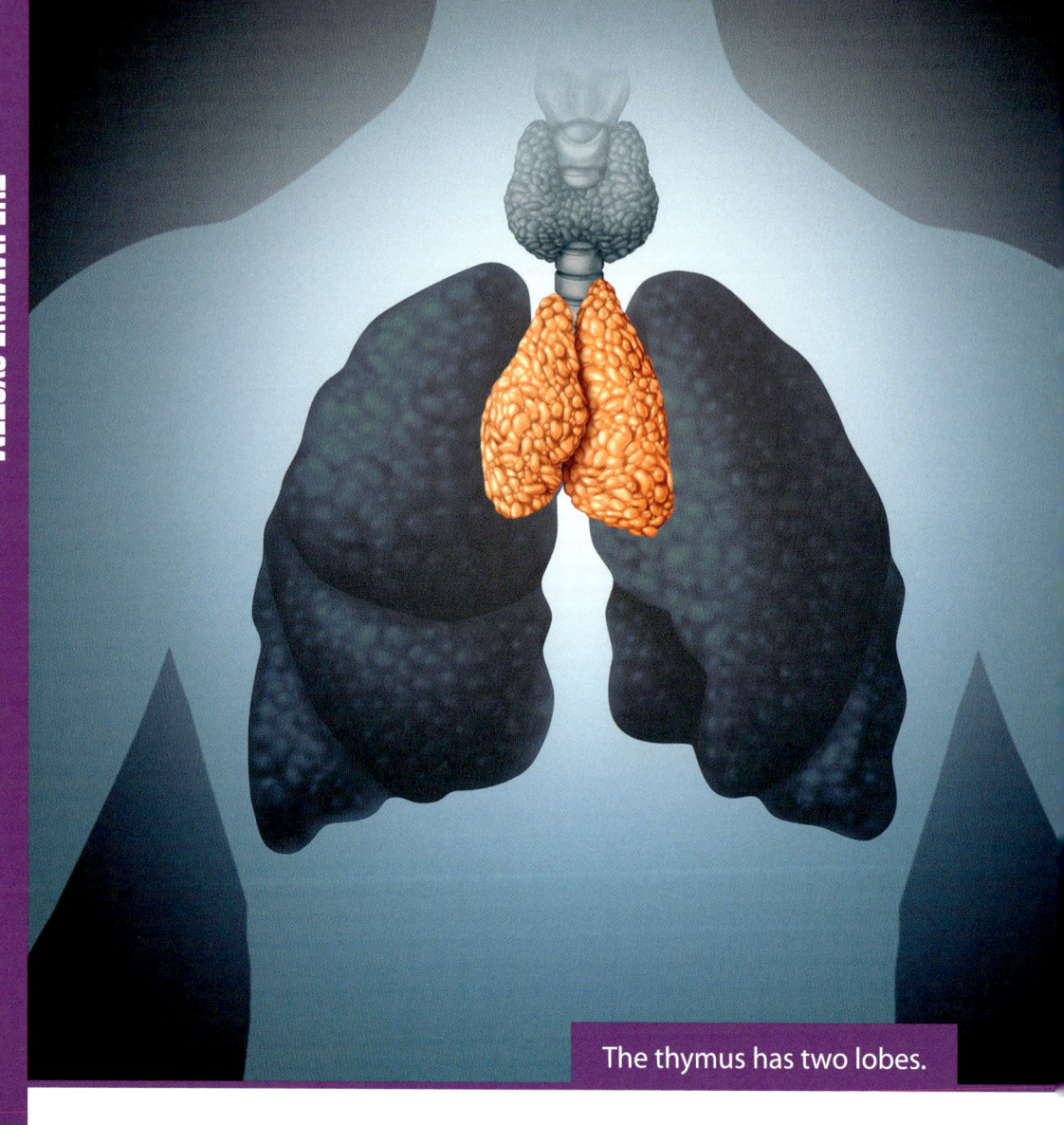

The thymus has two lobes.

The thymus is another organ in the immune system. It is located in the upper chest. The thymus produces T cells. These are a special type of white blood cell. The thymus is active only until puberty. It has produced all the T cells a person needs at this point. After puberty, the thymus stops producing T cells. It begins to shrink. It is one of the few organs in the body that is larger in children than adults. Over time the thymus is replaced with fatty tissue.

INNATE IMMUNITY

White blood cells protect the body from disease. Some white blood cells are produced in bone marrow. Bone marrow is found in the inner region of some bones. Some types of white blood cells only live for a short time. Because of this, bone marrow constantly produces new white blood cells. This keeps the body prepared to fight against disease. Other white blood cells are produced in the thymus and spleen. A person produces nearly 100 billion white blood cells every day.

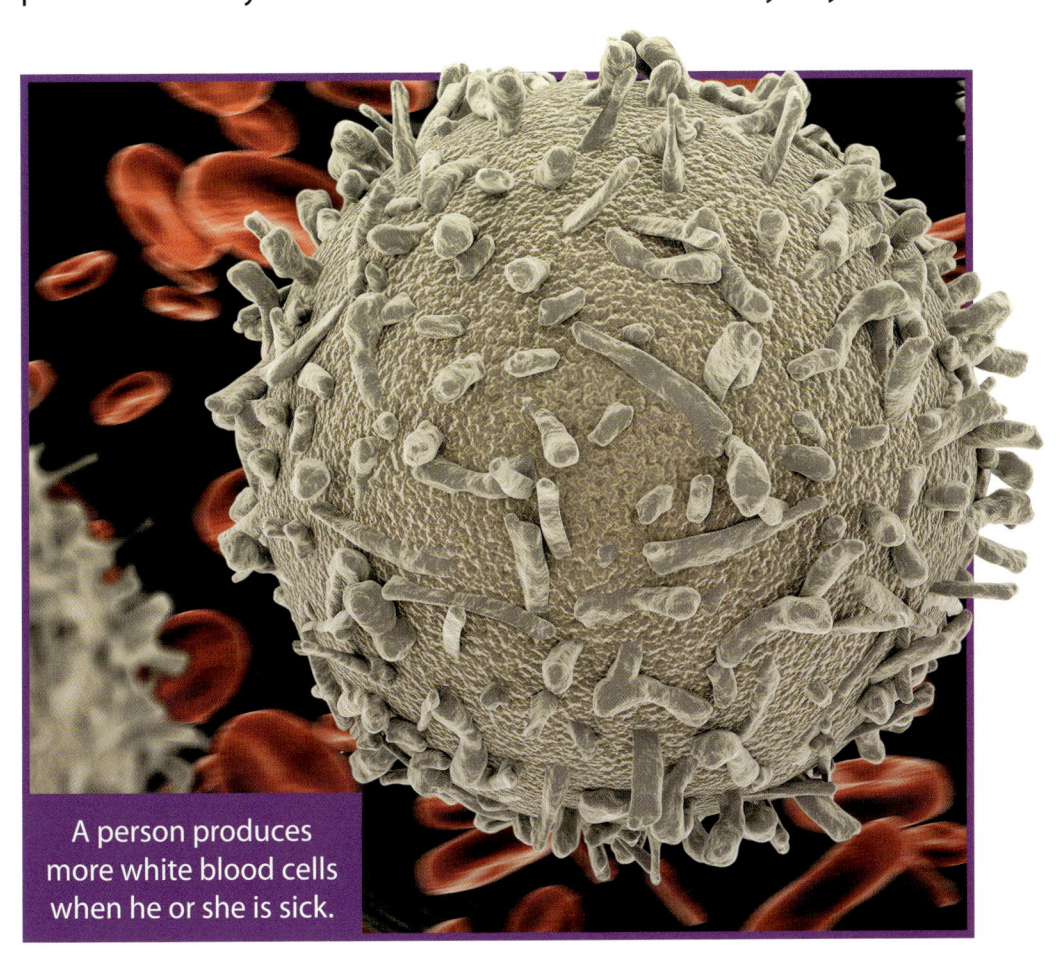

A person produces more white blood cells when he or she is sick.

White blood cells travel through the bloodstream. They destroy pathogens. They locate infections. They alert more white blood cells if there is an infection. They work together to stop the infection from spreading.

The body has many types of white blood cells. Some types of white blood cells are parts of the innate immune system. This is the immunity a person is born with. White blood cells that form innate immunity respond to any type of foreign material.

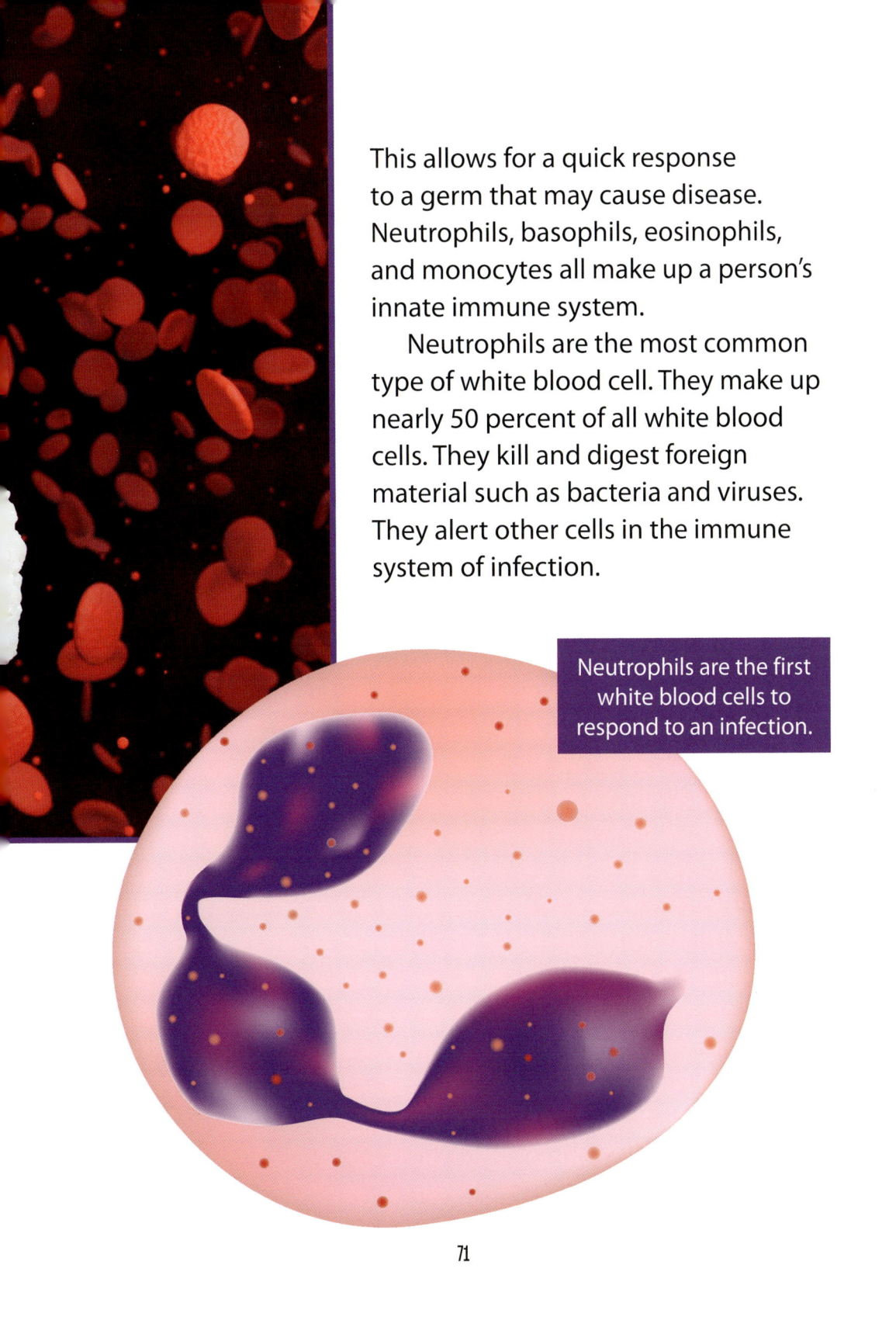

This allows for a quick response to a germ that may cause disease. Neutrophils, basophils, eosinophils, and monocytes all make up a person's innate immune system.

Neutrophils are the most common type of white blood cell. They make up nearly 50 percent of all white blood cells. They kill and digest foreign material such as bacteria and viruses. They alert other cells in the immune system of infection.

Neutrophils are the first white blood cells to respond to an infection.

Basophils and eosinophils also respond to any type of germ. They stop the germ before it can infect the body. But these white blood cells may trigger an immune response to a harmless particle, such as pollen. This is called an allergic reaction. Basophils release a substance called histamine. This substance causes inflammation, or swelling. It widens capillaries, making it easier for white blood cells to access the infection site. But too much histamine can cause airways to swell shut.

Monocytes are another common type of white blood cell. They make

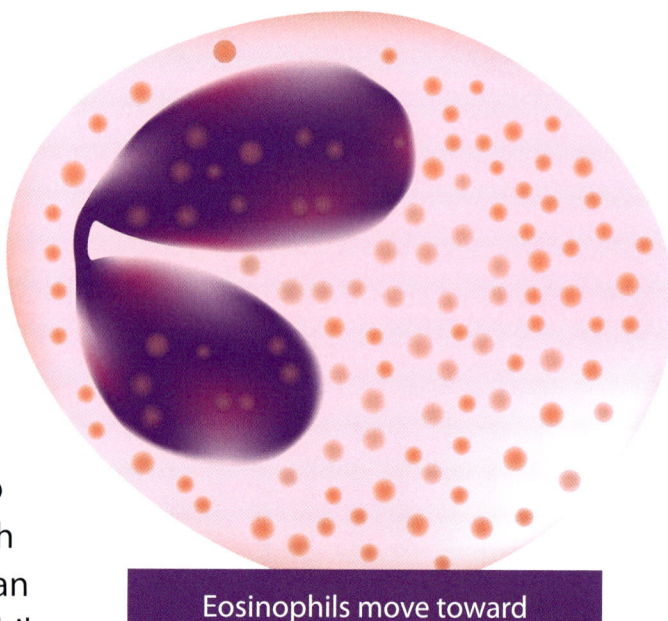

Eosinophils move toward swollen areas and destroy germs.

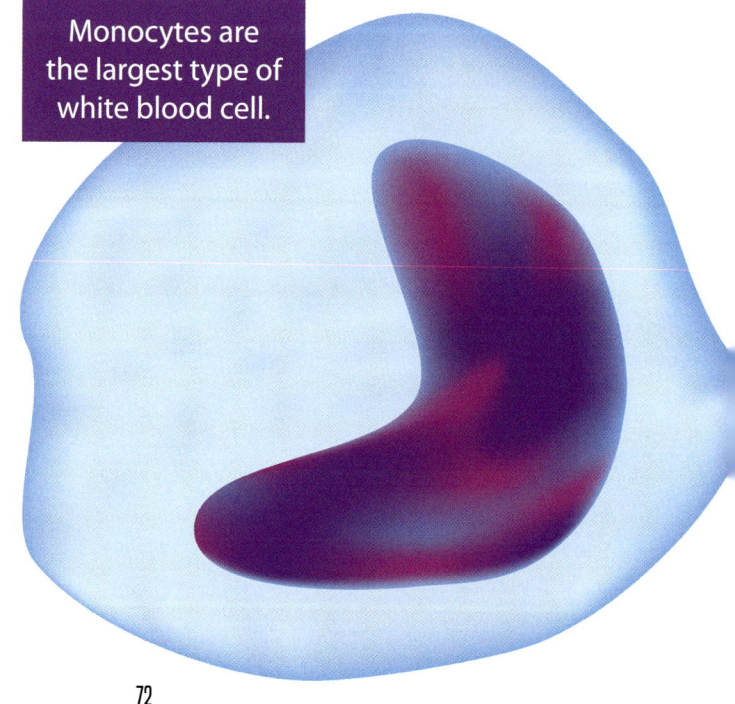

Monocytes are the largest type of white blood cell.

up approximately 12 percent of a person's white blood cell count. Monocytes destroy dead and damaged cells of the body. It is important to get rid of damaged cells. Damaged cells can cause cancer. A high monocyte count can be a sign of some types of cancer.

LEARNED IMMUNITY

The immune system continues to develop as a person grows older. It gets better at detecting and destroying pathogens. It recognizes pathogens that have previously entered the body. It is better able to fight against these pathogens when they enter the body again. This is called learned immunity.

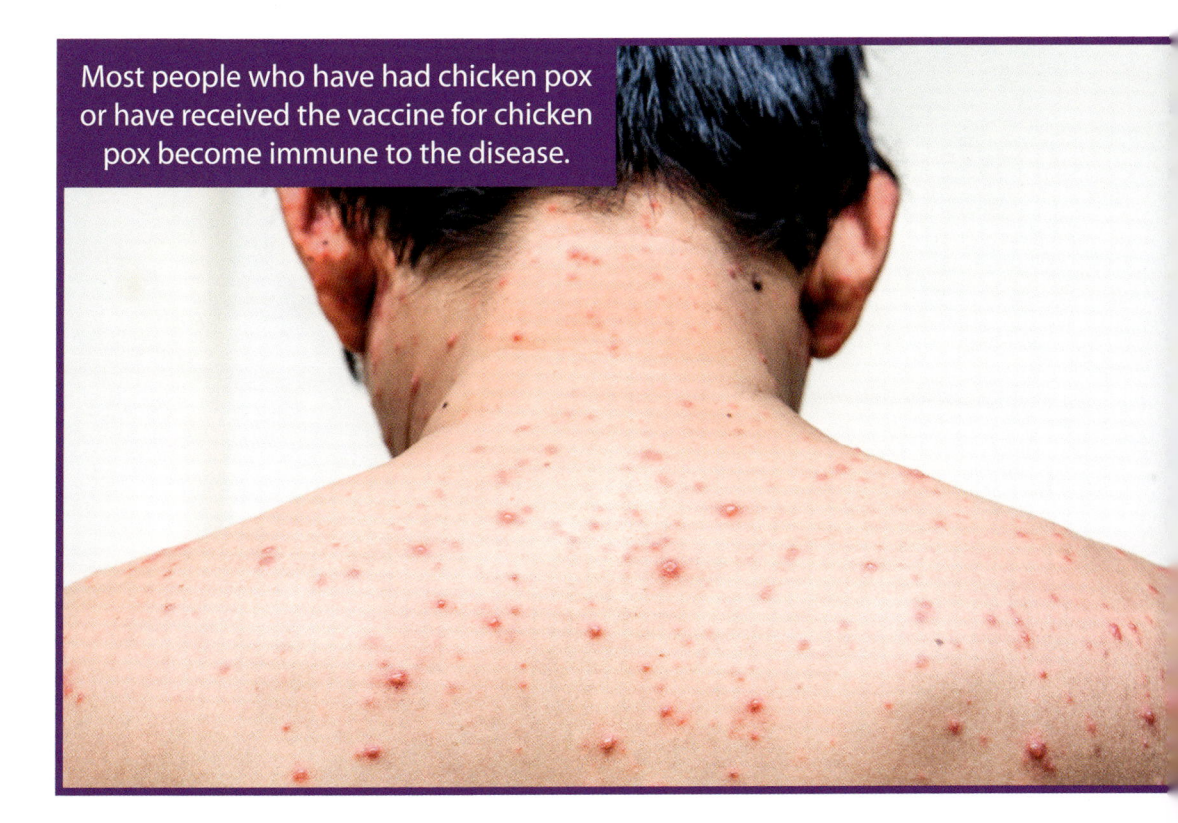

Most people who have had chicken pox or have received the vaccine for chicken pox become immune to the disease.

Certain white blood cells play a major role in learned immunity. They are B cells and T cells. Each type of bacterium and virus has a unique shape. B cells and T cells respond to the shape. These white blood cells fit together with the pathogen like puzzle pieces. If a B cell or T cell matches with the pathogen, it alerts the immune system.

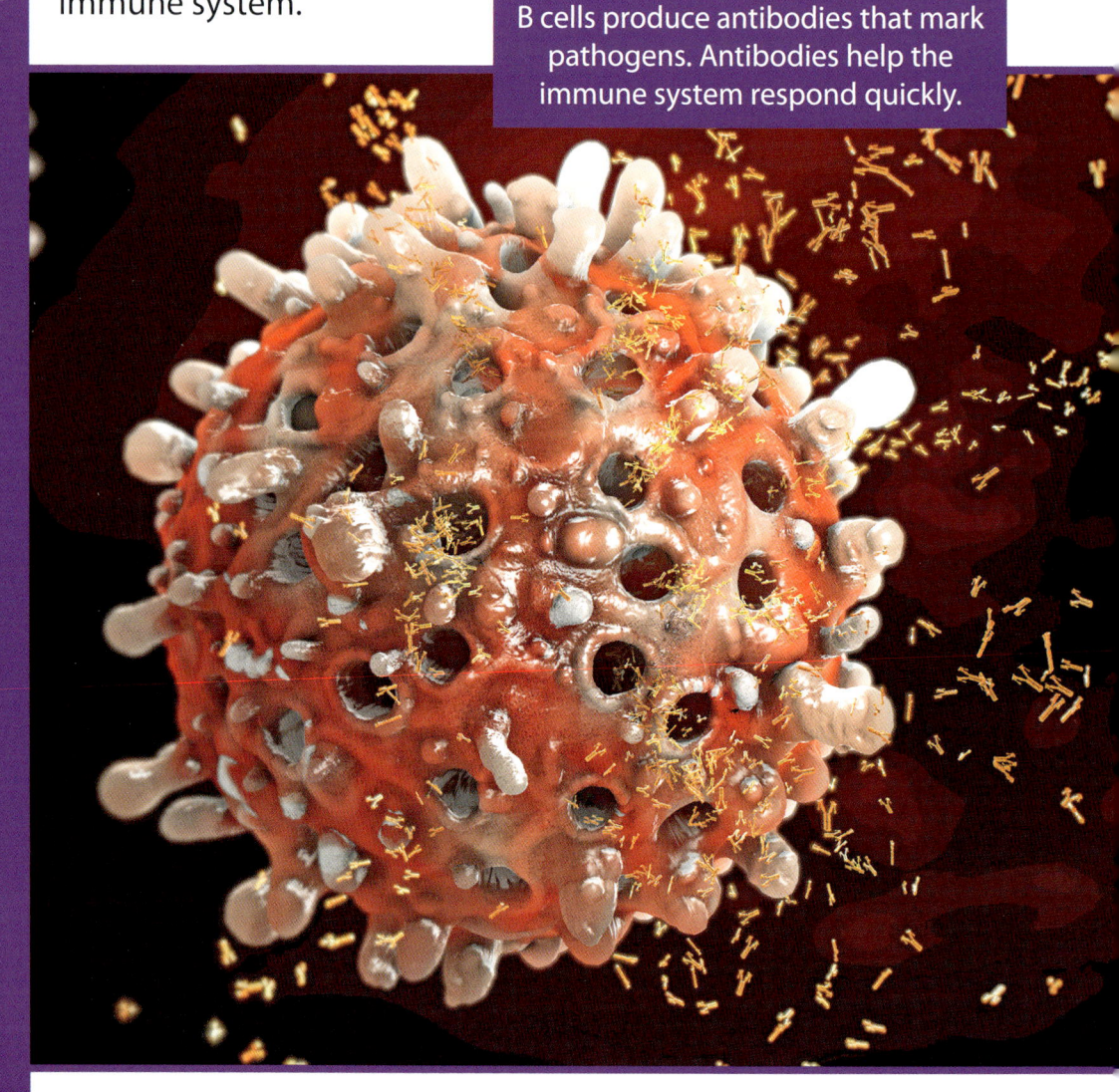

B cells produce antibodies that mark pathogens. Antibodies help the immune system respond quickly.

An antibody (green) responds to a specific pathogen (pink). A person may be able to produce 1 quintillion types of antibodies.

When a B cell matches with a pathogen, it begins to produce antibodies. Antibodies are small, *Y*-shaped proteins. They bind to a specific pathogen. B cells can make millions of types of antibodies. Each type responds to a single type of pathogen. Antibodies act as markers. They let the immune system know the pathogen should be destroyed. Binding to the pathogen may also keep it from spreading. B cells continue to produce large amounts of antibodies until the infection is stopped.

Sneezing into one's arm prevents germs from flying through the air.

Afterward, some B cells and antibodies remain in the bloodstream. They serve as memory cells. They are able to recognize the pathogen if it enters the body again. For example, a person produces antibodies to fight against the virus that causes COVID-19. The person still has these antibodies after he or she recovers. If he or she comes in contact with the virus again, antibodies recognize the virus. They help the immune system respond quickly. The illness will not be as severe.

Handwashing and good hygiene can help protect people from disease.

A cytotoxic T cell (left) releases chemicals to kill a cancer cell (right).

A newborn baby has some antibodies from his or her mother. But the baby loses these antibodies a few months after being born. This is why it is important for babies to receive vaccines. They cause the baby to produce his or her

78

own antibodies. These antibodies last for many years.

The learned immune system has two types of T cells. Helper T cells strengthen the immune response by increasing the production of white blood cells. There are also cytotoxic T cells. These cells release substances that kill a specific pathogen. They also destroy cells that are infected with that pathogen.

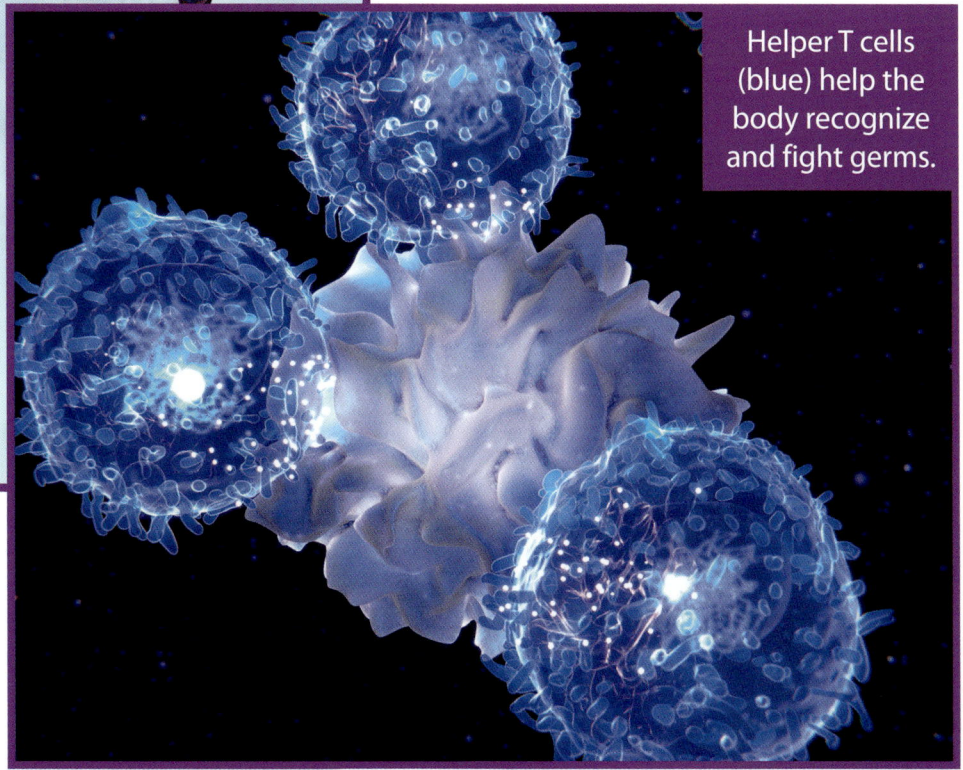

Helper T cells (blue) help the body recognize and fight germs.

THE MUSCULAR SYSTEM

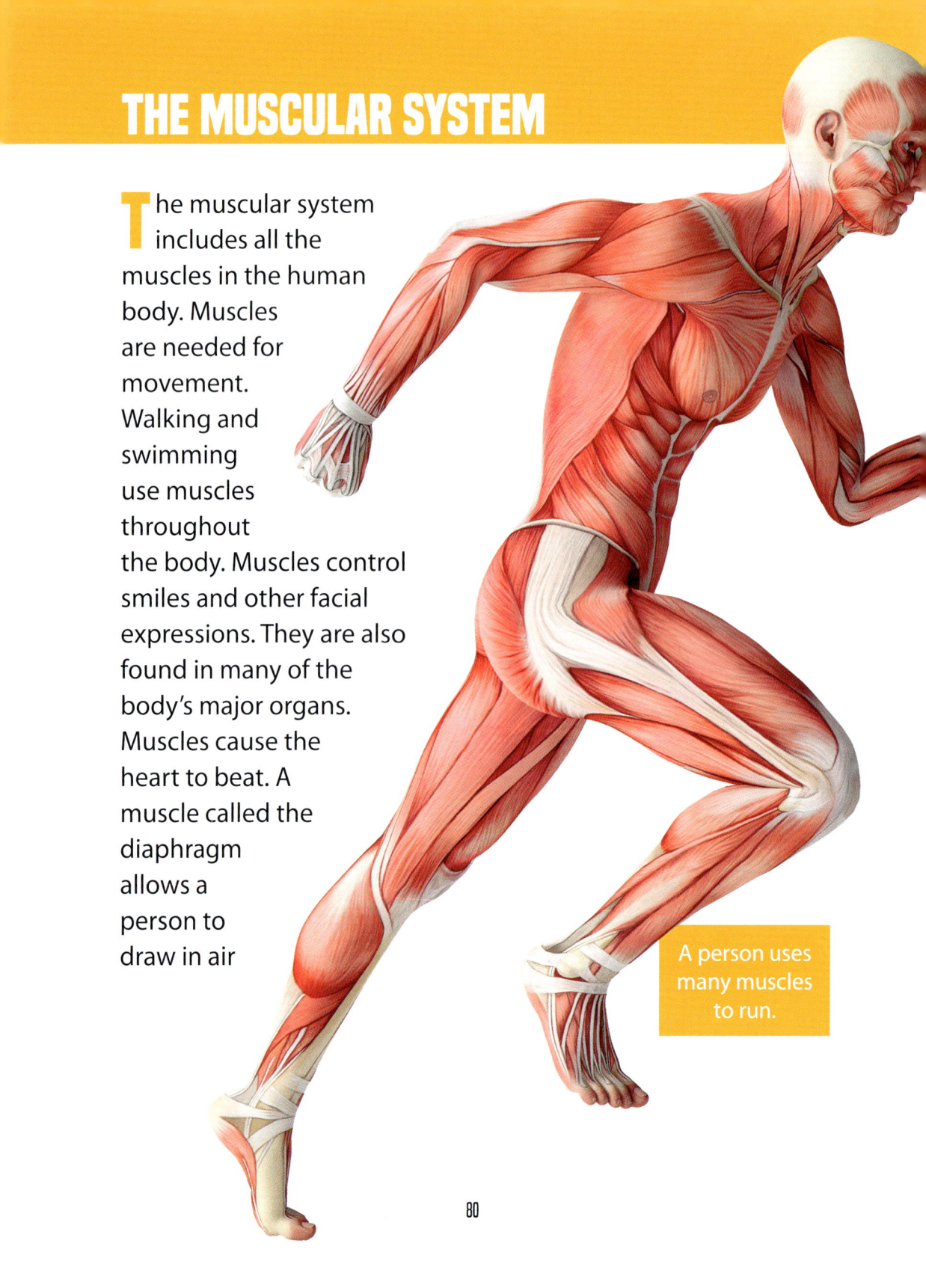

The muscular system includes all the muscles in the human body. Muscles are needed for movement. Walking and swimming use muscles throughout the body. Muscles control smiles and other facial expressions. They are also found in many of the body's major organs. Muscles cause the heart to beat. A muscle called the diaphragm allows a person to draw in air

A person uses many muscles to run.

to breathe. Muscles in the digestive system move food through the digestive tract. Without muscles, people could not survive.

The human body has more than 600 muscles. They come in different shapes and sizes. The gluteus maximus is the largest muscle. It is located in the buttocks. This muscle helps move the legs and hips. It's used to stand, squat, and walk. The smallest muscle is located in the inner ear. It is less than 0.04 inches (0.1 cm) in length. It provides stability to tiny bones in the ear that help a person hear.

Muscles in the back help control a person's posture.

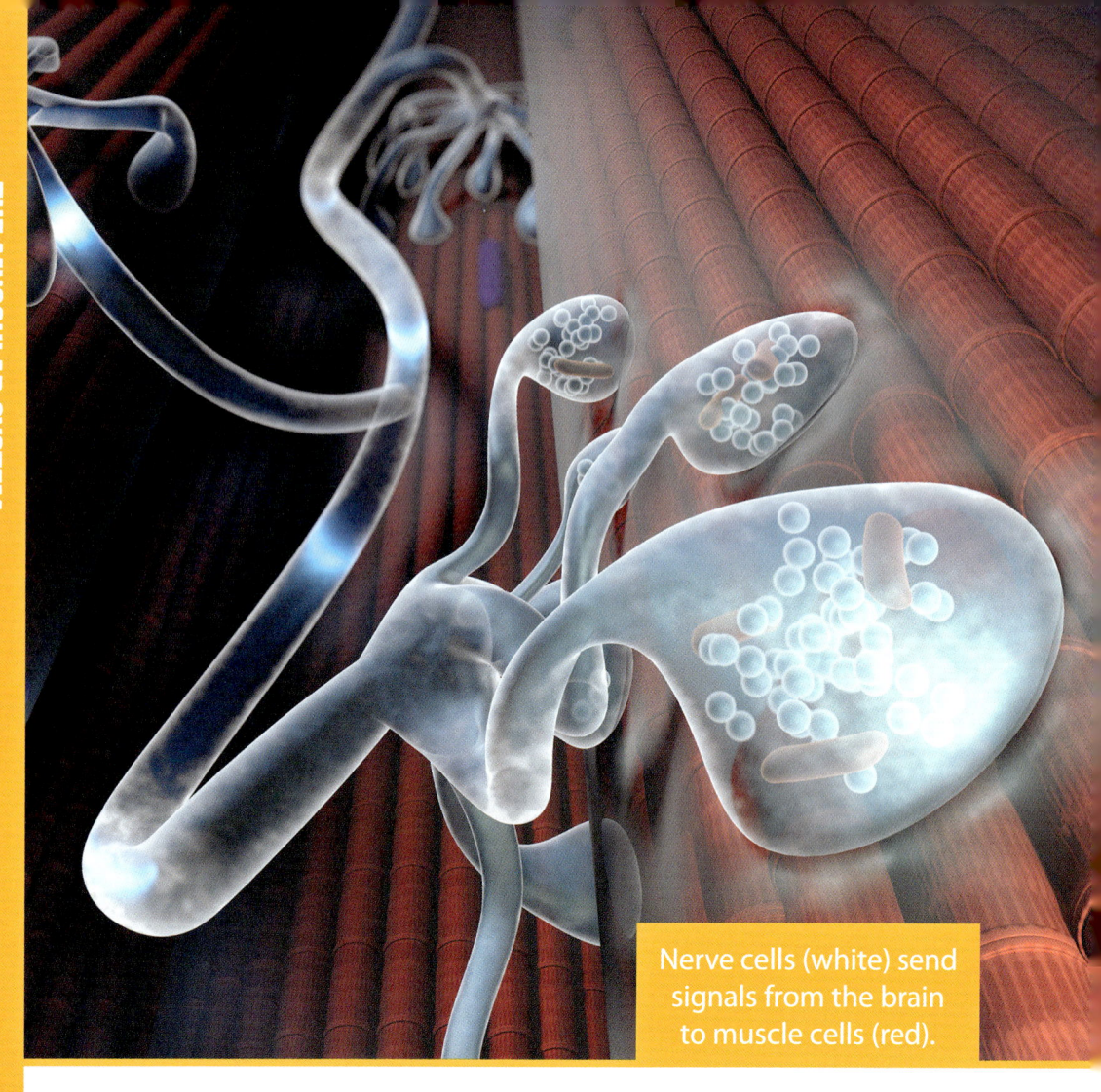

Nerve cells (white) send signals from the brain to muscle cells (red).

All muscles receive signals from the brain. The signals cause muscles to contract. When muscles contract, movement occurs.

Muscles belong to two main groups. They are voluntary muscles and involuntary muscles. People can consciously control voluntary muscles. These muscles move when people think about moving them. For example, a person can think about waving his or her hand. The brain sends signals to the arm and hand. Then the person can wave.

People cannot control involuntary muscles. Muscles in this grouping move without a person having to think about it. Involuntary muscles include those that cause the heart to beat. A person does not have to think about controlling the heart muscles. The brain sends signals automatically. These signals cause the heart muscles to contract.

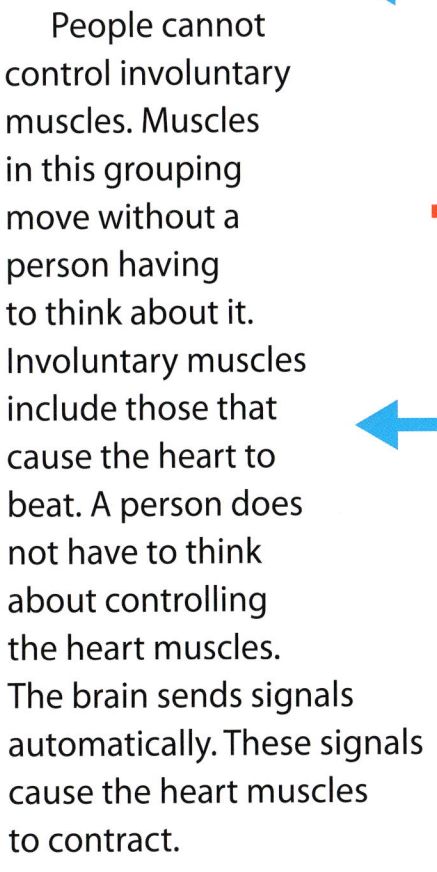

The esophagus is an example of an involuntary muscle. It contracts and relaxes without a person having to think about swallowing.

Muscles in the heart communicate through electrical signals. These signals can be measured using an electrocardiogram.

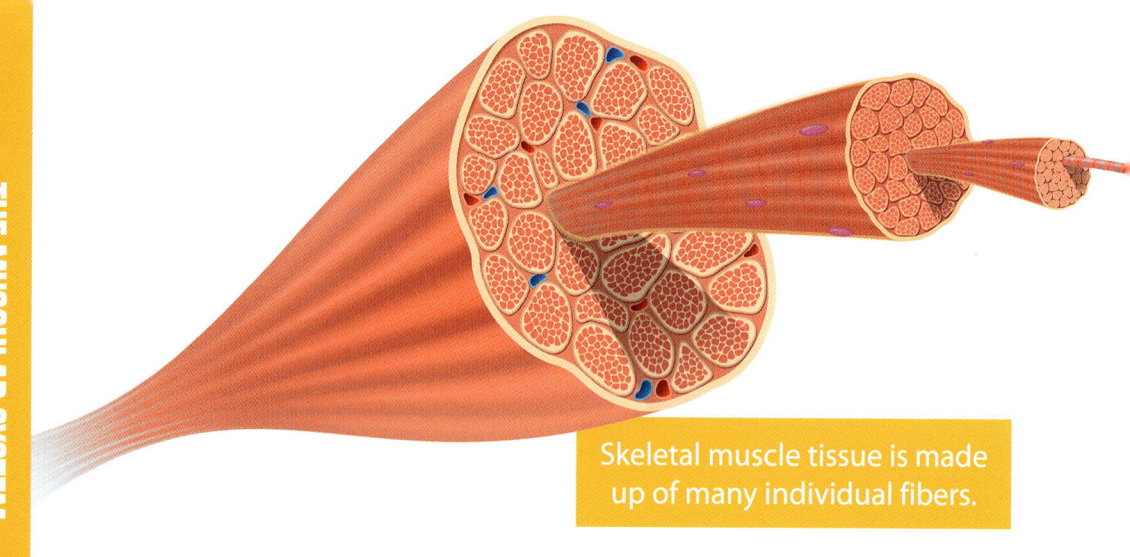

Skeletal muscle tissue is made up of many individual fibers.

TYPES OF MUSCLE CELLS

Muscles are made of muscle tissue. There are several types of these tissues. The type of tissue depends on the types of actions the muscle is used for. Skeletal muscle tissue makes up voluntary muscles. Smooth muscle tissue makes up many organs. Cardiac tissue makes up the heart.

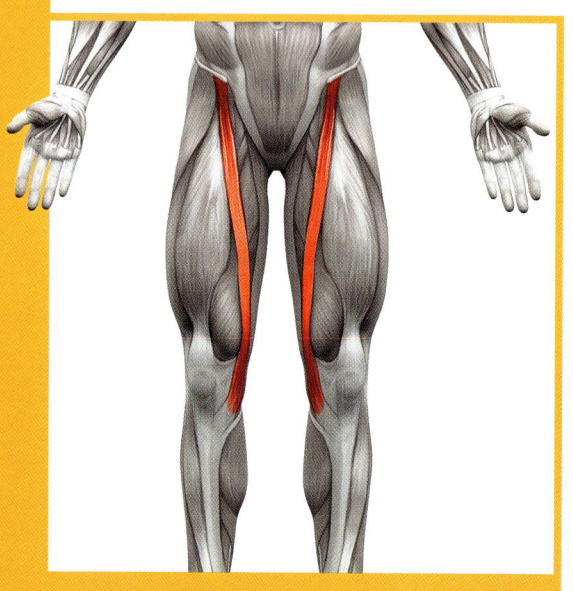

The sartorius muscle, which is located in the inner thigh, is the longest muscle in the human body.

Skeletal muscles make up about 40 percent of a person's weight. These muscles are located throughout the body. They help a person walk, talk, and do other actions. They also help maintain posture. Skeletal muscles in the back help a person stay upright while standing or sitting. Muscles in the jaw are some of strongest muscles in the human body. They can clamp down at a force of about 200 pounds (90 kg). Muscles in the eyes allow for fine movements. The eyes make approximately 240 small movements each minute. These movements help people see their surroundings and do tasks like reading.

Red muscle fibers appear red because they are rich in a protein called myoglobin.

Skeletal muscles are made of red and white fibers. That gives these muscles a striped appearance. The fibers are flexible and allow the muscles to contract.

Smooth muscles are involved with involuntary movements. They are called smooth muscles because they have a smooth appearance under a microscope. They are made of a thin layer of fibers.

Smooth muscles are located throughout the body. They help control many important functions. Smooth muscles in the intestines help food move through the digestive tract.

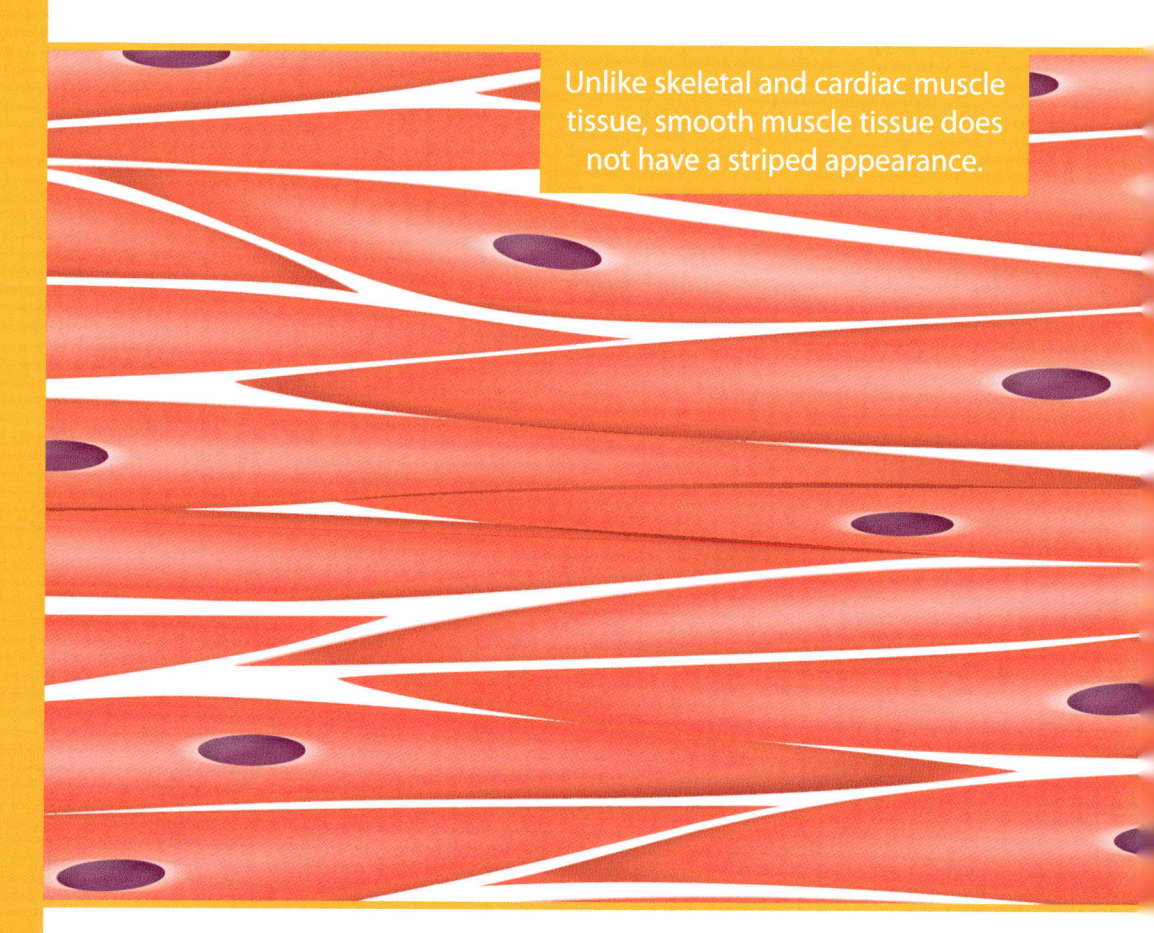

Unlike skeletal and cardiac muscle tissue, smooth muscle tissue does not have a striped appearance.

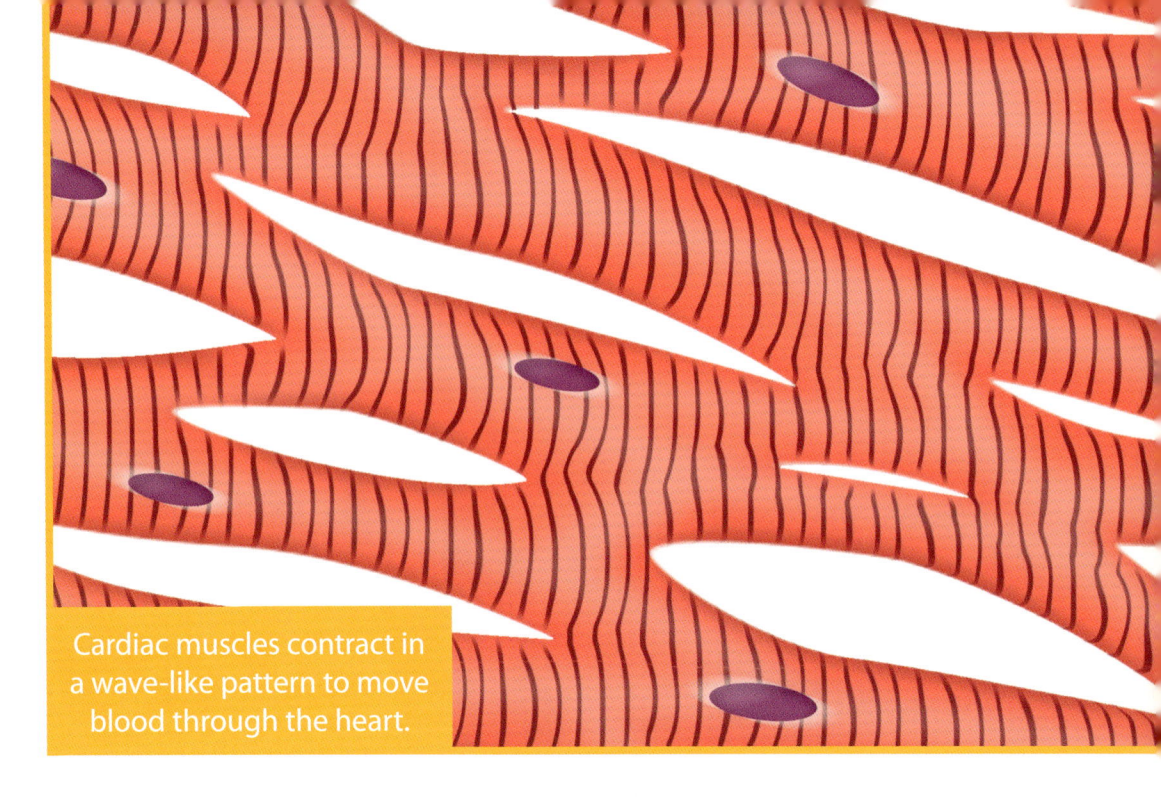

Cardiac muscles contract in a wave-like pattern to move blood through the heart.

Smooth muscles also line the blood vessels. They control the width of these vessels and affect blood flow. The iris is the colored part of the eye. It is made of two layers of smooth muscles. When the muscles contract or expand, they change the size of the pupil. They determine how much light is let into the eye. Smooth muscles under the skin contract when a person is cold. This creates goosebumps.

Cardiac muscles are another type of involuntary muscle. They are found only in the heart. Like skeletal muscles, they have a striped appearance. Signals from the brain cause the cardiac muscles to contract. But the heart also has pacemaker cells. These cells send a cascade of electrical signals throughout the heart. This produces a heartbeat. Pacemaker cells allow the heart to beat without input from the brain. They regulate themselves. Even if the heart is removed from the chest, cardiac muscles can remain active for a short period of time.

TENDONS

Tendons are part of the muscular system. They are thick connective tissue. They attach muscles to bones. Tendons make sure bones move together with the muscle. They also help reduce the shock of sharp movements. They absorb some of the

The Achilles tendon helps control movement of the foot.

Individual tendon fibers can be seen under a microscope.

stress caused by running and jumping.

Tendons come in many shapes and sizes. A tendon in the inner ear is only about 0.07 inches (0.2 cm) long. The Achilles tendon is located at the back of the ankle. It connects the heel bone to the calf muscles in the lower leg. This tendon is the longest in the human body. In adults, the tendon is about 6 inches (15 cm) long. This tendon is also incredibly strong. It can withstand around 1,100 pounds (500 kg) of force.

Tendons are made of a protein called collagen. This protein is tough and flexible. But injuries to tendons can still occur. These injuries can take a long time to heal. Tendons do not receive a lot of blood flow. This means they do not get nutrients in the blood that help injuries heal. People must also keep the injured area still. Movement and pressure can cause additional strain to the tendon.

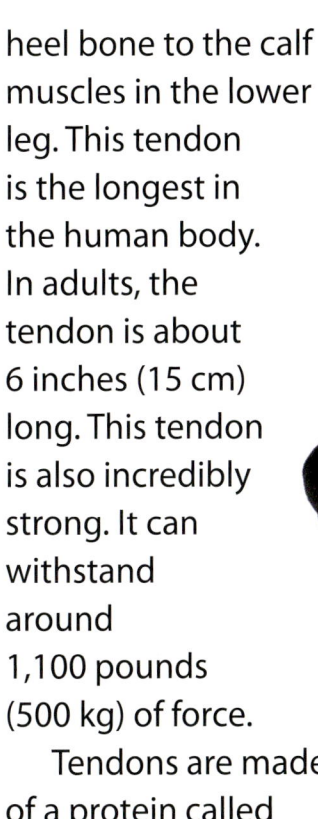

A muscle or tendon injury is called a strain.

Muscles must work together for smooth movement.

HOW MUSCLES WORK

Skeletal muscles work in pairs. Muscles can only produce a force in one direction. When a muscle contracts, it pulls on the bone it is attached to. But it cannot push the bone back. Another muscle must pull back on the bone to move it to the original position. Muscles that work together like this are called antagonistic pairs. As one muscle in the pair contracts, the other relaxes. These pairings can be seen throughout the body.

The biceps and triceps are examples of an antagonistic pair. Tendons attach these muscles to bones in the arm. The biceps is at the front of the upper arm. The triceps is at the back. These muscles work together to bend and straighten the elbow. When the

When the arm is straight, the biceps is relaxed.

biceps contracts, the triceps relaxes. This causes the elbow to bend. When the biceps relaxes, the triceps begins to contract. This straightens the arm.

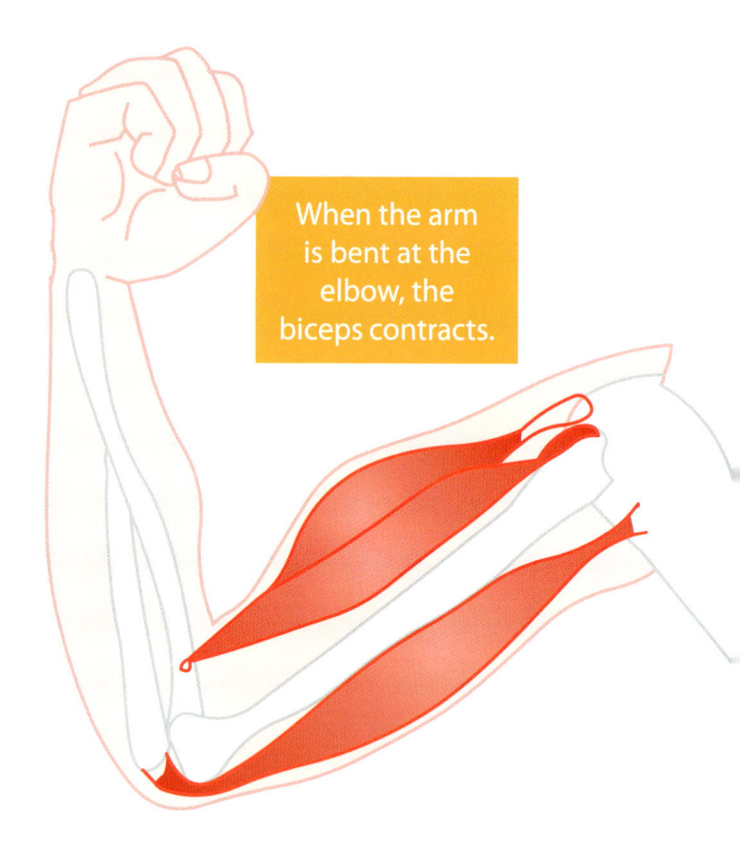

When the arm is bent at the elbow, the biceps contracts.

Antagonistic pairs are also seen in the legs. Large muscles are located in the front and back of the upper thigh. The quadriceps are at the front of the leg. The hamstrings are at the back. They work together to bend and straighten the knee. When one of the muscles is contracted, the other is relaxed.

MUSCLES AND EXERCISE

Like all cells in the body, muscles require oxygen to function. Oxygen is necessary to produce energy. When exercising, muscles require a lot of oxygen and energy. This is why people breathe harder while exercising. The body takes in more oxygen to be delivered to the muscles in use. The heart also beats more rapidly. It pumps blood quickly, allowing oxygen and nutrients to be delivered to the muscles. As muscles use up energy, they produce carbon dioxide as a waste product. People then exhale carbon dioxide while breathing.

Muscles use up oxygen quickly during exercise, which can cause someone to feel out of breath.

Swimming is a low-impact aerobic exercise. It puts little stress on the joints.

Aerobic exercise is exercise in which muscles receive a constant supply of oxygen. It strengthens muscles in the heart. It improves blood circulation and lowers the risk of certain diseases. Doctors recommend about 30 minutes of aerobic exercise every day. This keeps the heart healthy. Aerobic activity includes walking, swimming, and cycling. During aerobic activity, people are able to hold a conversation without feeling out of breath. They can perform these activities for extended periods of time.

Though oxygen is required for muscles to work, they are able to function for a short time without oxygen. Instead of

using oxygen for fuel, muscles burn fat. This occurs during anaerobic exercise. People burn more calories with this type of exercise. But they are unable to perform these exercises for long periods of time. The muscles become tired. Anaerobic exercises include weightlifting and sprinting.

Muscles create a sudden burst of speed while a person sprints.

When muscles do not have enough oxygen, they produce lactic acid. High intensity workouts cause muscles to feel sore while working out. This is because of the buildup of lactic acid. This soreness is a signal to lower the intensity of the workout. It goes away as more oxygen is supplied to the muscles. As the body becomes stronger, lactic acid does not build up as quickly. People are able to continue doing anaerobic activities for longer periods of time.

Muscles may cramp when they are tired or if a person is dehydrated.

Stretching after exercise is important. It keeps muscles healthy and flexible.

Muscles may feel sore for a few days after intense exercise. This is not caused by lactic acid. Exercise creates microscopic tears in the muscles. Muscles become stronger as they repair themselves. They become larger and more toned. They are better able to handle more intense exercise.

THE NERVOUS SYSTEM

The nervous system includes the brain, spinal cord, and nerves. The brain sits on top of the spinal cord. The spinal cord branches into hundreds of nerves. These nerves connect to all parts of the body, such as the muscles, heart, and other organs.

The nervous system is the control center of the human body. It is connected to all other body systems. The brain produces electrical signals. The spinal cord and nerves act as a highway system. They carry the signals to other parts of the body. The signals tell the body what to do. The brain

Billions of nerve cells make up the nervous system.

controls many bodily processes. It controls heart rate and breathing. It sends signals to the digestive system. The brain sends signals that cause muscles to move. It also processes sensory information, such as sight and hearing. The brain is in charge of memory, emotion, and thinking.

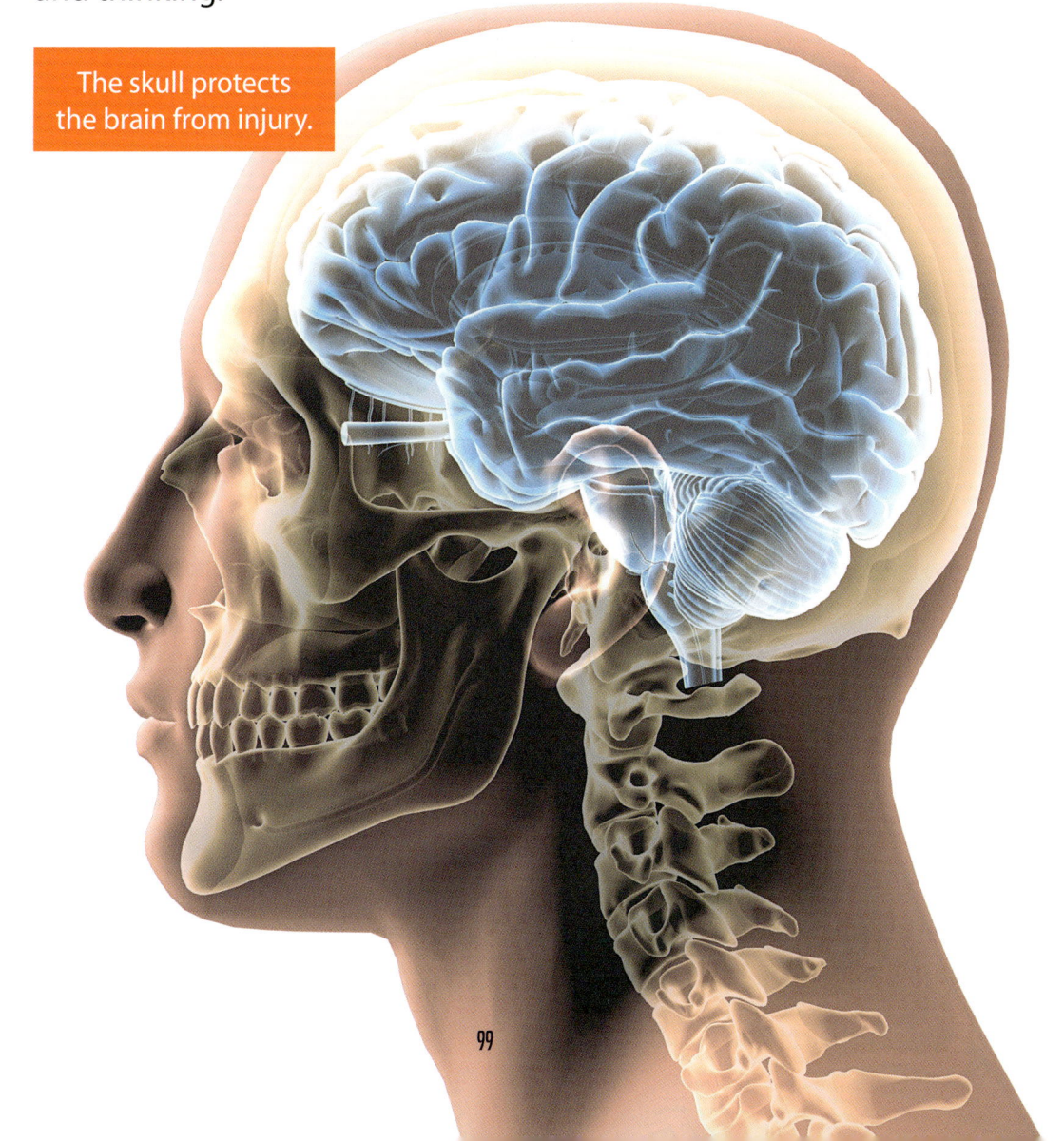

The skull protects the brain from injury.

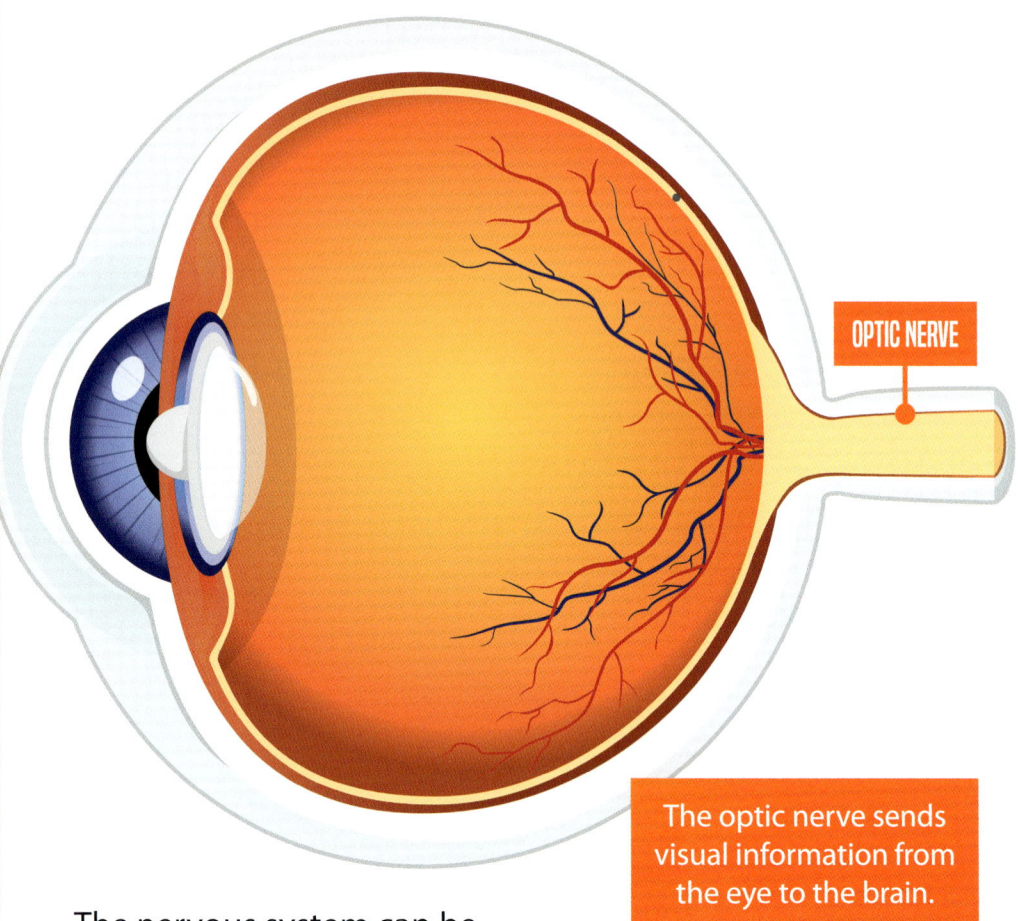

OPTIC NERVE

The optic nerve sends visual information from the eye to the brain.

The nervous system can be divided into two main parts: the central nervous system and the peripheral nervous system. The central nervous system includes the brain and the spinal cord. The peripheral nervous system includes all other nerves in the body. The peripheral nervous system can be divided even further. The somatic nervous system includes nerves related to movement. These nerves are connected to muscles that people can control by thinking. The somatic nervous system allows people to move their arms and legs. The autonomic nervous system includes nerves that control automatic processes. These nerves regulate digestion and heartbeat. People do not have to think about these actions.

NEURONS

The nervous system is made of nerve cells, which are called neurons. Neurons may be linked to other neurons. They may also be linked to a muscle or a gland. The body has billions of neurons.

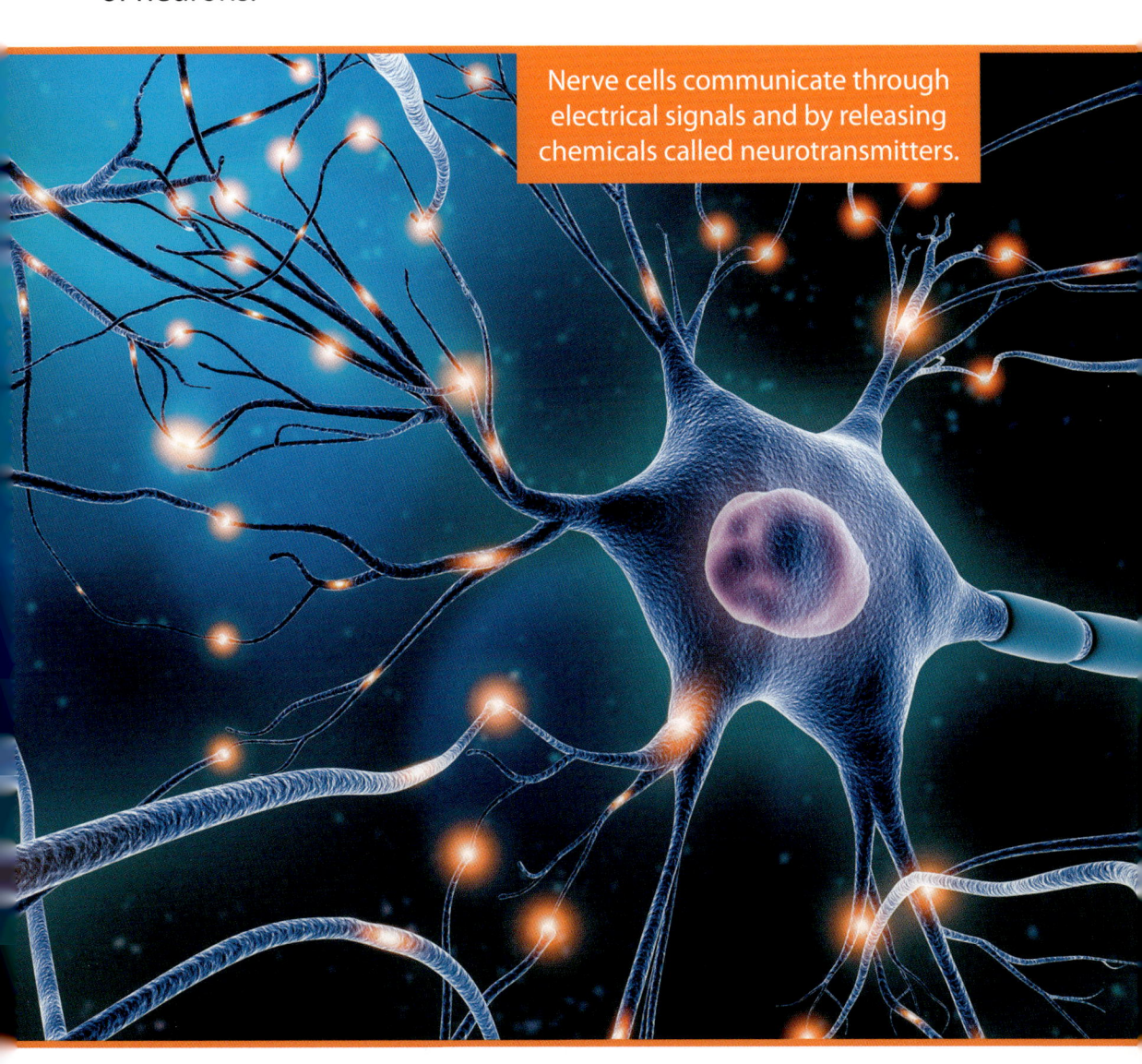

Nerve cells communicate through electrical signals and by releasing chemicals called neurotransmitters.

Most neurons have a similar basic structure. They have a rounded cell body with many branches. These branches are called dendrites. The cell body has another long branch called the axon.

Neurons send messages in the brain. They also send signals to the rest of the body. The signal from the brain first reaches the dendrites. Dendrites connect to other neurons. Signals pass from one neuron to the dendrite of another. The signal continues through the cell body. Then it travels along the axon. The signal transfers from the axon to the dendrites of the next neuron.

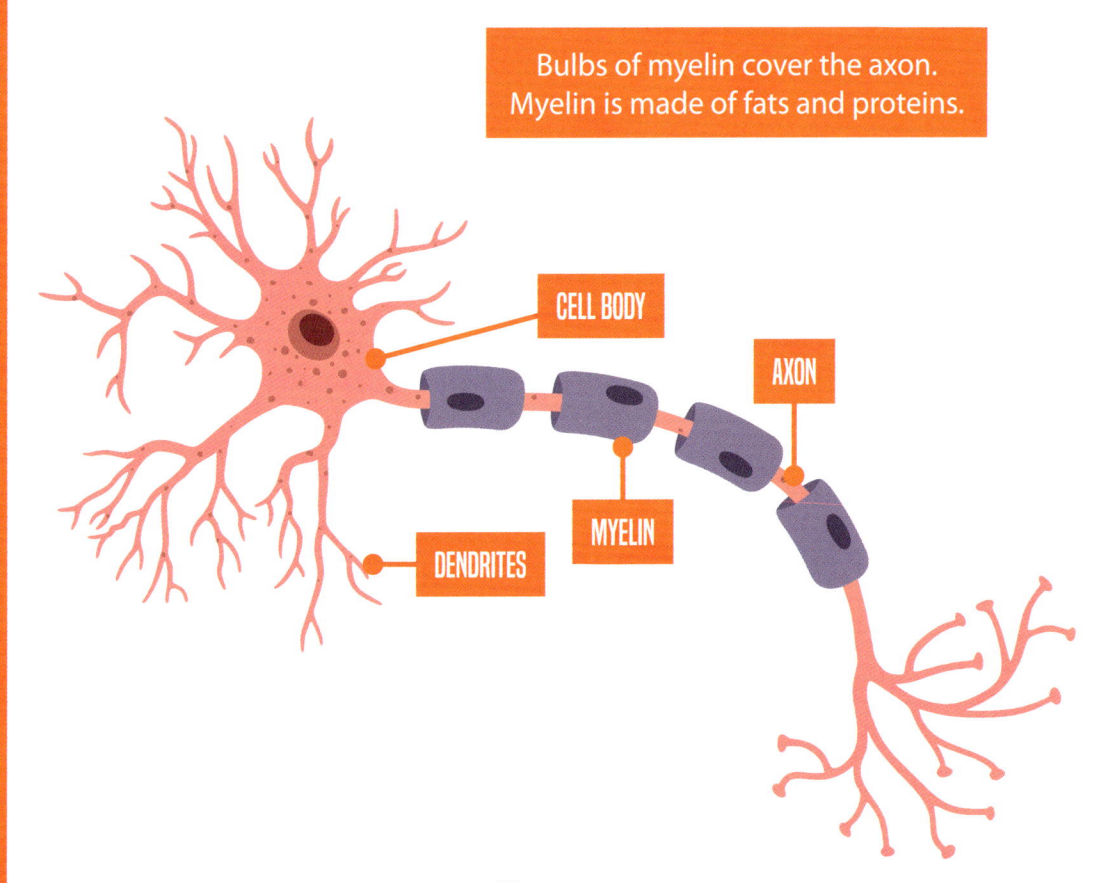

Bulbs of myelin cover the axon. Myelin is made of fats and proteins.

CELL BODY

AXON

MYELIN

DENDRITES

Neurons come close to each other but do not touch. The gap between neurons is called the synapse.

Signals from the brain travel quickly throughout the nervous system. They can travel as fast as 395 feet per second (120 m/s). Bulbs of fat and protein on the axon make this fast speed possible. Electrical signals skip over these bulbs. This allows the signal to move quickly along the axon.

There are three main types of neurons. The first are sensory neurons. They allow people to see, hear, smell, taste, and sense touch. Sensory neurons pick up information from the environment. They send information to be processed in the brain.

The hands have many sensory neurons dedicated to touch. These neurons send information about pressure, temperature, vibration, and more.

Motor neurons are the second type of neuron. They respond to signals from the central nervous system. They connect the central nervous system to muscles. Motor neurons are involved with movement. Some motor neurons control voluntary movement. Other motor neurons control automatic processes.

Interneurons are the third type of neuron. They are located only in the central nervous system. Sensory neurons send information to the brain to be processed. Interneurons form a pathway between sensory neurons and motor neurons. They help the body react quickly and smoothly to sensory information. Interneurons send sensory information to the brain, which processes the information. The brain then sends a signal through motor neurons to cause movement.

Interneurons in the spinal cord play an important role in keeping the body safe. Without these interneurons, information from the sensory neurons would have to travel all the way to the brain to be processed. Interneurons in the spinal cord act like a shortcut. They can relay sensory information directly to motor neurons. They do not need input from the brain. This allows for a fast reaction called a reflex.

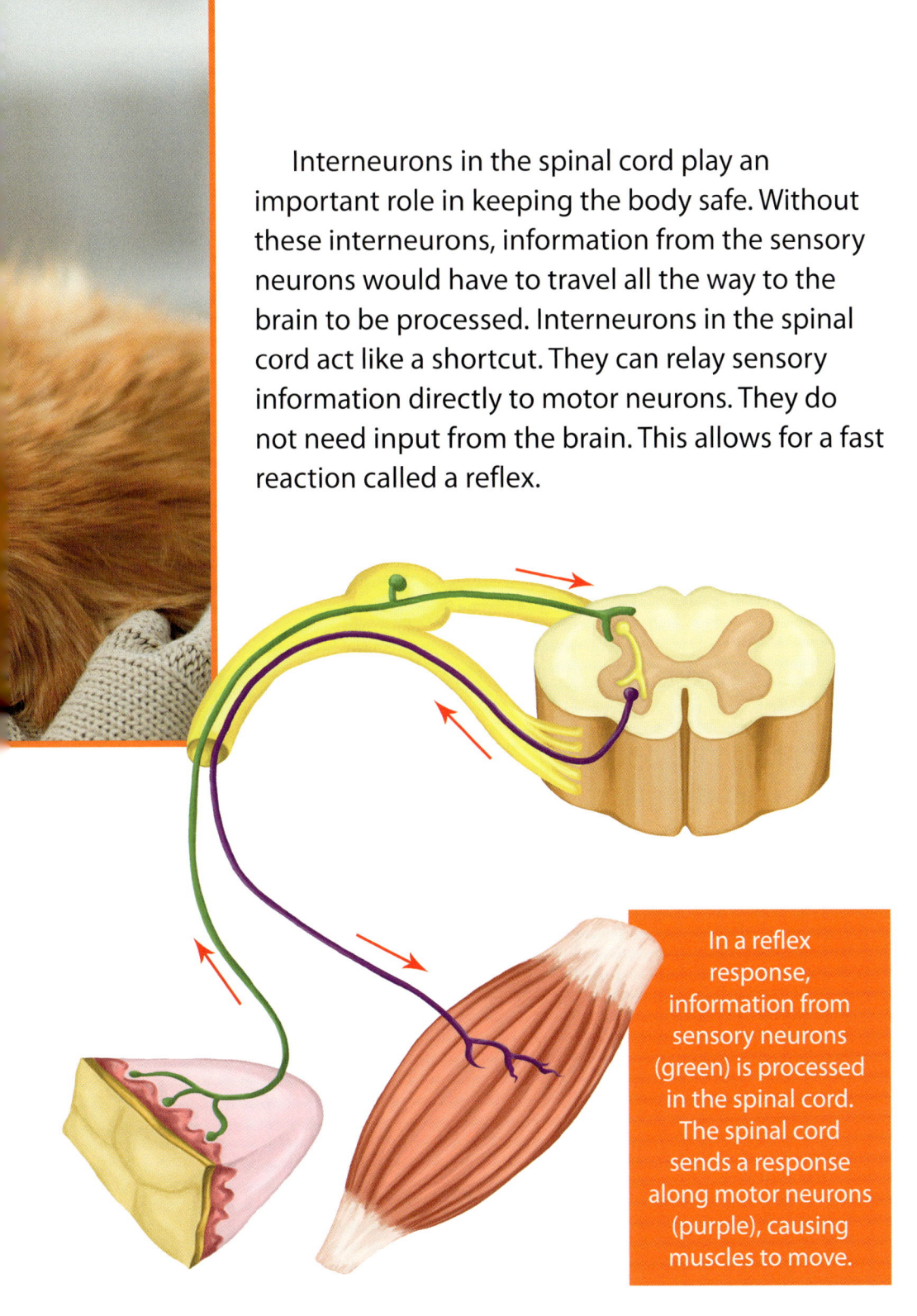

In a reflex response, information from sensory neurons (green) is processed in the spinal cord. The spinal cord sends a response along motor neurons (purple), causing muscles to move.

For example, touching a hot stove triggers a reflex response. Sensory neurons sense the extreme temperature. They send a message to the brain. Some of this information is sent to interneurons. Interneurons quickly get motor neurons in the hand to respond. They tell motor neurons to pull the hand away from the stove. This action occurs even before the brain processes the heat. The person moves his or her hand away before feeling pain.

Striking part of the knee triggers a reflex. The leg automatically kicks out.

THE BRAIN

The brain is the main organ in the nervous system. It sends signals that control many bodily processes. It directs the lungs to breathe. It controls digestion, hormone release, movement, and much more. The brain is also the center of thought and emotion.

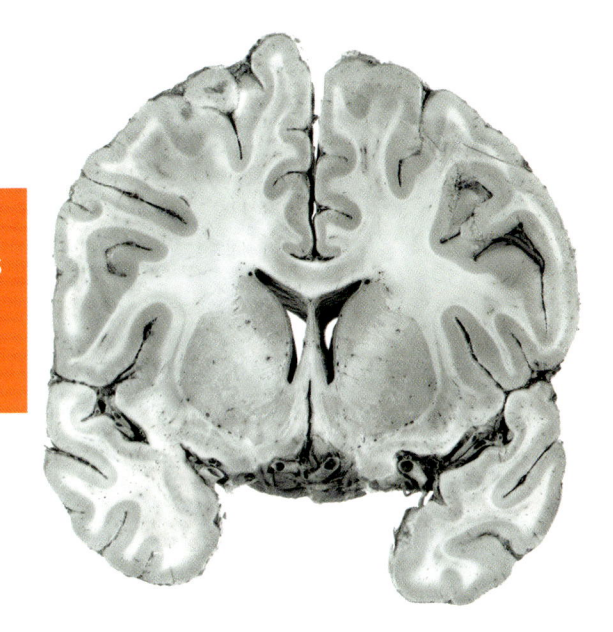

The average adult brain weighs approximately 3 pounds (1.4 kg). It is about the size of two fists. The brain has billions of neurons. New neurons grow and connect to each other as a person develops. When a person learns something, these connections become stronger.

The brain can be divided into three main regions. The first is the brain stem. This is the stalk at the bottom of the brain. It connects to the spinal cord. The brain stem controls many of the body's automatic processes. It regulates breathing and heart rate. It monitors blood pressure. A person does not have to think about these behaviors. The brain stem is also responsible for swallowing and sleeping.

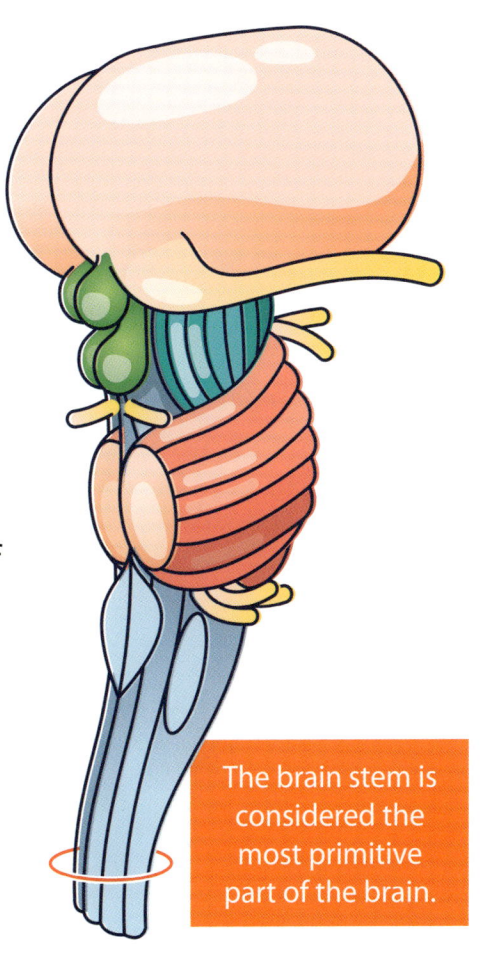

The brain stem is considered the most primitive part of the brain.

The inside of the cerebellum is made of white matter.

The cerebellum is another brain region. It is located near the back and base of the brain. The cerebellum plays a major role in coordination and movement. It helps a person keep his or her balance. It controls eye movement. It also makes sure that movements throughout the body are smooth. Muscles need to work together in order for people to walk and speak. People who have problems with their cerebellums have jerky movements. Certain actions can be difficult for them.

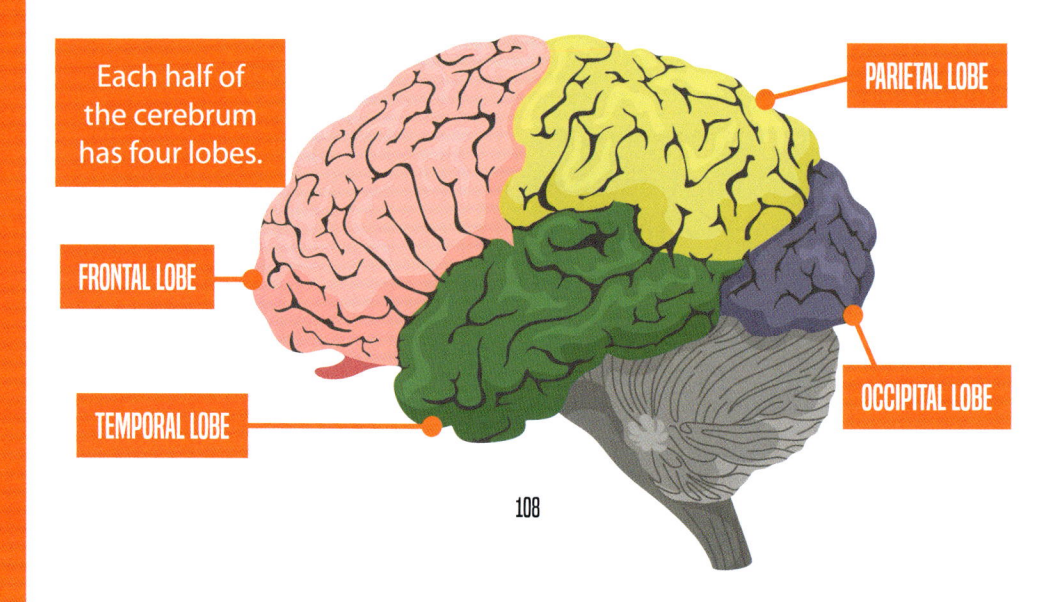

Each half of the cerebrum has four lobes.

PARIETAL LOBE

FRONTAL LOBE

OCCIPITAL LOBE

TEMPORAL LOBE

108

The cerebrum is the largest region of the brain. It is covered in wrinkles and folds. This gives the brain a large surface area. If flattened, the cerebrum would be larger than a page of a newspaper. The large surface area gives space for new neurons to form.

The cerebrum has two hemispheres, or halves. A large fissure divides the left and right sides of the brain. A cord of nerve fibers connects the halves deep within the brain. These fibers allow signals to cross from one side of the brain to the other. The right hemisphere controls the left side of the body. The left hemisphere controls the right side of the body.

CORPUS CALLOSUM

The corpus callosum is the band of nerve fibers that connects the left and right hemispheres.

The cerebrum has many responsibilities. These responsibilities are divided among different regions of the cerebrum, which are called lobes. The lobes relay information to each other. The cerebrum has four lobes on each hemisphere. The frontal lobe is the largest. As its name suggests, it is located at the front of the brain. This brain region influences personality. It plays a role in decision-making and attention. Part of the frontal lobe plays a role in planning movement. It sends signals to the cerebellum to help activate muscles throughout the body.

Part of the frontal lobe plays a role in a person's ability to speak.

The parietal lobe is located on the side of the brain. It is the sensory hub of the brain. It processes touch, sight, sound, taste, and smell. Some areas of the body are extremely sensitive. For example, the fingers can pick up details about texture. The back is not as sensitive. It is difficult for the back to sense texture. This is because the fingers have many more sensory neurons than the back. As a result, a large part of the parietal lobe is dedicated to sensory information from the fingers. The section that processes information from the back is much smaller. The parietal lobe also plays a role in spatial awareness. It allows a person to sense where his or her body is without looking at the body part.

This illustration shows approximately how the parietal cortex is divided. Larger parts of the parietal lobe are needed to process information from sensitive body parts, like the hands.

The temporal lobe can help with empathy and understanding other people's emotions.

The temporal lobe is located under the parietal lobe. It processes sound. The temporal lobe helps a person understand spoken language. It also processes music and other sounds. The temporal lobe plays a role in memory. It helps a person remember instructions. It also memorizes nonverbal information, such as melodies. A small portion of the temporal lobe is dedicated to processing faces. It groups facial features together into a single image. Damage to this part of the temporal lobe makes it difficult to recognize faces. A person may focus too much on a single part of the face. It is difficult to look at the face as a whole.

The occipital lobe is at the back of the brain. It processes all aspects of sight. The occipital lobe is responsible for color recognition. It tracks movement. It helps a person recognize forms and shapes. This allows a person to pick out an object from a background.

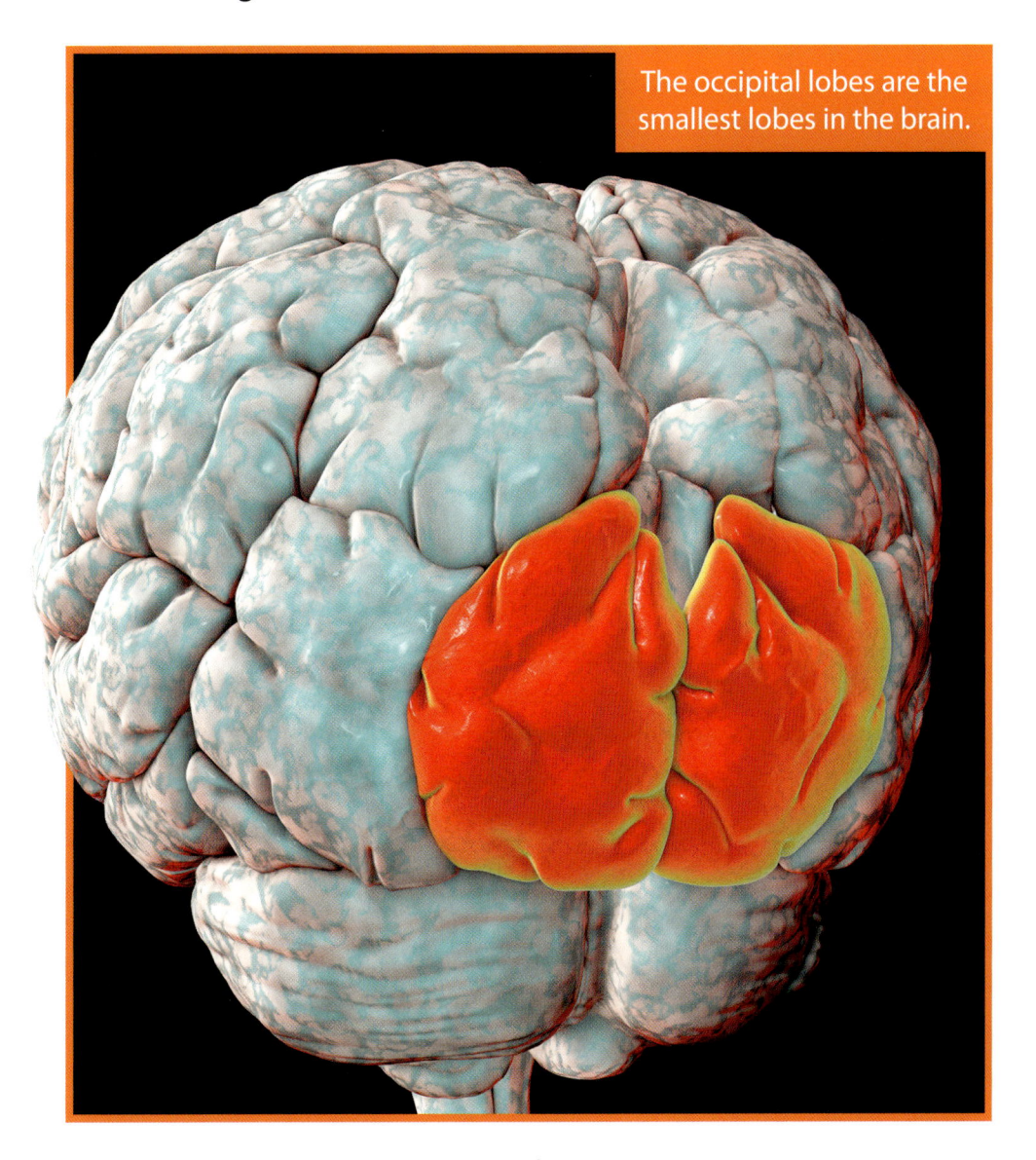

The occipital lobes are the smallest lobes in the brain.

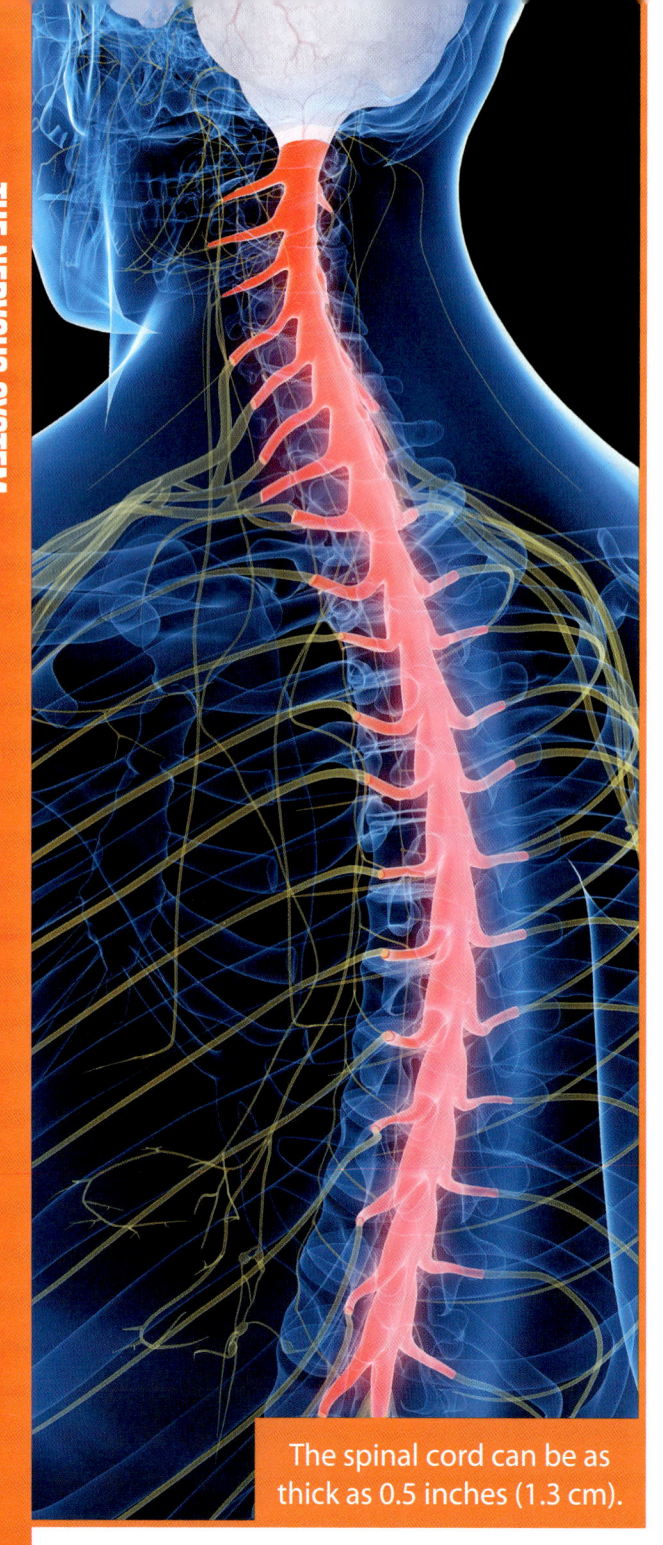

The spinal cord can be as thick as 0.5 inches (1.3 cm).

THE SPINAL CORD

The spinal cord is a rope-like structure that is made of neurons. It connects the brain with nerves in the peripheral nervous system. The spinal cord runs through a person's back. It is protected by bones that make up the spine. The brain sends information for movement through the spinal cord. The spinal cord passes sensory information back to the brain. The spinal cord also quickly processes reflexes that help people stay safe.

The spinal cord branches into 31 pairs of nerves that extend throughout the body. Nerves in the neck control head and neck movement. They also help people move their fingers and shoulders. Nerves in the chest and upper back control balance and posture. Nerves in the lower back are responsible for movement in the legs.

Damage to the spinal cord can affect a person's ability to sense touch. It can also cause paralysis, or make a person unable to move parts of the body. A spinal cord injury affects the function of the nerves at the site of the injury. It also affects all the nerves below the injury. Signals cannot travel past the injury site. For instance, a spinal cord injury at the neck affects the arms and legs.

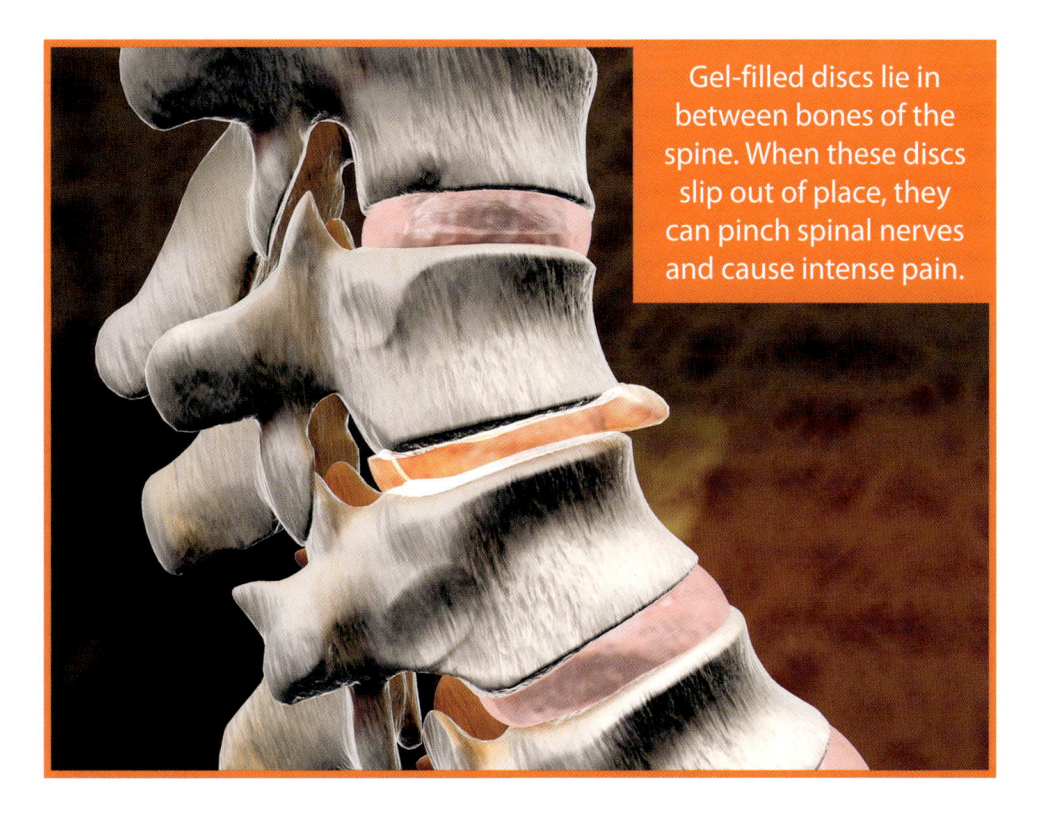

Gel-filled discs lie in between bones of the spine. When these discs slip out of place, they can pinch spinal nerves and cause intense pain.

THE REPRODUCTIVE SYSTEM

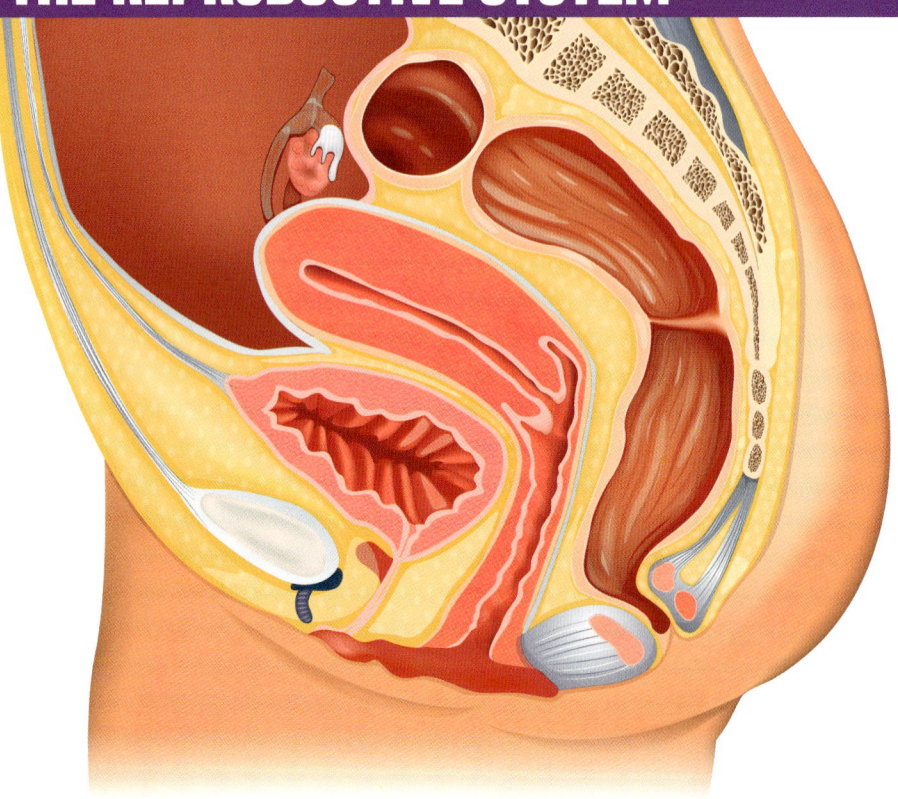

The reproductive system is responsible for producing children. It includes sex organs called the gonads. It also includes tissues and glands that play a role in reproduction. This is the only organ system that differs between males and females.

The gonads in both the male and female reproductive systems produce sex cells called gametes. The male gametes are called sperm. The female gametes are called egg cells. The gametes contain genes. These are the instructions that the cells use to make a person. They determine things like height and eye color. A male and female gamete combine in a process called

Gametes contain genetic information called DNA. DNA has a spiral shape.

fertilization. The genes mix together. After fertilization, it is possible that the combined gametes will result in the creation of a child. The developing child will have some genes from the mother and some genes from the father.

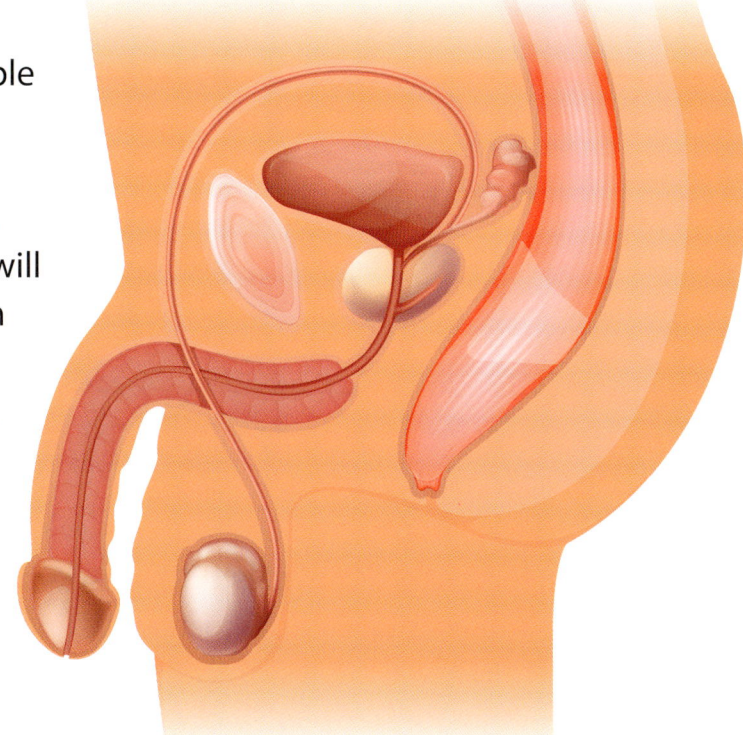

The male reproductive system has more noticeable external organs than the female reproductive system.

Reproduction is only possible after puberty. Puberty usually happens before the age of 16 in males. It begins slightly earlier in females. Most females reach puberty around 13 years of age. Bodies begin to change during puberty. This is caused by changing hormone levels. The gonads reach maturity. Males begin to grow facial hair. Their voices deepen. Females develop breasts and wider hips.

THE MALE REPRODUCTIVE SYSTEM

The male reproductive system includes organs that produce and store sperm. It also includes tubes that sperm travel through. Sperm move through these tubes and can

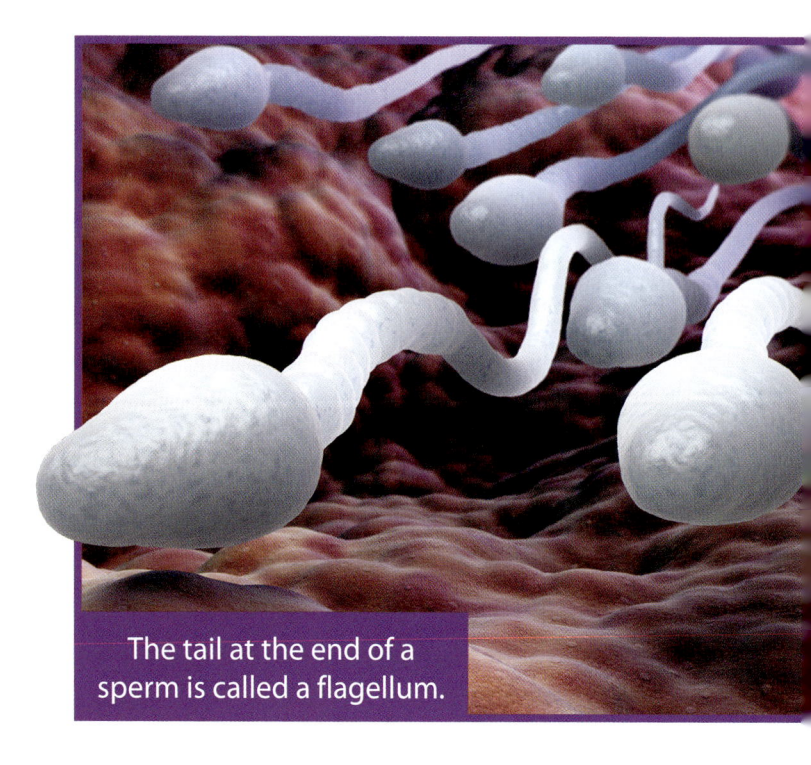

The tail at the end of a sperm is called a flagellum.

be released from the male body. If sperm enter the female body and encounter an egg, fertilization may occur. Sperm are microscopic cells. A sperm cell has an oval-shaped head and a long tail. The tail helps sperm move through the male and female reproductive systems.

Males begin producing sperm after puberty. Sperm production occurs in the testes. These are small, oval-shaped organs. The testes also produce a hormone called testosterone that helps with the

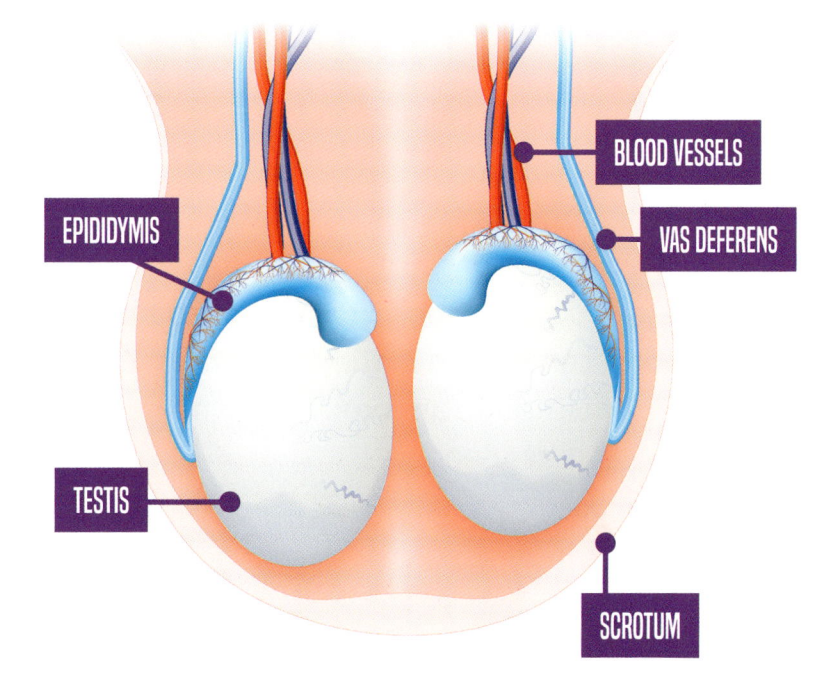

Testosterone produced in the testes is carried in blood and delivered to other body parts.

development of the male reproductive system. The testes are located outside of the body in a sack of skin called the scrotum.

Because the scrotum is outside the body, it is a cooler temperature than the rest of the male body. This is important for sperm development. Sperm die if they overheat. Long-term exposure to heat can lead to abnormal sperm development. The sperm may be shaped incorrectly. They cannot travel through the reproductive system.

A male may produce as many as 525 billion sperm cells in his lifetime.

From the testes, sperm move into the epididymis. The epididymis is a long, coiled tube. Stretched out, it would be 20 feet (6 m) long. Sperm mature while in the tube. It takes two to four days for sperm to swim through the epididymis, but sperm can remain in the epididymis for about 74 days. After this time, sperm are broken down and reabsorbed by the body.

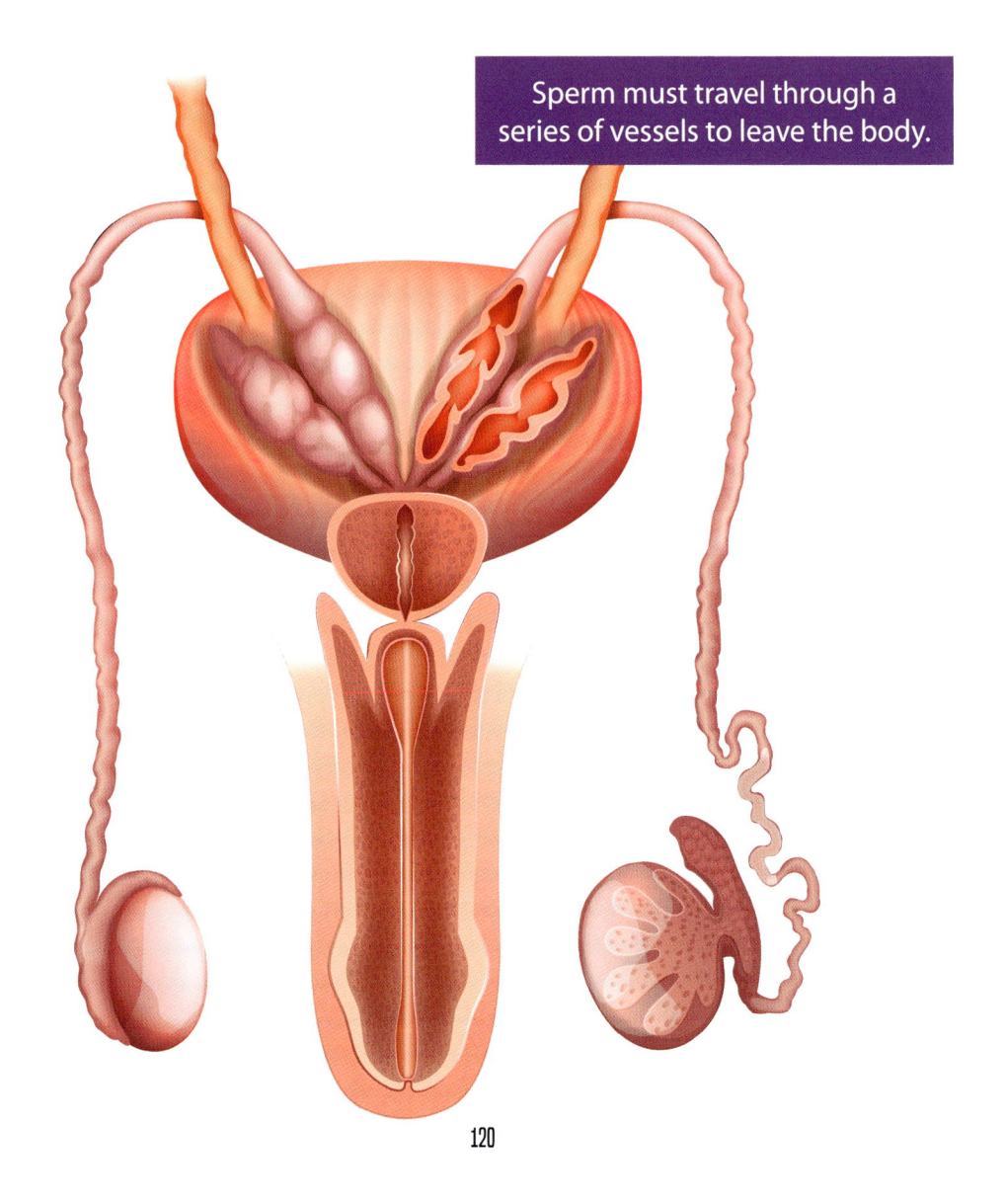

Sperm must travel through a series of vessels to leave the body.

The epididymis connects to another tube called the vas deferens. The sperm move into the vas deferens as a part of ejaculation. Ejaculation may occur as a result of sex. As the vas deferens contracts, sperm move to the penis. There, the sperm combine with several fluids. The seminal vesicles and prostate gland are located below the bladder. They provide energy-rich substances that help the sperm swim.

The sperm swim through a tube in the penis called the urethra. Urine also flows through the urethra. But the flow of urine is blocked during ejaculation. Sperm are eventually released through an opening at the end of the penis. The sperm may then continue to swim into the female reproductive system if the partners are engaging in sex.

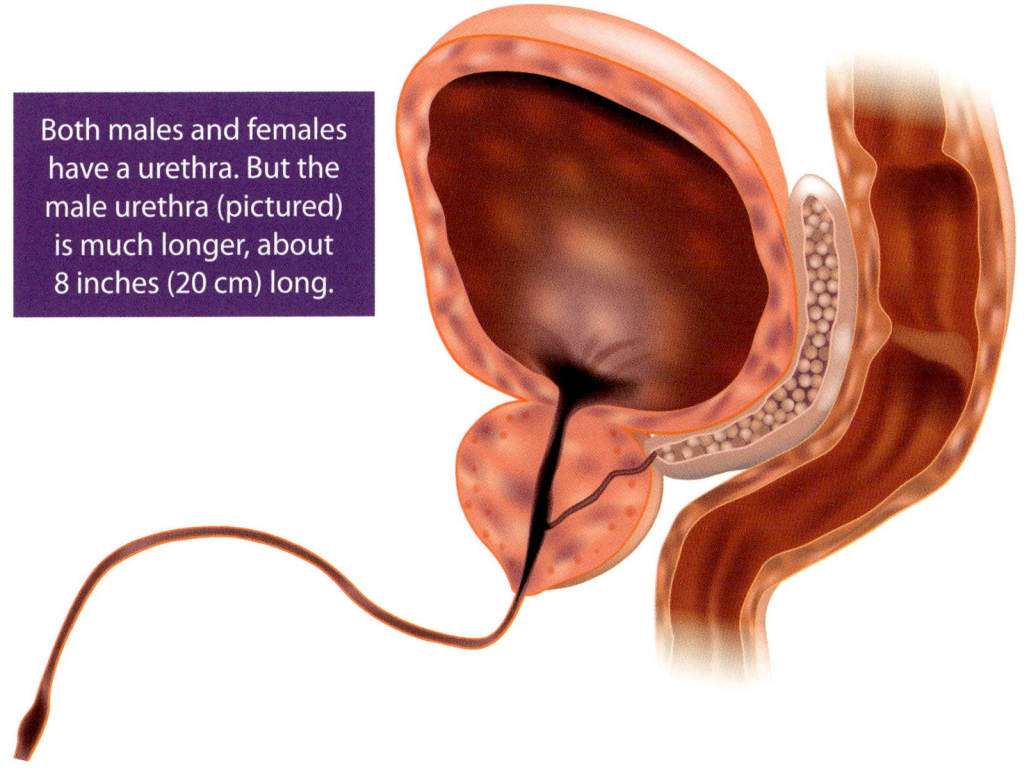

Both males and females have a urethra. But the male urethra (pictured) is much longer, about 8 inches (20 cm) long.

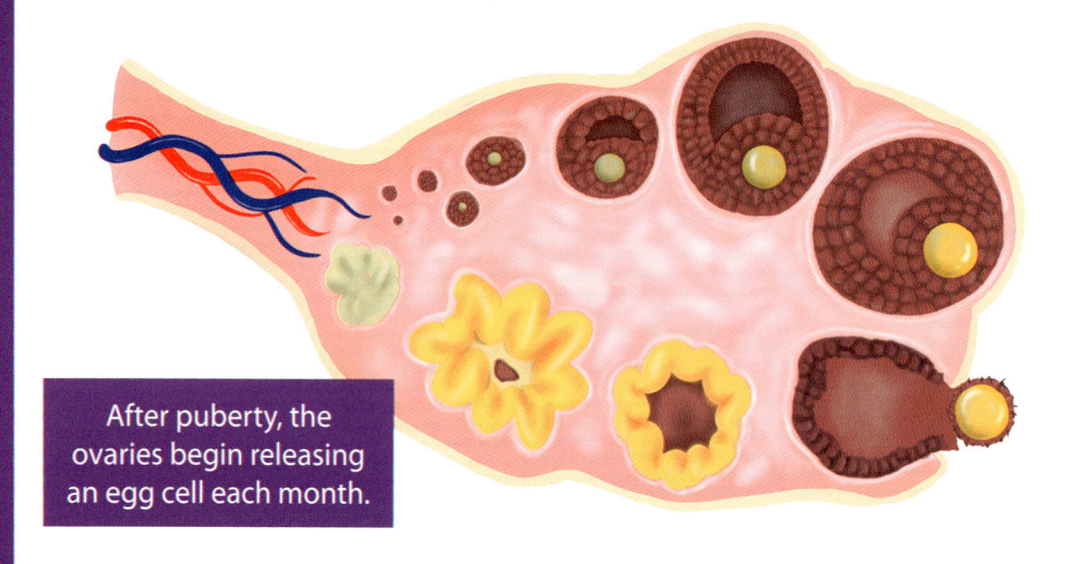

After puberty, the ovaries begin releasing an egg cell each month.

THE FEMALE REPRODUCTIVE SYSTEM

Females are born with about two million egg cells. This is the total amount of egg cells they will have in their bodies. They do not produce any more after they are born. Hormones help maintain the egg cells. But the female body does not produce large amounts of these hormones until reaching puberty.

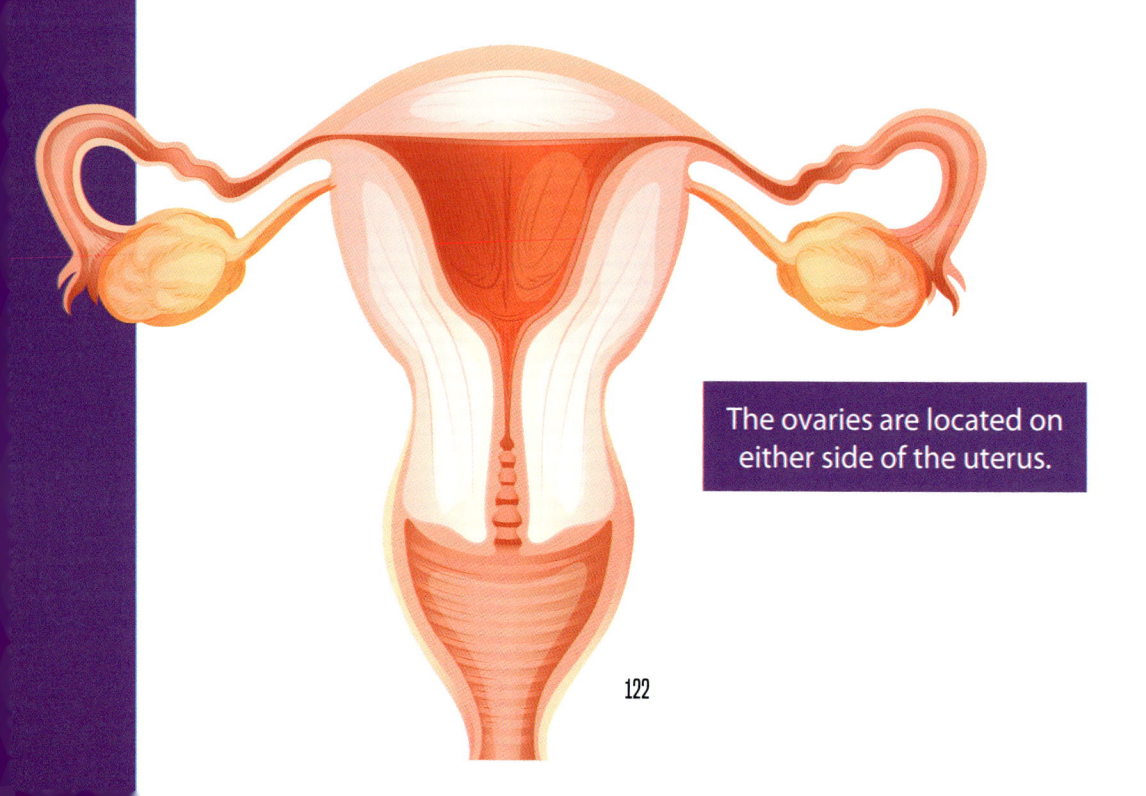

The ovaries are located on either side of the uterus.

By that point, many of the egg cells have died. When females reach puberty, only about 400,000 egg cells remain.

Females have a pair of ovaries. One ovary is on the left side of the body, and the other is on the right. The ovaries are located in the lower abdomen, near the pelvis. They are the organs that produce and release egg cells. The ovaries also produce hormones such as estrogen and progesterone.

An ovary releases an egg cell approximately every 28 days as part of the menstrual cycle. The timing varies for each female. After the egg is released, it enters the fallopian tubes. These are muscular tubes that connect the ovary to the uterus. The end of the fallopian tube that is near the ovary is brush-like. It is covered in small hairs called cilia. The cilia sweep the egg cell toward the uterus. Unlike sperm, the egg cannot move by itself. It depends on the cilia to transport it to the uterus.

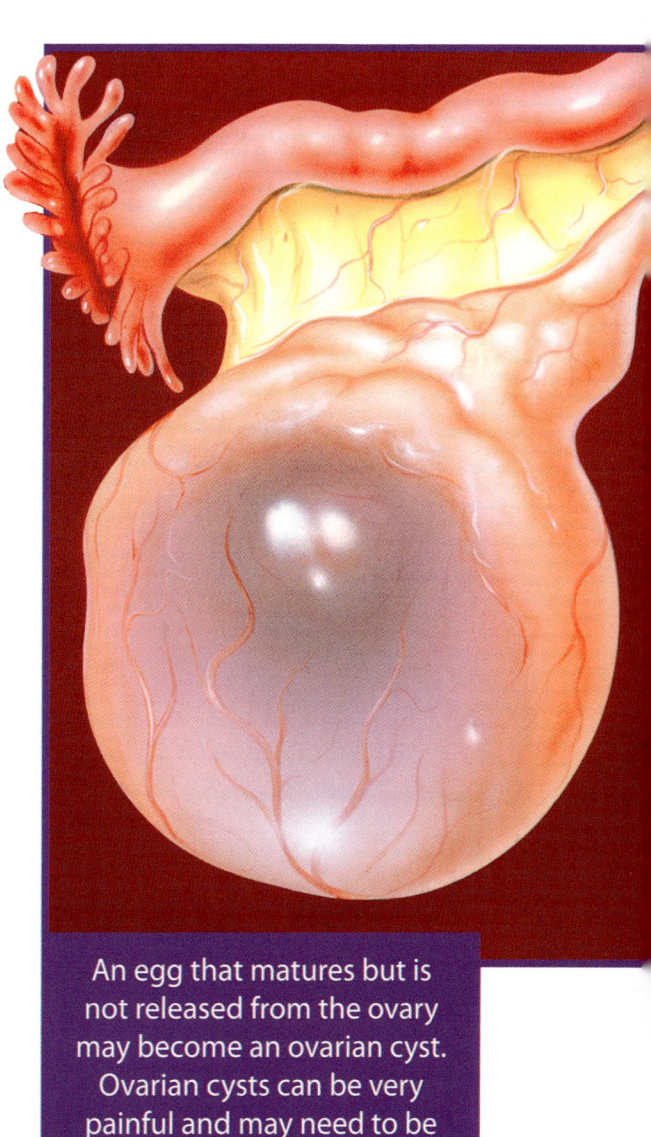

An egg that matures but is not released from the ovary may become an ovarian cyst. Ovarian cysts can be very painful and may need to be removed with surgery.

A woman may experience a headache and abdominal cramps in the days leading up to her period.

The fallopian tube is where fertilization occurs. Regardless of whether the egg is fertilized, it continues to the uterus. It takes several days for the egg to reach the uterus.

If the egg cell has been fertilized by a sperm, it implants into the uterus's thick lining. The egg cell may develop into a fetus. If the egg is unfertilized, it is eventually expelled from the body through an opening called the vagina. The body also gets rid of the lining of the uterus. The shedding of these tissues is known as a period. Periods typically last between two and seven days.

The menstrual cycle restarts after the period.

If the egg cell is fertilized, it implants in the lining of the uterus. The uterus begins producing a hormone after implantation. High levels of this hormone indicate that the female is pregnant. The hormone prevents the body from getting rid of the uterine lining. It maintains the lining as the fertilized egg develops into a fetus. It stops the female from having a period.

An ectopic pregnancy occurs when the egg implants anywhere other than the uterus. The embryo cannot safely develop anywhere other than the uterus. These labels represent the different types of ectopic pregnancies.

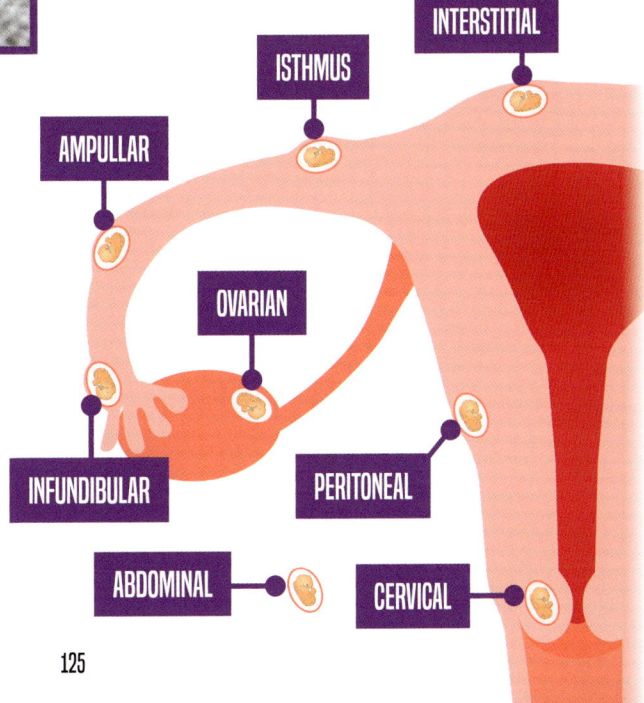

INTERSTITIAL

ISTHMUS

AMPULLAR

OVARIAN

INFUNDIBULAR

PERITONEAL

ABDOMINAL

CERVICAL

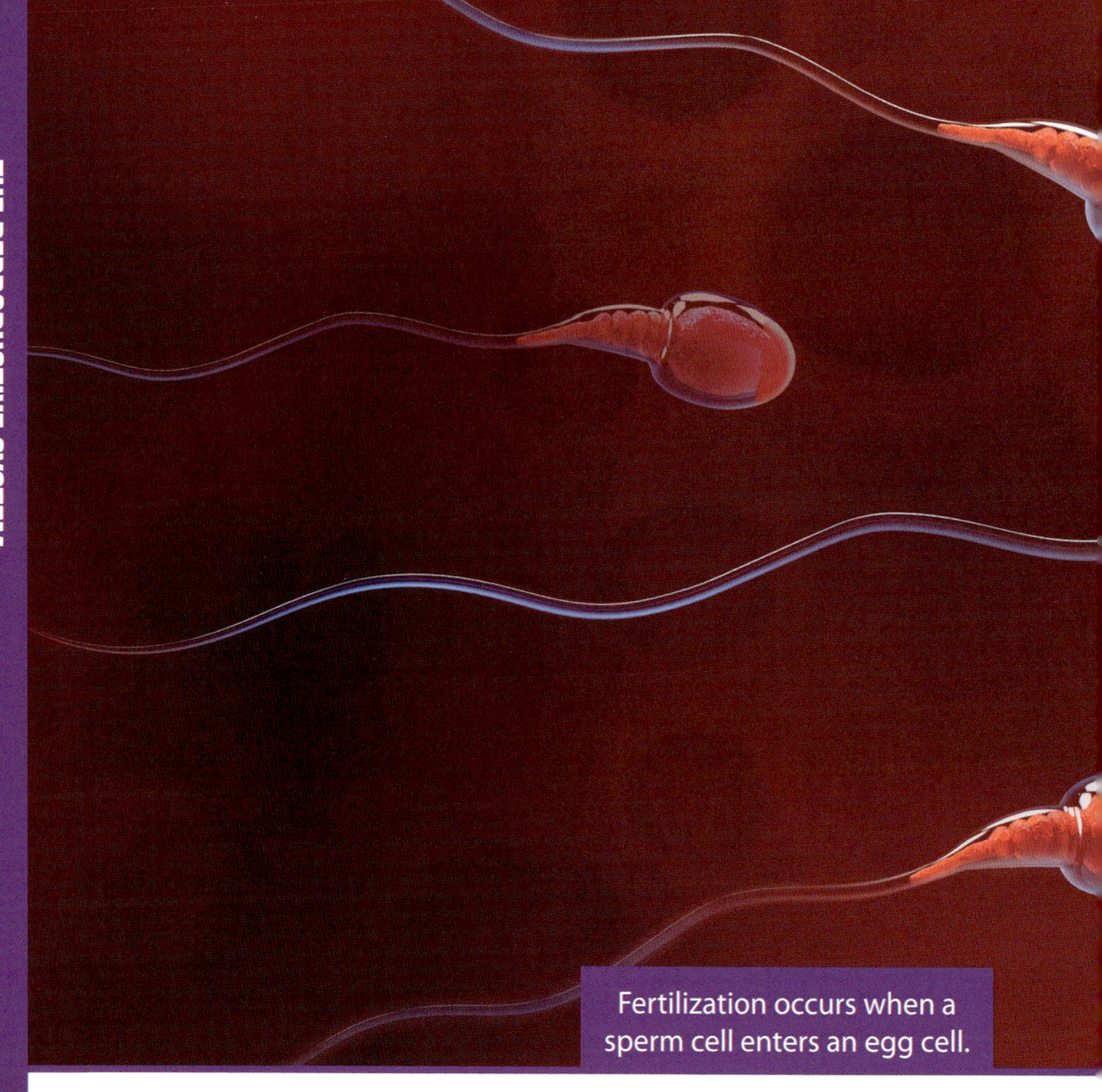

Fertilization occurs when a sperm cell enters an egg cell.

FERTILIZATION

In order for fertilization to occur, sperm must enter the female body. This may occur after sex. Sperm are ejaculated from the penis. They enter the female body through the vagina. The vagina is connected to the uterus by the cervix. Sperm swim up the vagina and through the cervix. They continue to travel through the uterus before entering the fallopian tubes, where fertilization occurs.

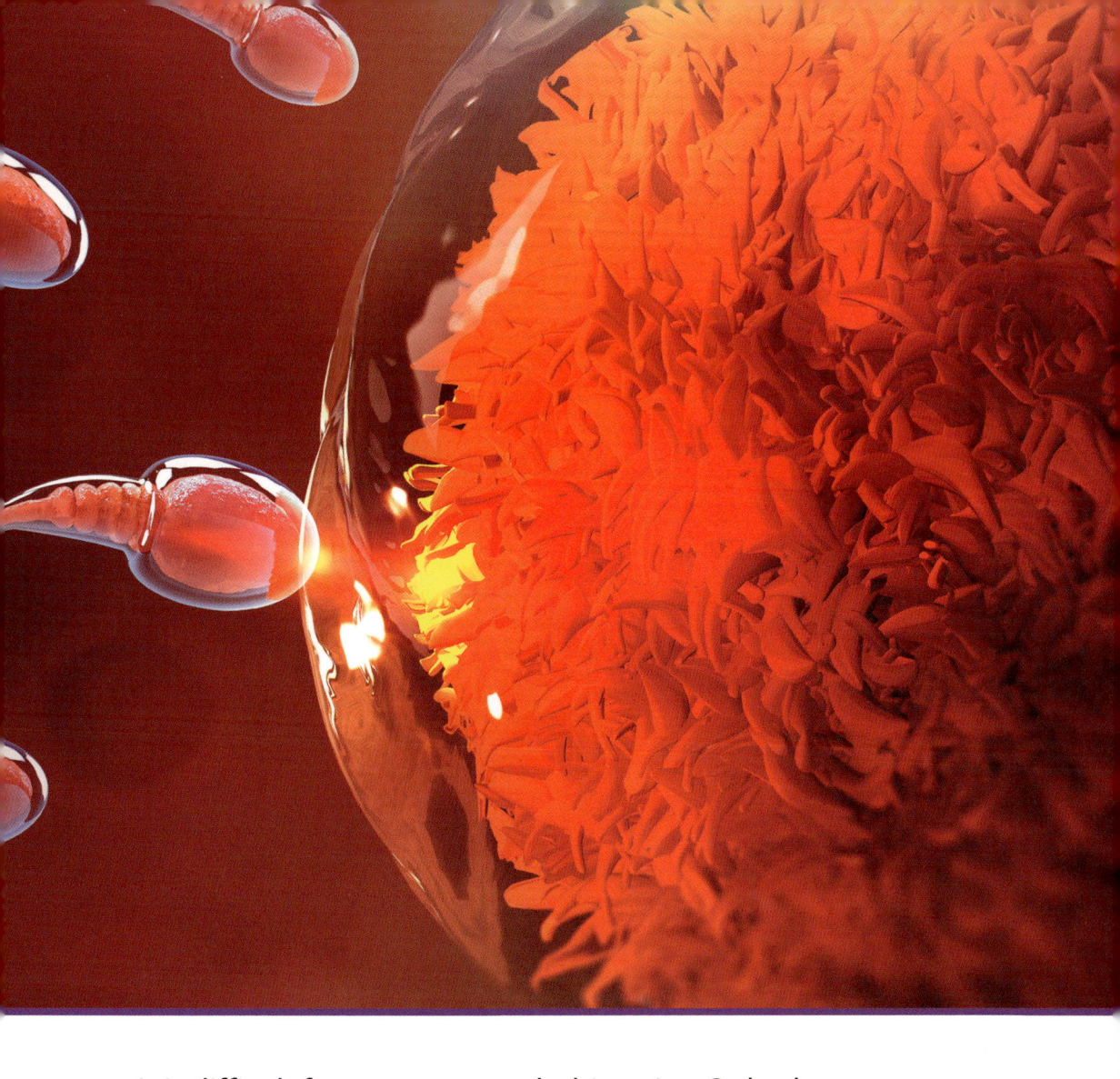

It is difficult for sperm to reach this point. Only about one in 14 million ejaculated sperm reach the fallopian tubes. The egg cell secretes chemicals that help sperm locate it. Sperm can survive in the female reproductive system for several days. This helps increase the chances of fertilization. An egg may be released into the fallopian tube during this time.

A sperm cell enters into the egg cell. Only one sperm can enter and fertilize the egg. The sperm and egg fuse together after fertilization. The outer layer of the egg becomes hardened. This prevents other sperm from entering the egg. The genes from the sperm and egg combine. The fertilized egg begins to divide. It develops into an embryo. The embryo continues to grow and develop in the uterus. It eventually becomes a fetus.

After the egg has been fertilized, it begins to divide.

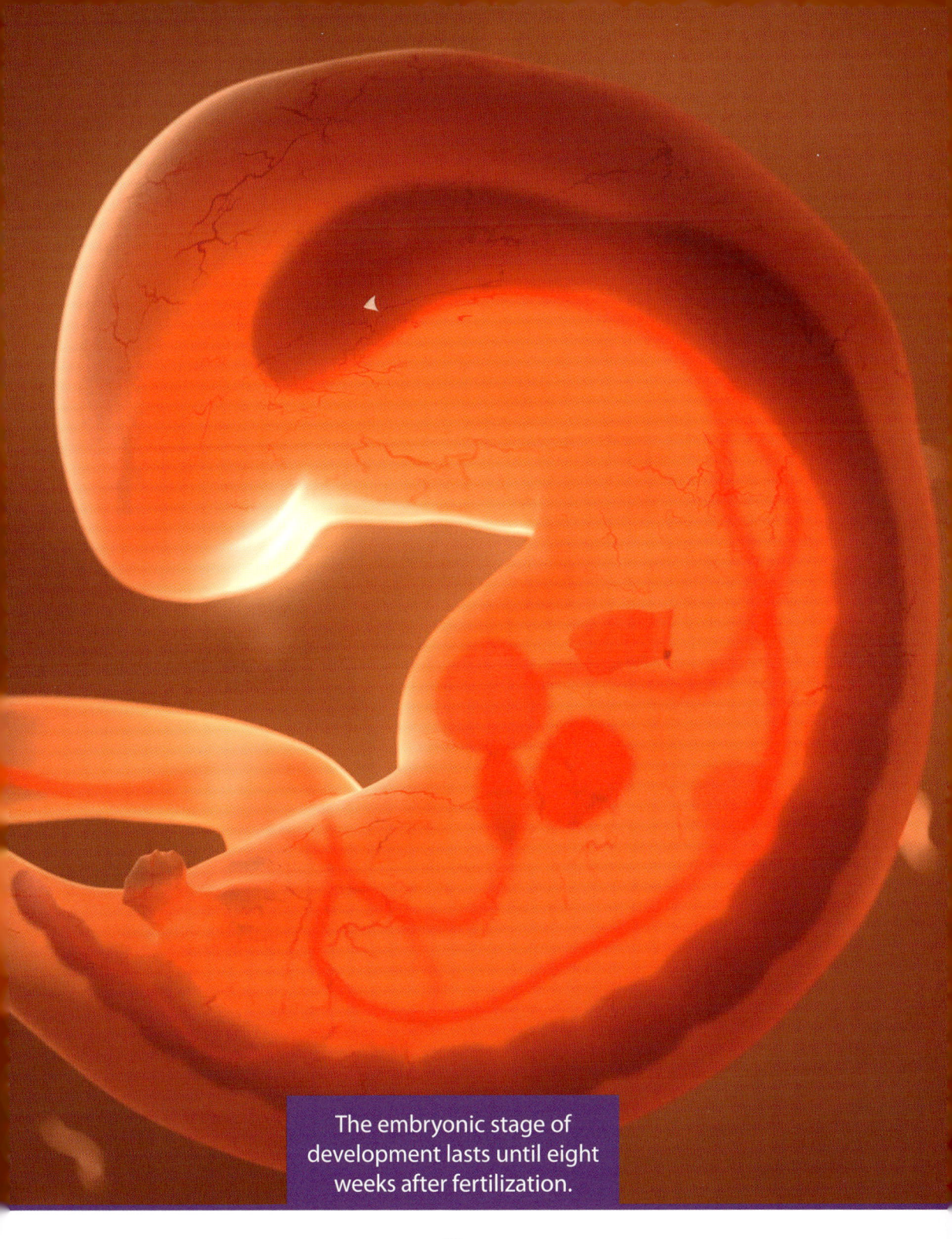

The embryonic stage of development lasts until eight weeks after fertilization.

PREGNANCY AND BIRTH

A typical pregnancy lasts for 40 weeks. During this time, the fetus grows. Bones and organs develop. These organs and organ systems continue to mature over the 40 weeks. After this

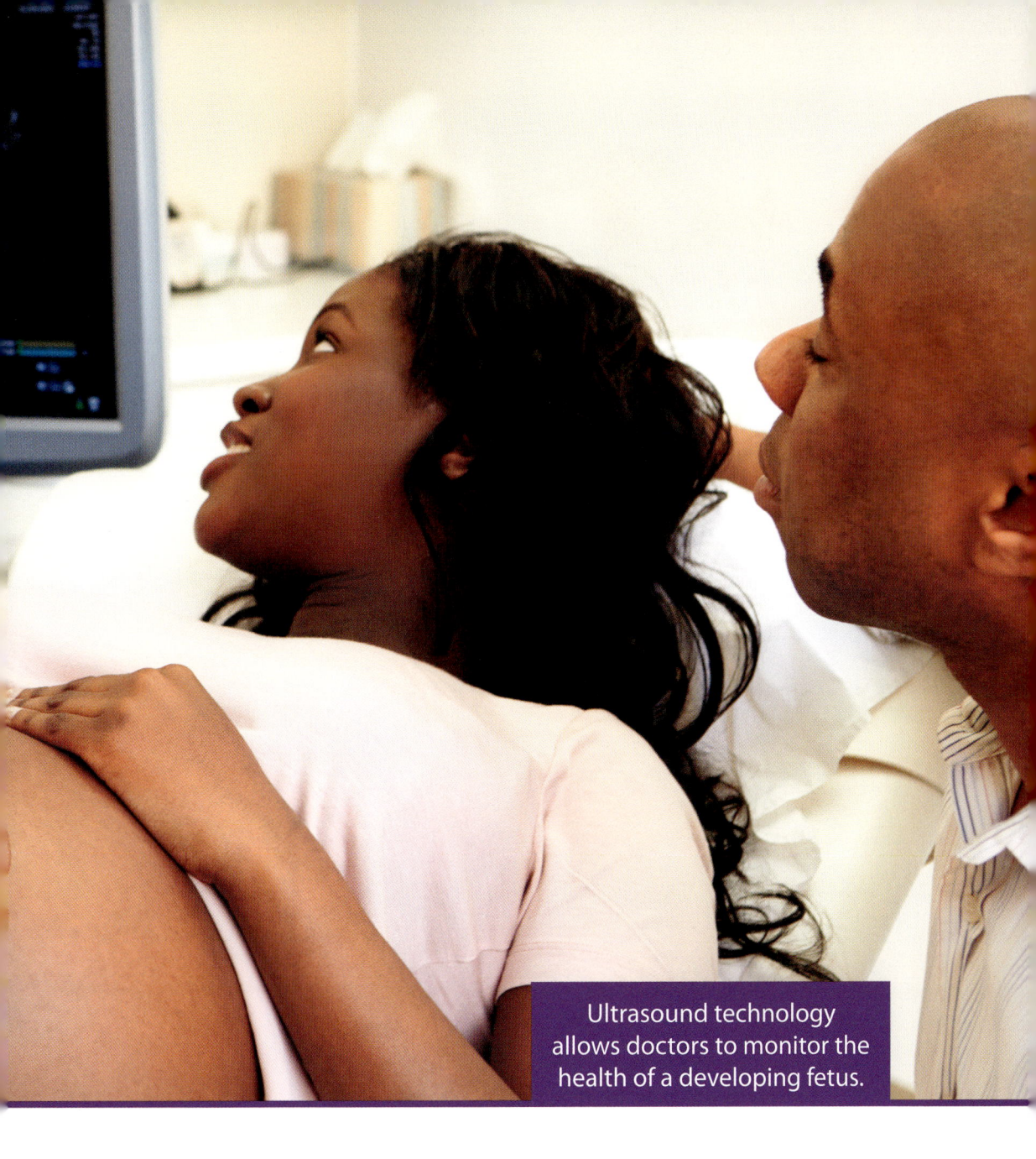

Ultrasound technology allows doctors to monitor the health of a developing fetus.

point, the lungs and other organs are well-developed. The fetus is able to survive outside of the uterus.

The developing fetus requires oxygen and other nutrients. It gets these nutrients from the placenta. The placenta is an organ

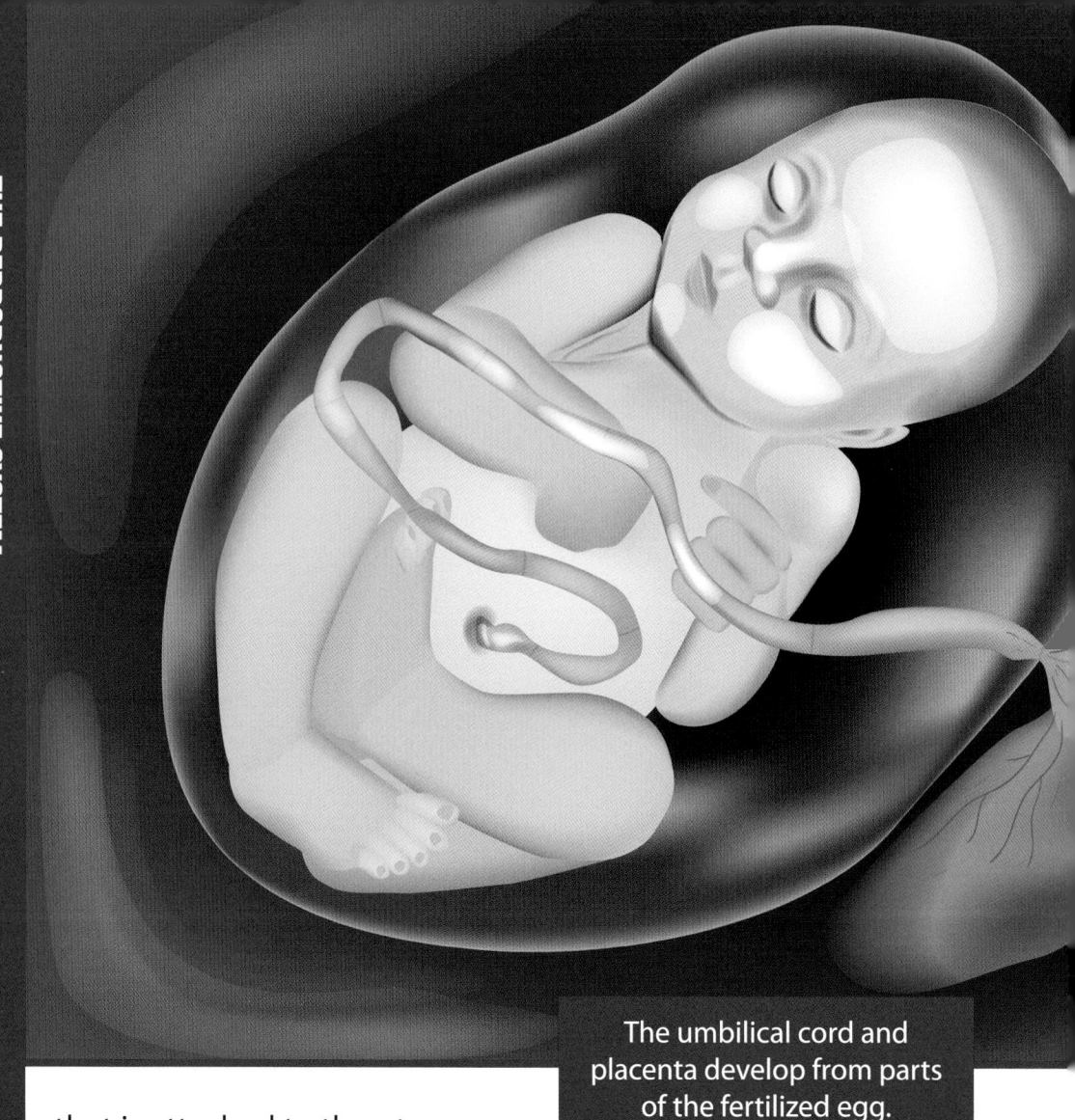

The umbilical cord and placenta develop from parts of the fertilized egg.

that is attached to the uterus. It is connected to the fetus by the umbilical cord. The umbilical cord carries nutrients from the mother to the fetus. It also removes waste such as carbon dioxide from the fetus.

After 40 weeks, the fetus is fully developed. It releases hormones that signal the start of the birthing process, or labor. The mother begins to experience contractions. The cervix changes shape. The baby moves through the uterus. The mother pushes the baby through the cervix. The cervix may expand to 4 inches (10 cm) in order to allow the baby to pass through. The placenta is also pushed out following the birth of the baby.

It may take several minutes to several hours to deliver a child after the cervix is fully expanded.

THE RESPIRATORY SYSTEM

The respiratory system supplies oxygen to the body. It also removes carbon dioxide. These gases are taken in or expelled as a person breathes. When people inhale, they receive a supply of oxygen. When they exhale, they release carbon dioxide.

All the cells in the human body require oxygen to function. Without oxygen, the cells die. Organ systems would stop working. Cells need oxygen to create energy. They produce carbon dioxide as a waste product. High levels of carbon dioxide in the bloodstream can lead to health problems such as muscle weakness and brain damage.

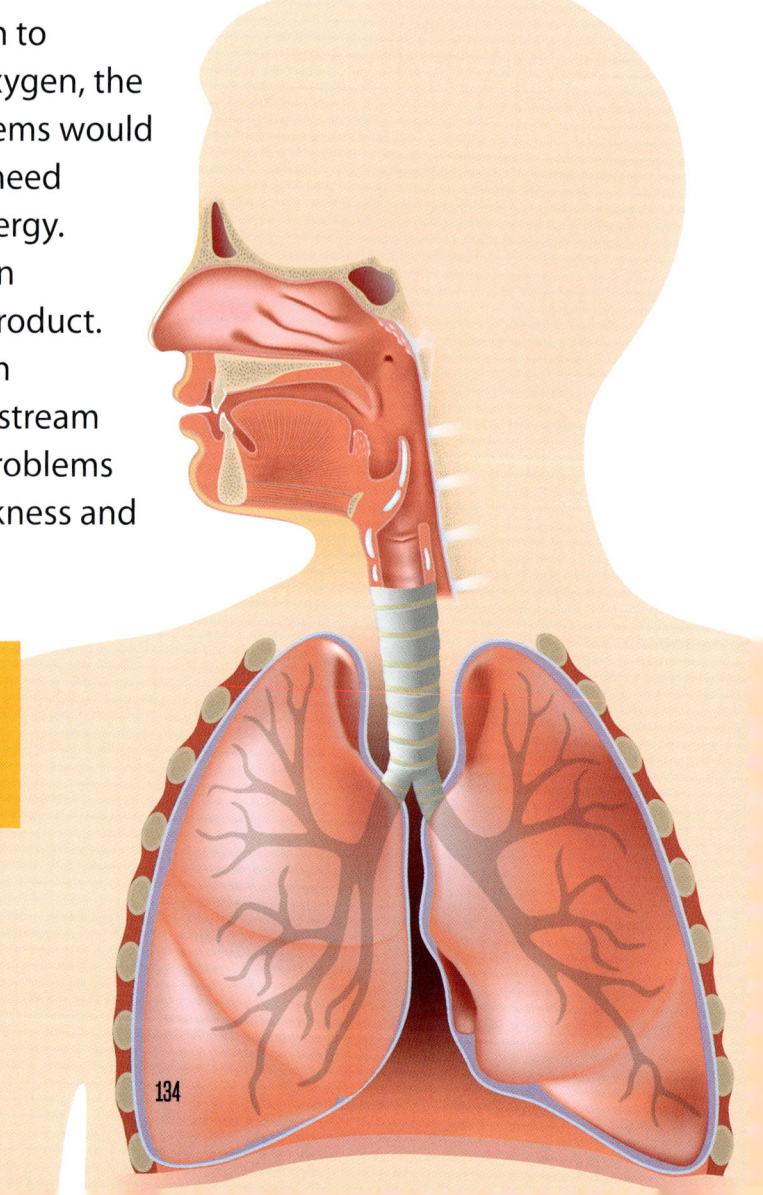

The lungs and airways take in oxygen that is used in all bodily processes.

The respiratory system regulates the levels of oxygen and carbon dioxide in the body. This organ system includes the airways, diaphragm, and lungs. It is closely connected to the circulatory system. The lungs deliver oxygen to the bloodstream, which carries oxygen throughout the body. In exchange for oxygen, the bloodstream releases carbon dioxide to the lungs. The lungs exhale this gas.

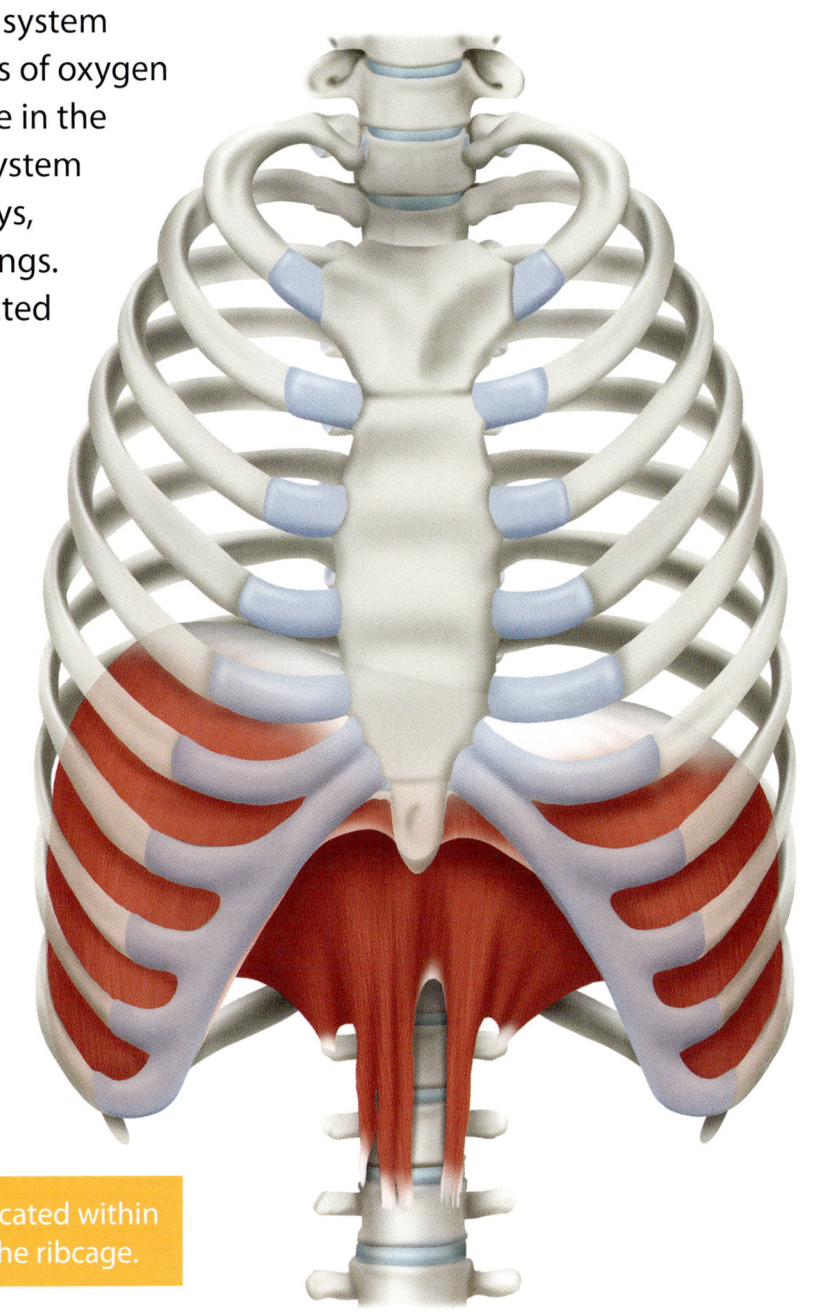

The diaphragm is located within the lower part of the ribcage.

Scents, like freshly baked cookies, enter the airways where they interact with sensory neurons.

In addition to regulating gas levels, the respiratory system has many other jobs. It makes sure that the air the body receives is warm and moist. It allows a person to smell. The respiratory system also plays a role in protecting the body from diseases.

THE AIRWAYS

Before air reaches the lungs, it flows through a series of airways in the nose, mouth, and throat. These passages are lined with small hairs called cilia. They are also covered in a layer of mucus. The cilia and mucus help protect the respiratory system from disease. Mucus traps bacteria and viruses before they can enter the lungs. It can trap other small particles that may irritate the lungs, such as dust and pollen. Cilia sweep the mucus and trapped particles out of the airways. Mucus is eventually coughed up or swallowed.

Cilia move in a wave-like pattern to clear the airways of germs and other particles.

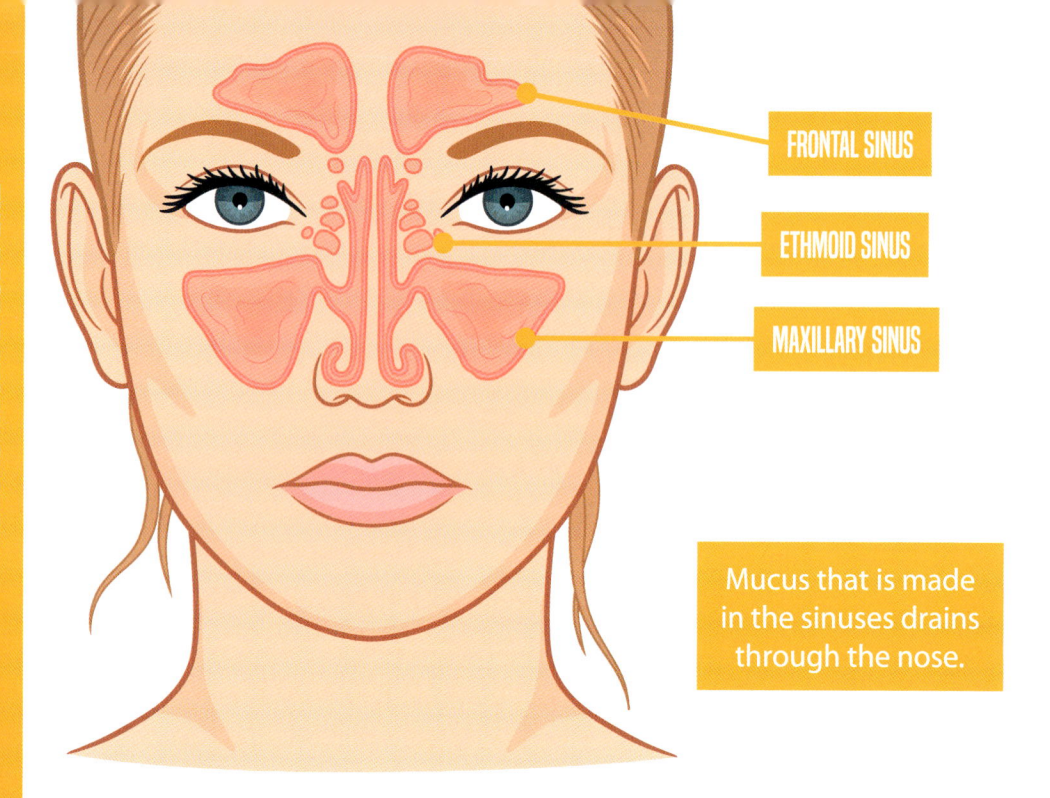

FRONTAL SINUS

ETHMOID SINUS

MAXILLARY SINUS

Mucus that is made in the sinuses drains through the nose.

Air first enters the nose and mouth. The nose is the primary entrance. It is lined with cilia. It is also connected to the sinuses. The sinuses are hollow spaces in the head. They produce mucus. They also regulate the temperature and moisture of the air people breathe. It is more comfortable to breathe air that is warm and moist. A person has four pairs of sinuses. The largest are behind the cheekbones. These can be about 1 inch (2.5 cm) in length.

Air that enters the mouth is not filtered by cilia. It also does not pass through the sinuses. This is why the lungs may hurt after exercise in cold weather. The air is chilly and dry. This can irritate the airways and lungs. But having this airway is important. The mouth allows a person to take in additional air during exercise. The nasal airway can become blocked when a person is sick. Being able to breathe through the mouth allows a person to continue receiving oxygen.

Allergies cause the sinuses to produce more mucus.

Air from the nose and mouth then enters the throat. The throat is divided into two tubes. The back tube is called the esophagus. Food travels down the esophagus. The front tube is the windpipe, or trachea. Air enters and exits through the trachea. The epiglottis is a flap of tissue that sits at the top of the trachea. This structure closes over the trachea when a person swallows. This prevents food and liquid from entering the trachea. If food or water does enter the trachea, a person may choke. He or she may be unable to breathe.

A US sergeant demonstrates the Heimlich maneuver, which can help someone who is choking. The Heimlich maneuver should only be performed by someone who has first aid training.

The trachea divides into two bronchial tubes. One tube connects to each lung. The bronchial tubes split into smaller and smaller tubes as they extend deeper into the lungs. The bronchial tubes are also lined with mucus and cilia. These serve as a line of defense to protect the lungs. Coughing and sneezing help clear mucus from the airways.

At its widest point, the adult trachea is about 1 inch (2.5 cm) in diameter.

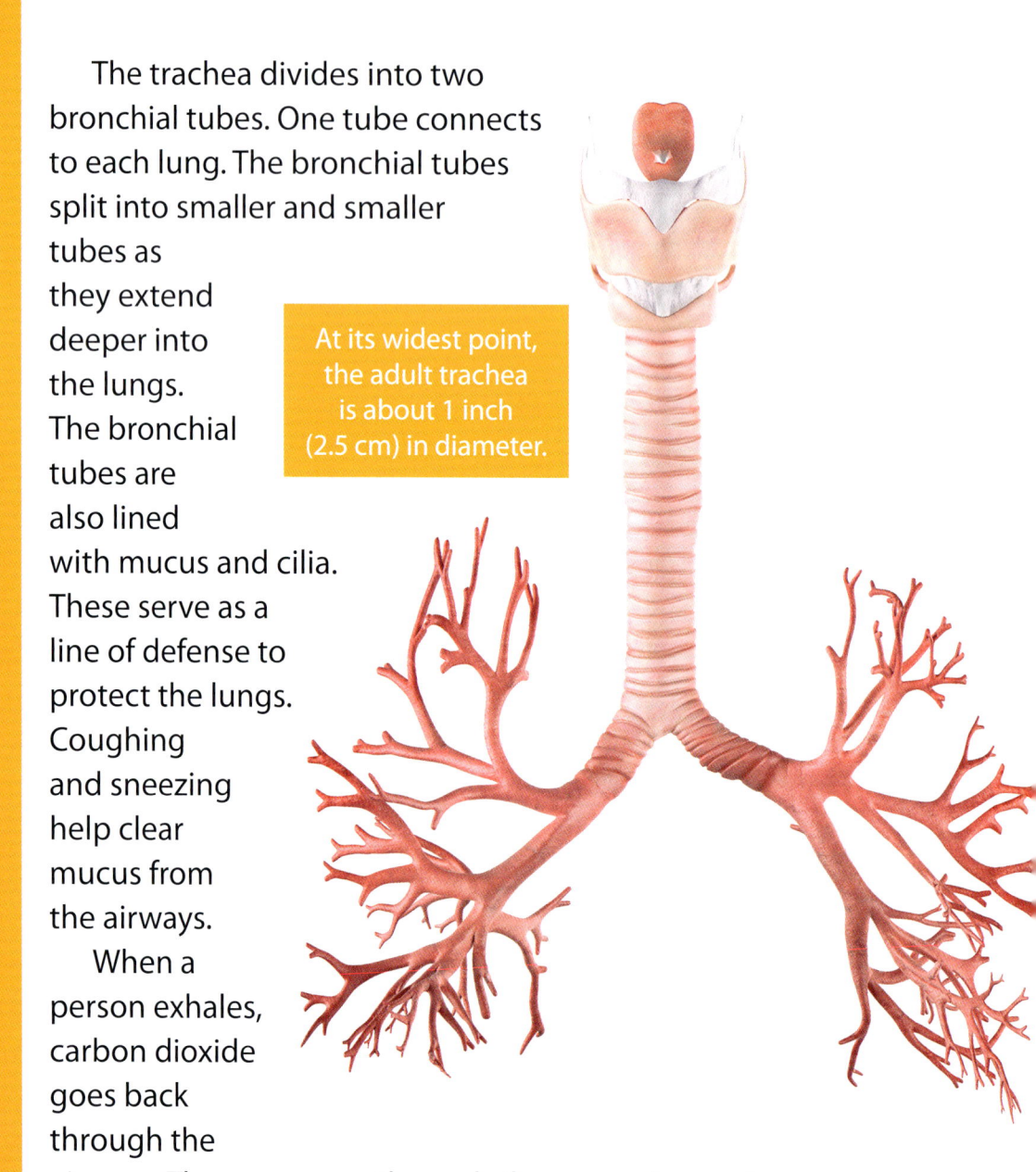

When a person exhales, carbon dioxide goes back through the airways. The gas moves through the same airways in reverse. When exhaled air passes over the larynx, speech is possible. The larynx is a group of muscles, tissues, and cartilage. It rests at the top of the trachea. The larynx contains the vocal cords.

The cords vibrate when air passes over them. This vibration produces sound. If the vocal cords are not vibrating properly, a person's voice may sound weak or raspy.

Vocal cords come together and vibrate to produce sound. This illustration shows vocal cords viewed from above.

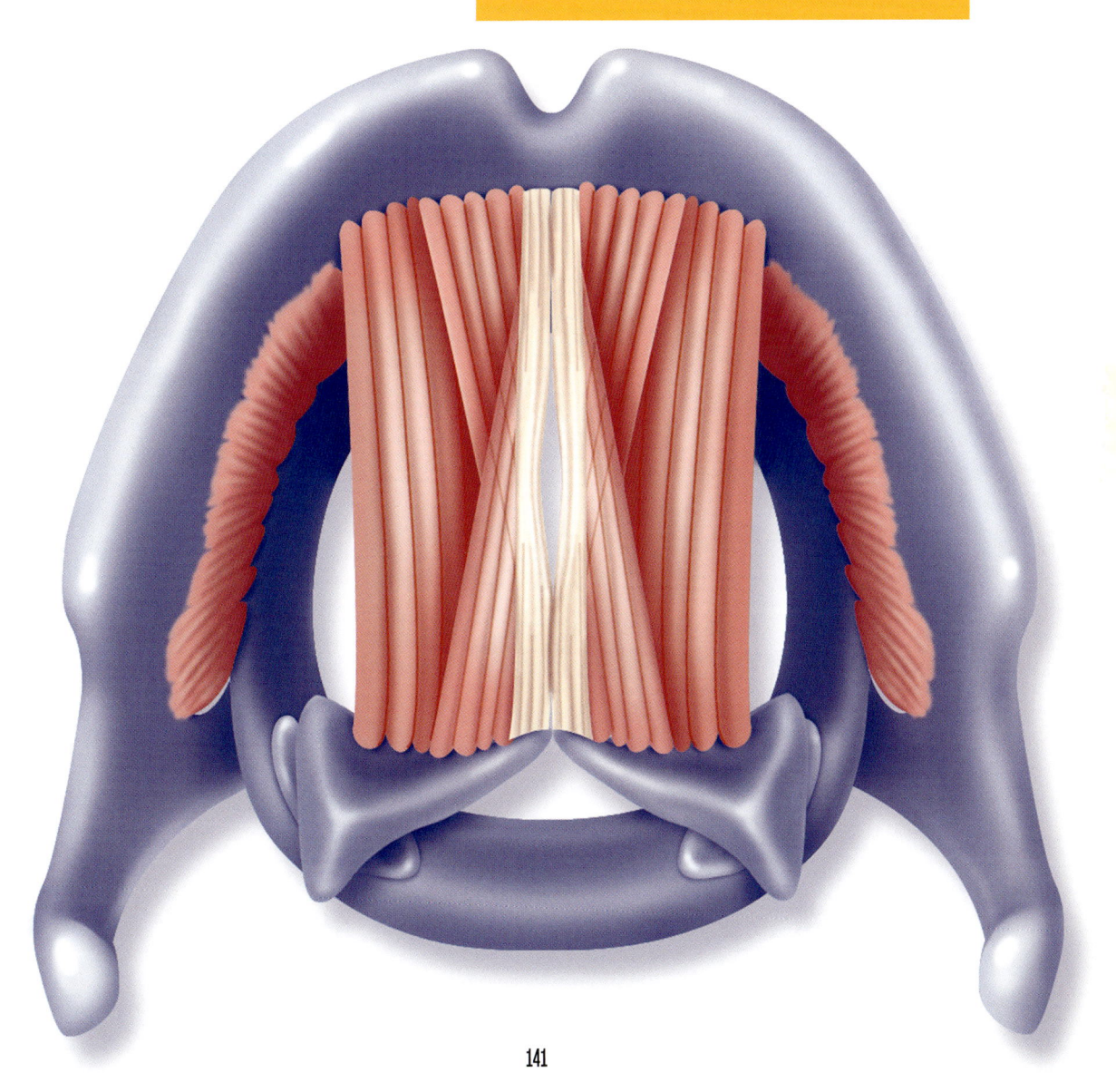

THE LUNGS AND BREATHING

The lungs are the major organs in the respiratory system. People have two lungs, one on each side of the body. The right lung is slightly larger than the left lung. It is divided into three sections called lobes. The left lung has only two lobes. It is smaller in size to make room for the heart. The lungs are made of flexible tissue. This allows the lungs to change shape and expand.

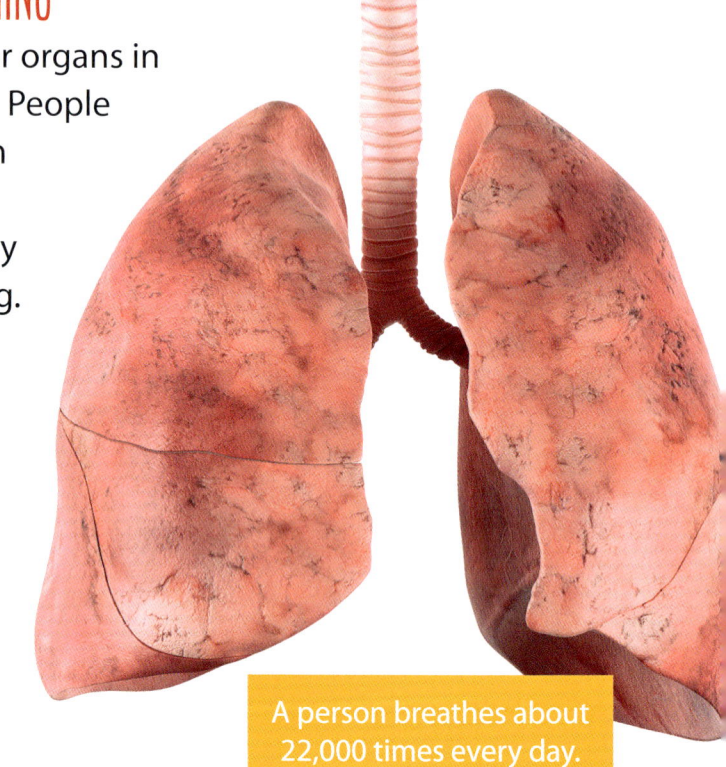

A person breathes about 22,000 times every day.

Healthy newborn babies are able to breathe on their own. But their lungs continue to develop until their teenage years. The lungs are filled with tiny air sacs called alveoli. A newborn has fewer than 50 million air sacs in the lungs. New air sacs grow rapidly during the first months of life. As an adult, the person will have about 300 million air sacs. The amount of air the lungs can hold also increases as a person grows up. The average adult has a lung capacity of about 1.5 gallons (6 L).

The lungs are located in the chest cavity. There is empty space surrounding the lungs, which gives the lungs room to

Premature babies may need a machine to support their breathing because their lungs have not developed enough to breathe on their own.

expand and contract. The diaphragm is a strong muscle at the bottom of the chest cavity. When the diaphragm contracts, it pulls the bottom of the chest cavity. The chest cavity becomes larger. When the diaphragm relaxes, the chest cavity becomes smaller. Air pressure inside the lungs changes as the chest cavity changes size. Air travels from high to low pressure. Air pressure is the reason why air moves in and out of the lungs.

Muscles attached to the rib cage allow the ribs to expand and contract with each breath.

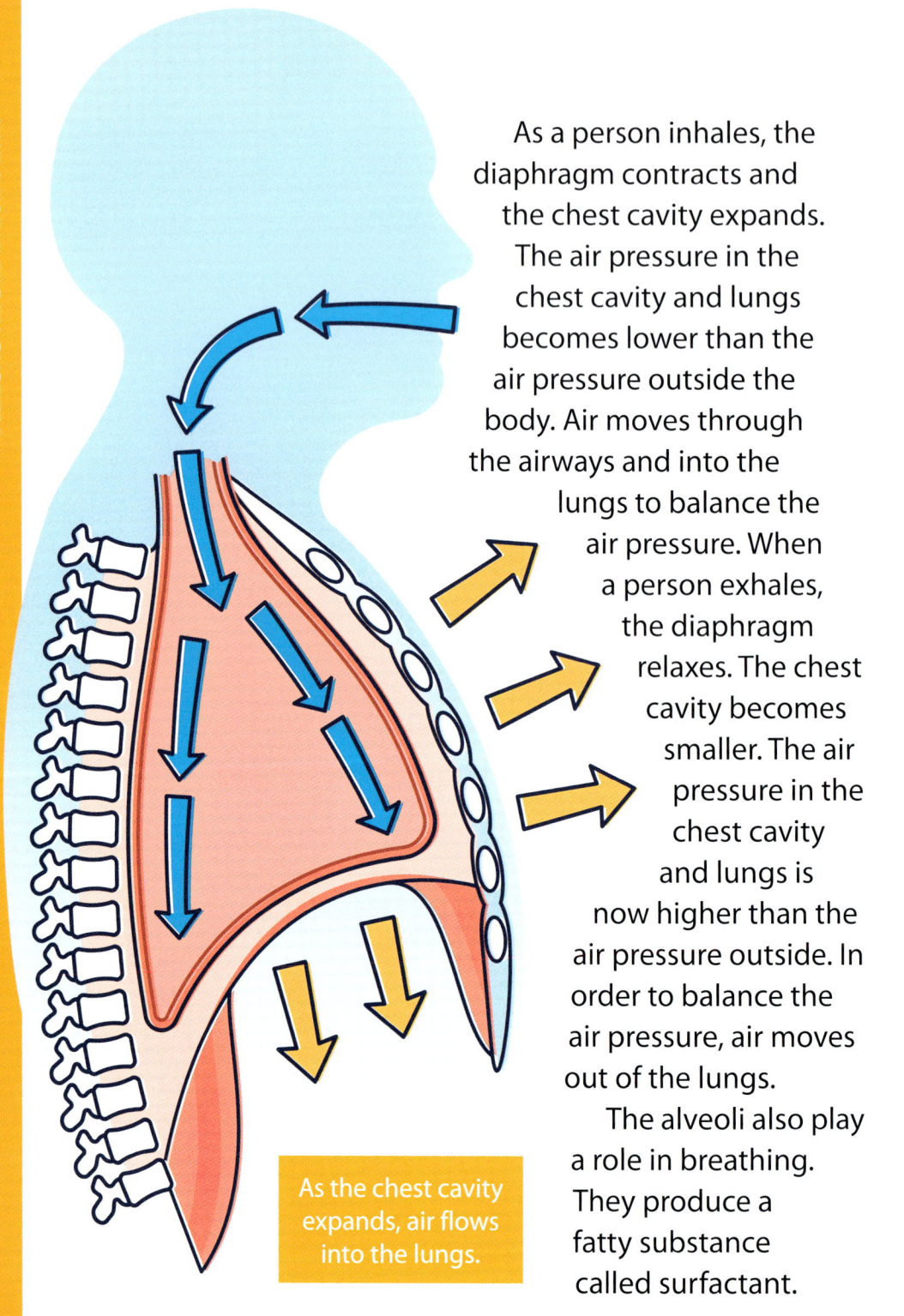

As a person inhales, the diaphragm contracts and the chest cavity expands. The air pressure in the chest cavity and lungs becomes lower than the air pressure outside the body. Air moves through the airways and into the lungs to balance the air pressure. When a person exhales, the diaphragm relaxes. The chest cavity becomes smaller. The air pressure in the chest cavity and lungs is now higher than the air pressure outside. In order to balance the air pressure, air moves out of the lungs.

The alveoli also play a role in breathing. They produce a fatty substance called surfactant.

As the chest cavity expands, air flows into the lungs.

144

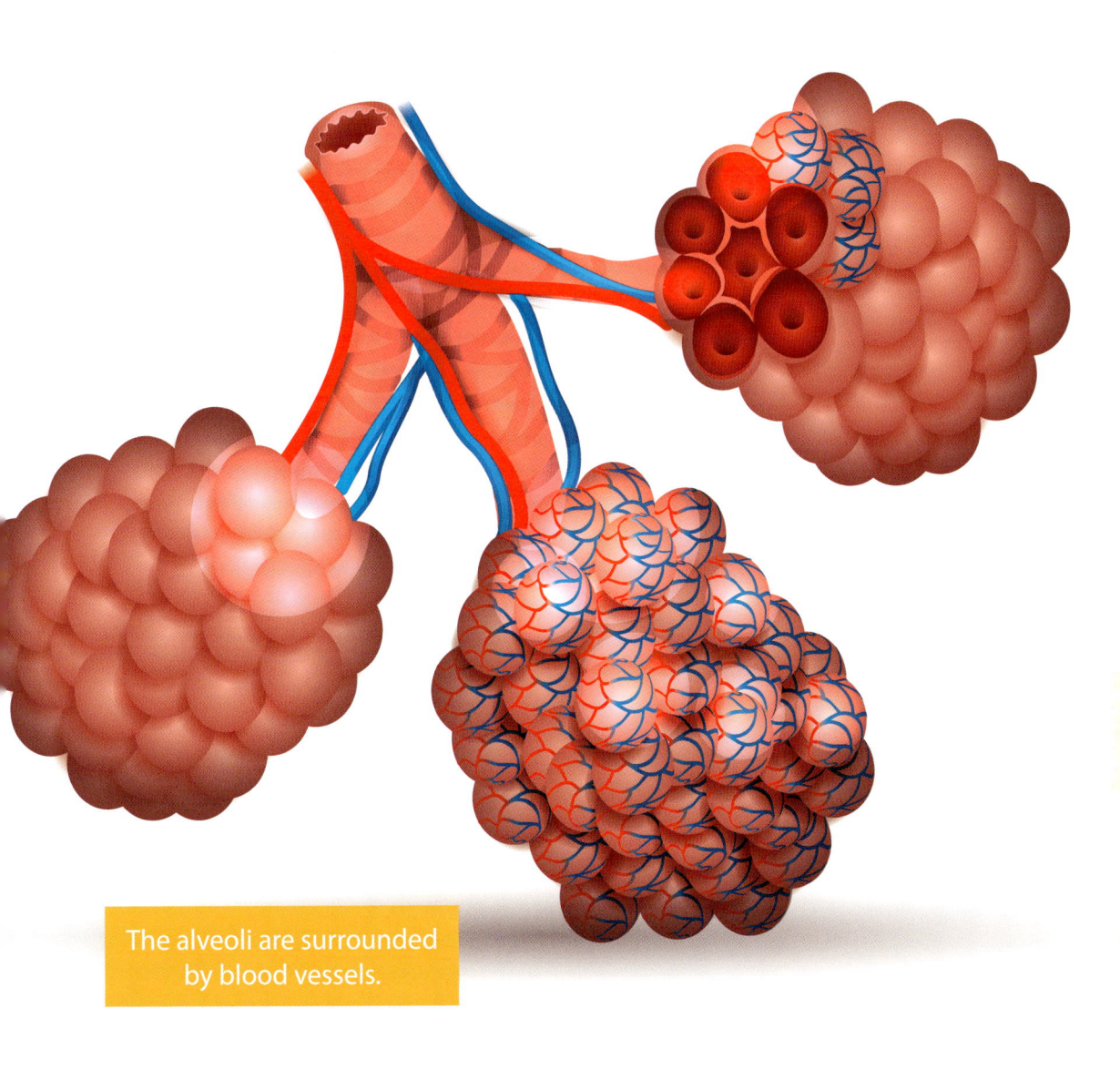

The alveoli are surrounded by blood vessels.

This substance coats the alveoli and the lungs. It makes breathing easier. It prevents the alveoli from collapsing due to changing air pressure. Without surfactant, it is impossible for the body to get oxygen. Fetuses begin producing surfactant at about 24 weeks. But they do not have enough surfactant to survive outside the womb until about 34 weeks.

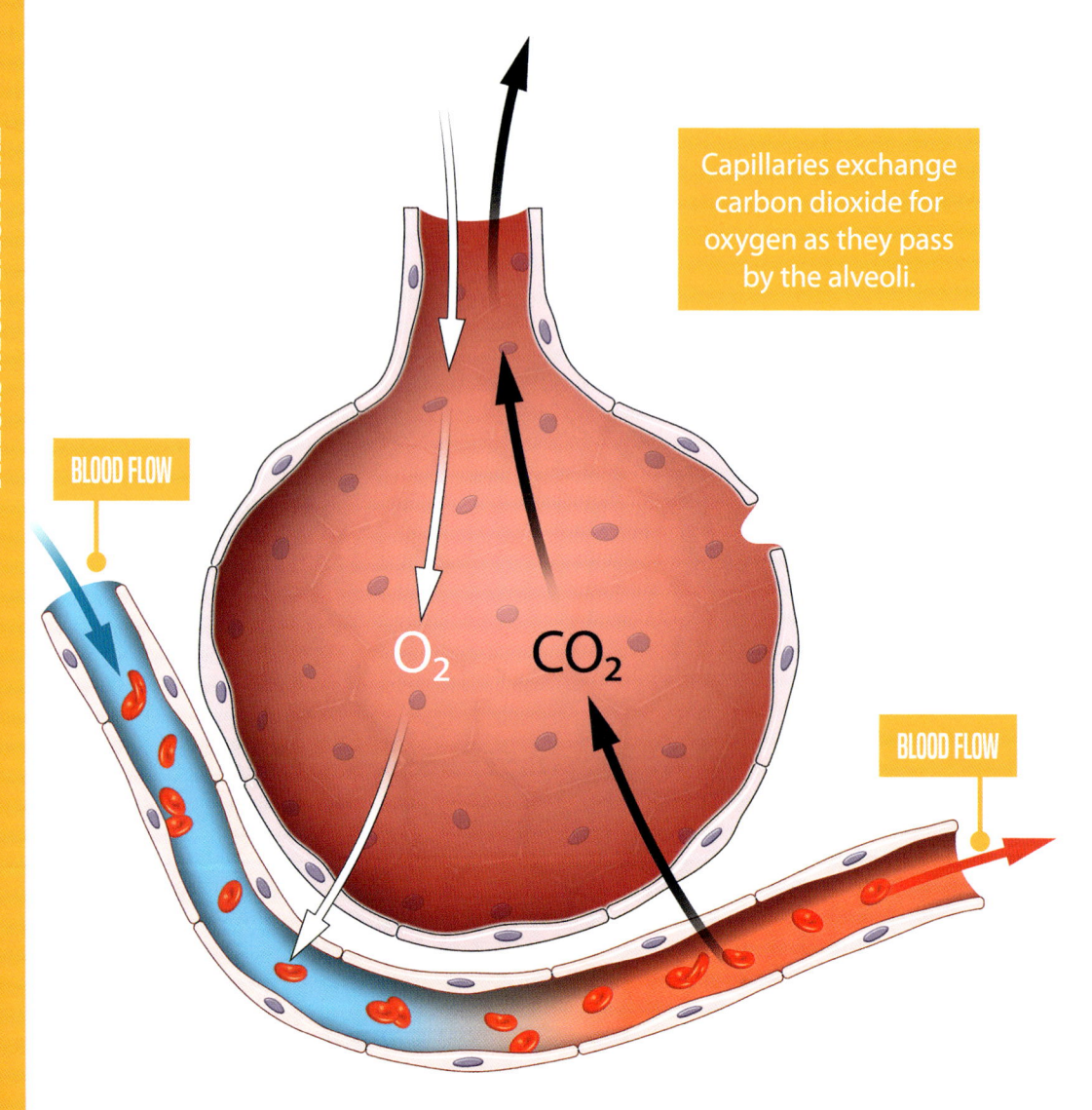

Capillaries exchange carbon dioxide for oxygen as they pass by the alveoli.

BLOOD FLOW

O_2

CO_2

BLOOD FLOW

GAS EXCHANGE

Alveoli are located throughout the lungs. They are where gas exchange occurs. Oxygen in the alveoli is transferred to the bloodstream. The alveoli pick up carbon dioxide from the blood to be exhaled. The walls of the alveoli are very thin. They are only one cell thick. This allows gases to pass easily between the alveoli and the bloodstream.

Alveoli are very tiny. But together, they have a large surface area. Stretched out, the alveoli could cover an area of more than 1,075 square feet (100 sq m). This large area is necessary for great amounts of oxygen to quickly enter the bloodstream. The alveoli can pass more than 10 fluid ounces (300 mL) of oxygen into the bloodstream each minute.

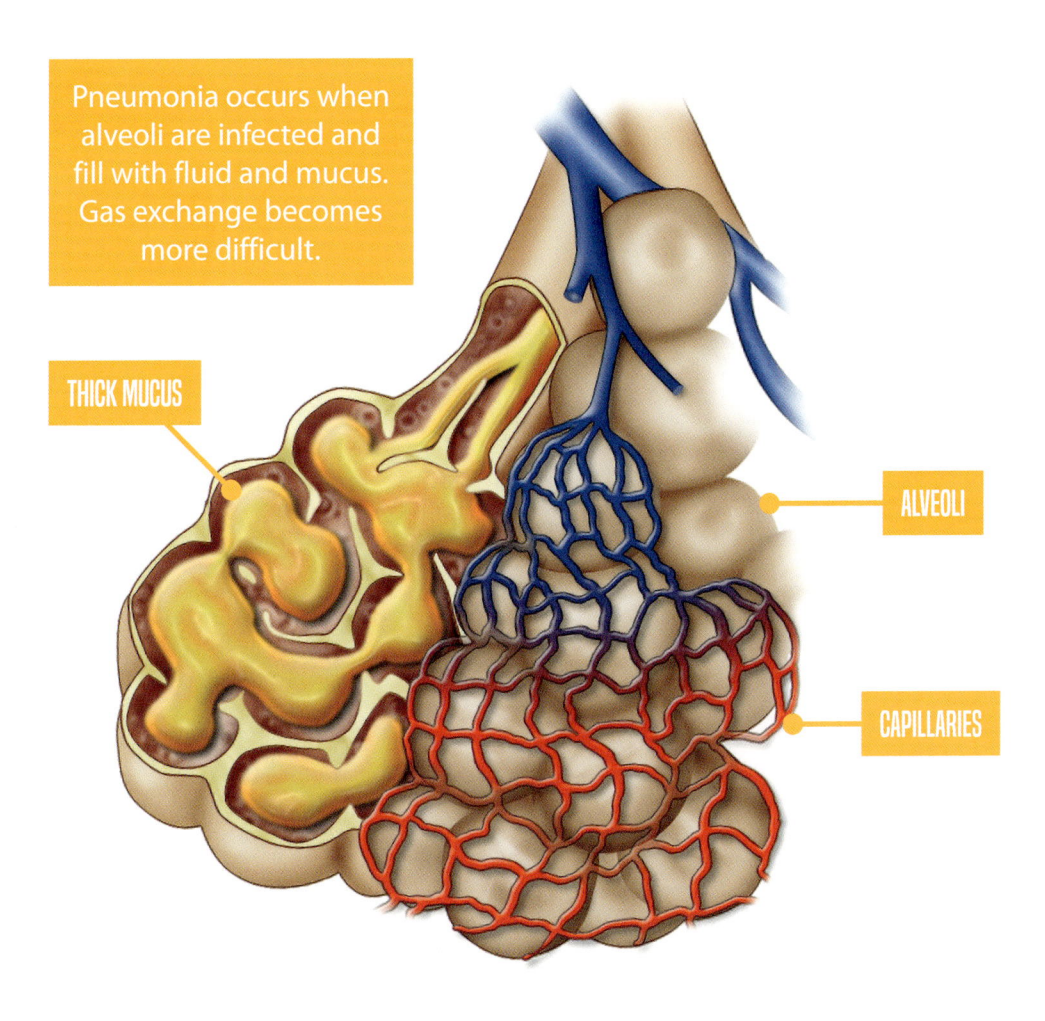

Pneumonia occurs when alveoli are infected and fill with fluid and mucus. Gas exchange becomes more difficult.

THICK MUCUS

ALVEOLI

CAPILLARIES

Smoking or being near someone who smokes can permanently destroy alveoli.

Thin blood vessels called capillaries branch into the alveoli. The capillaries carry blood that has high amounts of carbon dioxide. This gas passes from the capillaries and into the alveoli. The carbon dioxide moves through the body's airways and is exhaled. At the same time, oxygen passes through the thin walls of the alveoli. Oxygen enters the capillaries. The capillaries now carry oxygen-rich blood. The capillaries widen into larger blood vessels that return to the heart. The heart then pumps oxygen-rich blood throughout the body.

Alveoli health is very important. If the alveoli are damaged, gas exchange does not occur as efficiently. Alveoli begin to break down as a person gets older. But a person's lifestyle also affects alveoli health. Smoking damages the lungs. Even exposure to cigarette smoke can hurt the alveoli. Polluted air can be harmful. However, exercise can help improve lung health.

This photograph compares the lungs of a nonsmoker (left) to the lungs of a smoker (right). Smoking causes the lung to become darker and misshapen.

Wildfires cause poor air quality that is harmful to the lungs.

THE SKELETAL SYSTEM

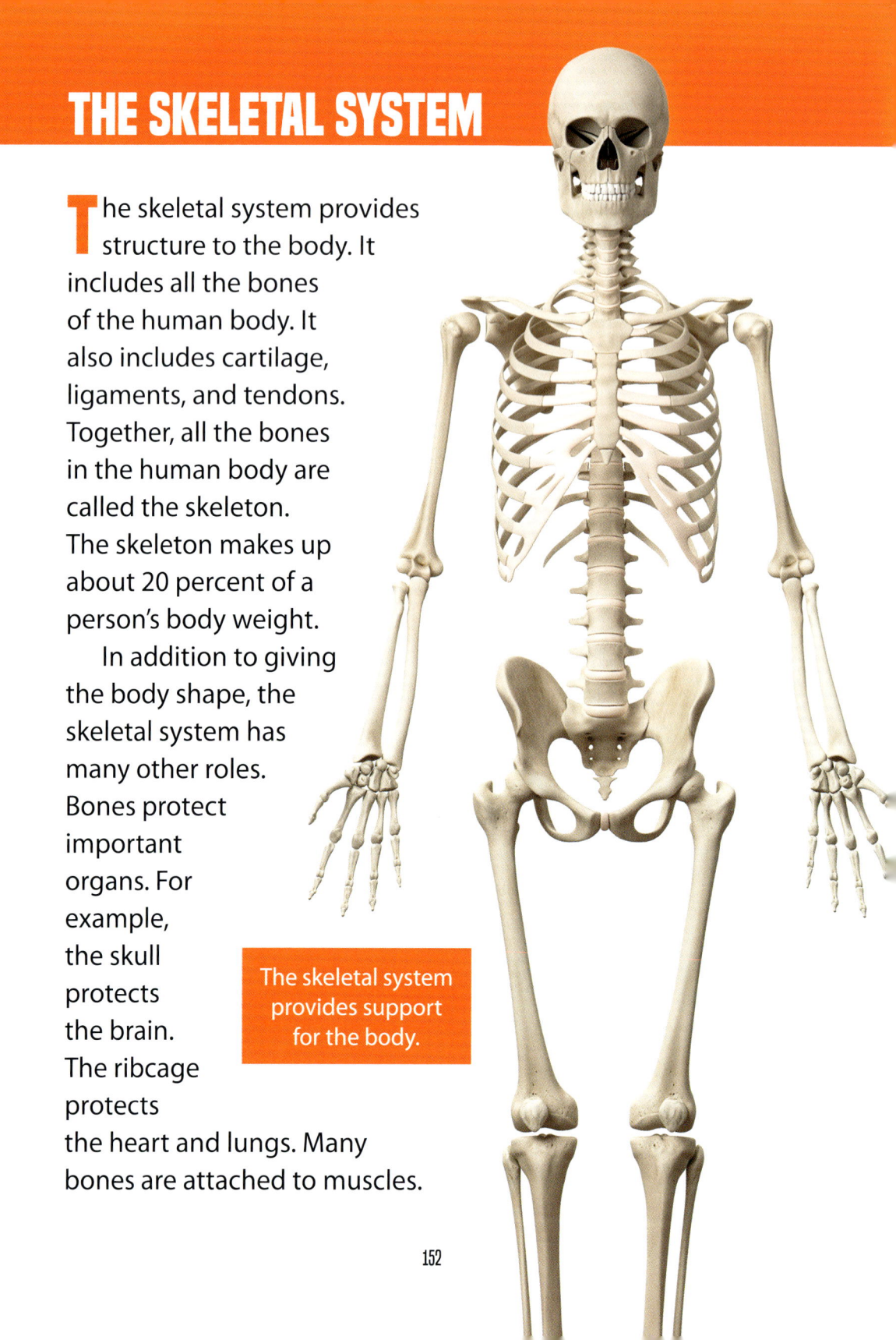

The skeletal system provides structure to the body. It includes all the bones of the human body. It also includes cartilage, ligaments, and tendons. Together, all the bones in the human body are called the skeleton. The skeleton makes up about 20 percent of a person's body weight.

In addition to giving the body shape, the skeletal system has many other roles. Bones protect important organs. For example, the skull protects the brain. The ribcage protects the heart and lungs. Many bones are attached to muscles.

The skeletal system provides support for the body.

The skeletal system and muscular system work together to make movement possible. Bones also produce blood cells. They store important minerals like calcium. Muscles need calcium to function. The nervous system also uses calcium to send messages throughout the body.

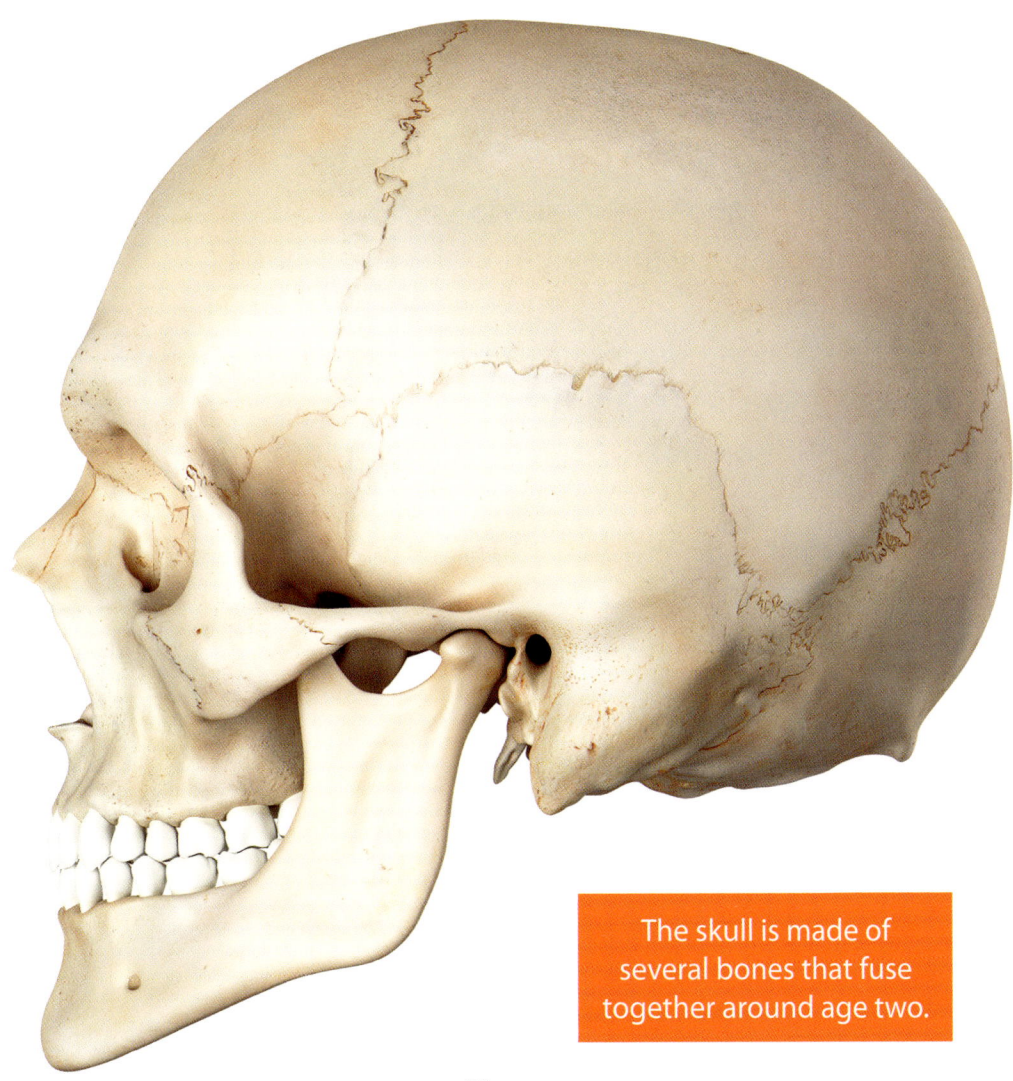

The skull is made of several bones that fuse together around age two.

Bones come in many shapes and sizes. The femur is the longest bone in the body. It is located in the upper thigh. The length of this bone varies depending on a person's height. On average, the femur is equal to about a quarter of a person's height. If a person is 4.6 feet (1.4 m) tall, the femur will be about 14 inches (36 cm) long. The bone supports the full weight of the body when a person stands.

The femur is one of the strongest bones in the human body. It can withstand forces that are approximately 30 times a person's weight.

The smallest bones in the human body are located in the inner ear. They are the malleus, incus, and stapes. These three bones are known as the ossicles. *Ossicles* means "tiny bones" in Latin. The ossicles work together to help a person hear. The stapes is the smallest of the ossicles. It is just 0.1 inches (0.3 cm) long.

The bones in the inner ear vibrate with the eardrum. They help make sounds seem louder.

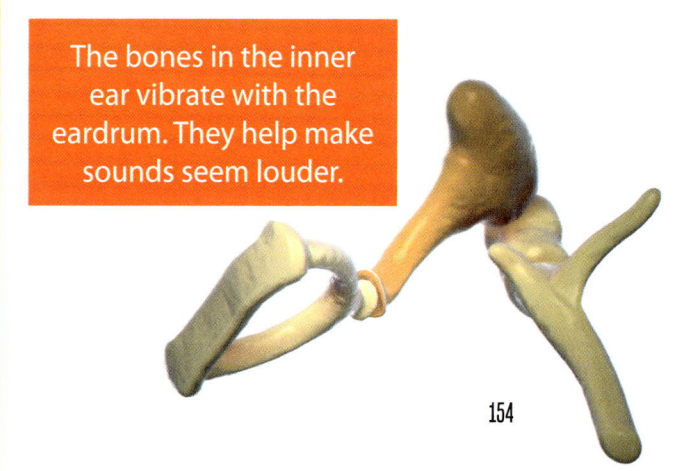

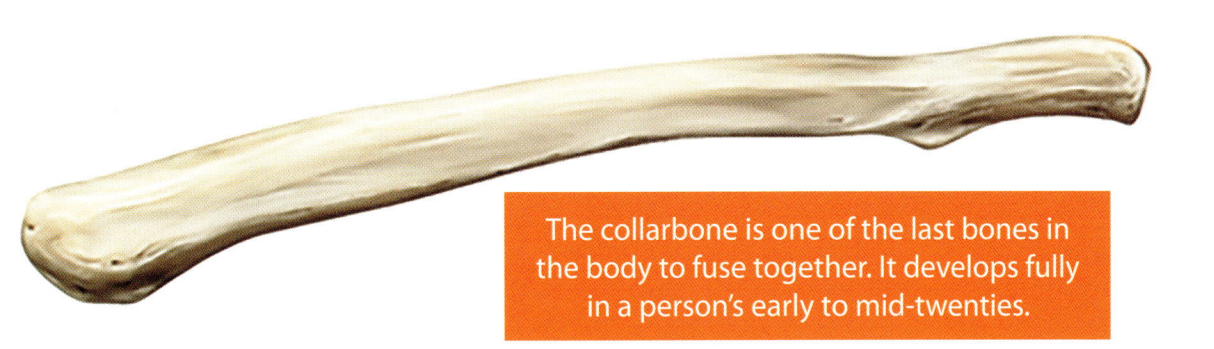

The collarbone is one of the last bones in the body to fuse together. It develops fully in a person's early to mid-twenties.

Babies are born with 300 bones. Their bones are softer and more flexible than adult bones. This allowed them to stay curled in the uterus for many months. But as they grow older, their bones become harder and more rigid. The bones also begin to fuse together. The adult skeleton has 206 bones.

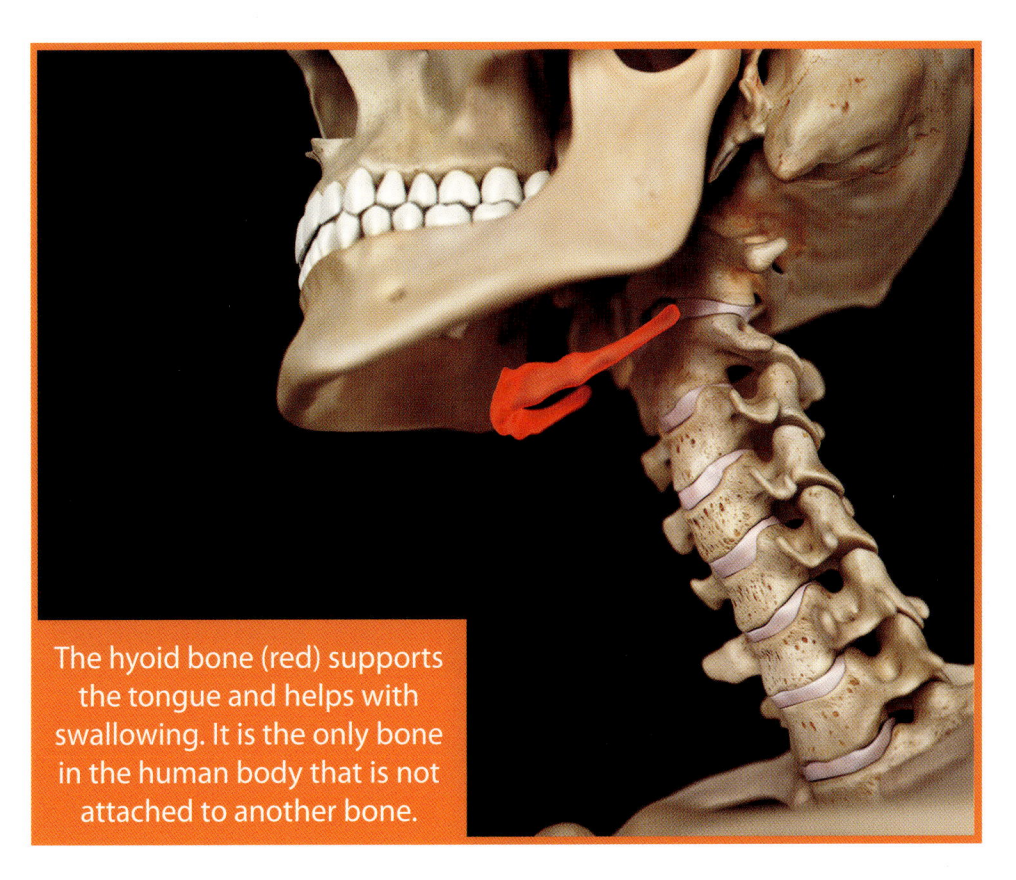

The hyoid bone (red) supports the tongue and helps with swallowing. It is the only bone in the human body that is not attached to another bone.

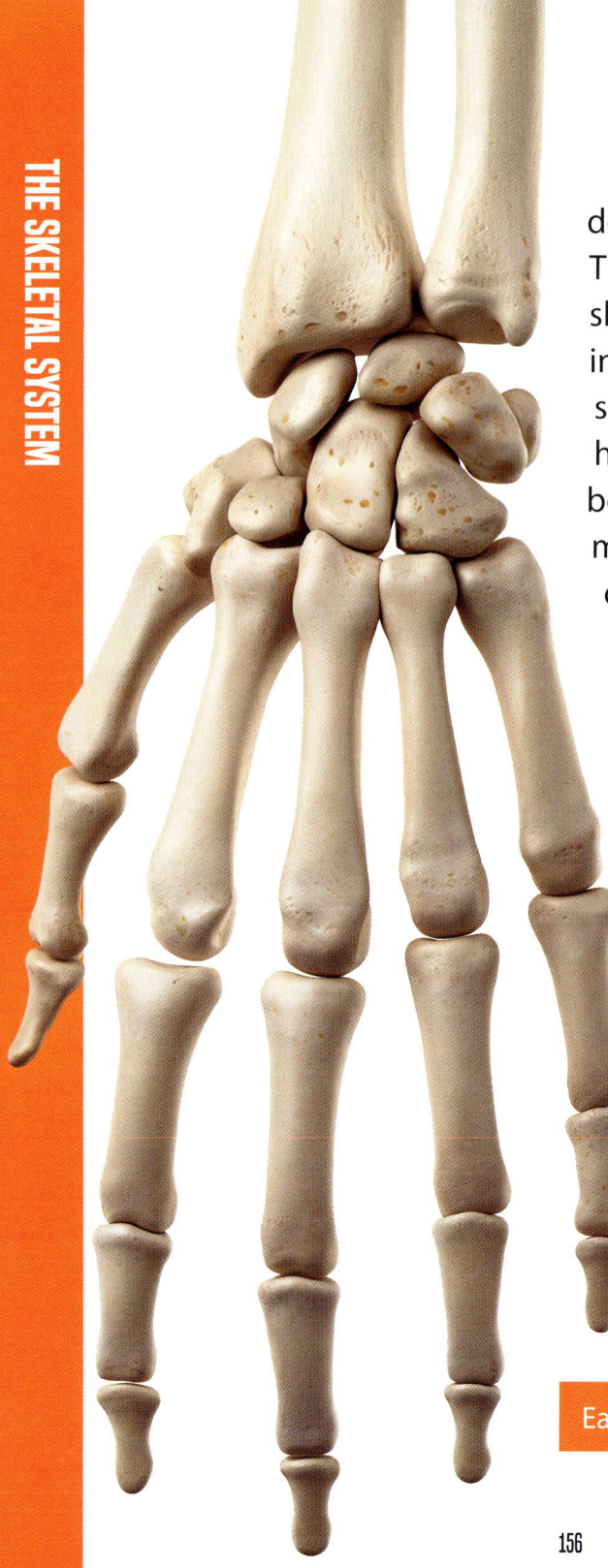

The skeleton can be broken down into two main groups. The first group is the axial skeleton. It includes bones in the head, neck, chest, and spine. The adult axial skeleton has a total of 80 bones. Major bones include bones that make up the skull. Bones called the vertebrae make up the backbone. The axial system also includes 12 pairs of ribs. These bones provide support for the upper body. Bones in the axial system also protect the brain, spinal cord, and organs in the chest.

The second group of bones make up the appendicular skeleton. Bones in the arms and legs belong to the appendicular skeleton. Adults have 126 bones

Each hand has 27 bones.

in the appendicular skeleton. Many of these bones are in the wrists and fingers. They make a wide range of movement possible. The humerus, radius, and ulna are major bones in the arms. The femur, tibia, and fibula are important bones in the legs. The appendicular skeleton also includes the collarbone and the pelvis, or hip bone. Bones in the appendicular skeleton are important for movement and support.

The bones that make up the hips and rear have an irregular shape.

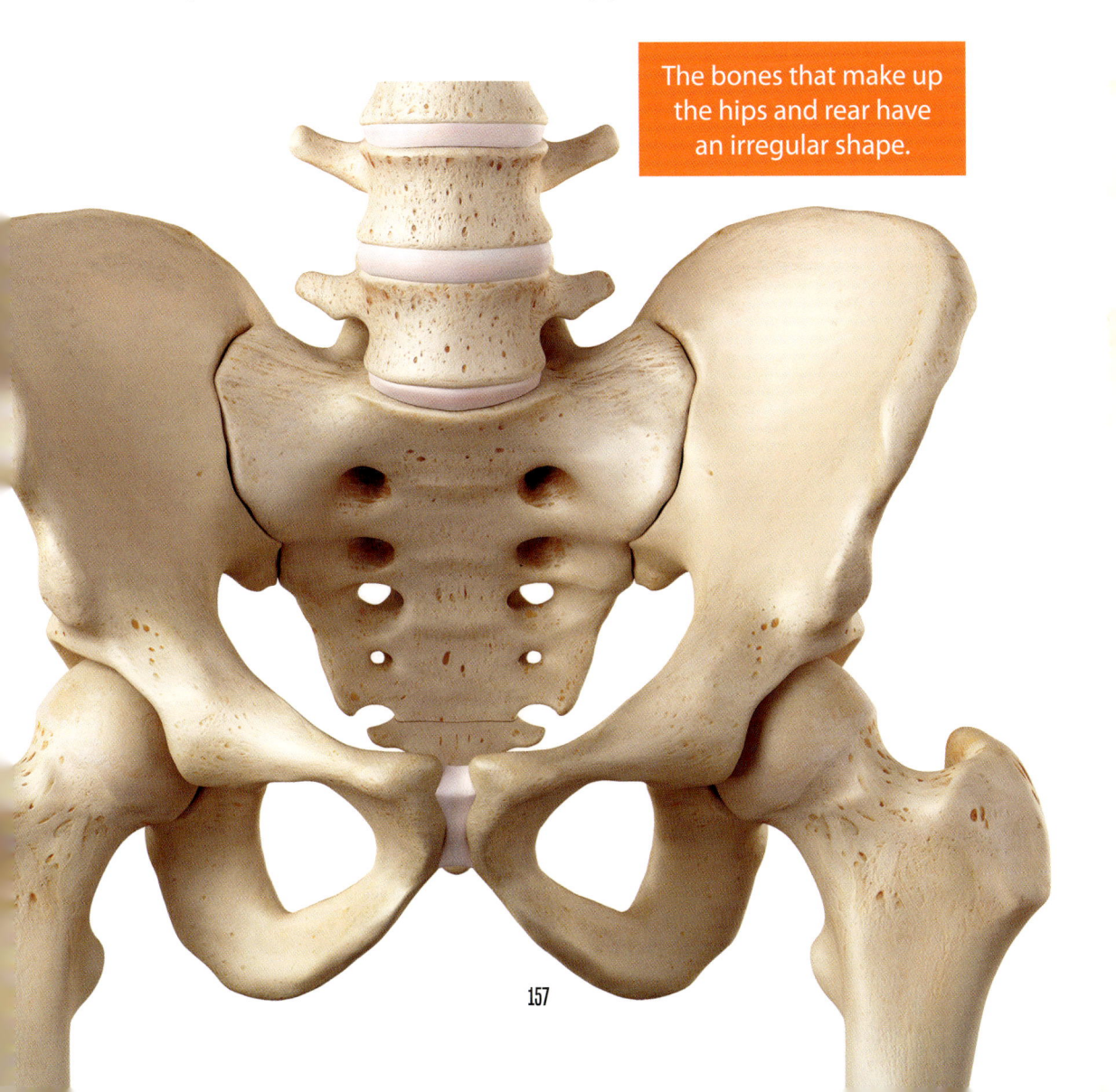

Bones come in four major shapes. Long bones are long and thin. They include bones like the humerus, femur, and other bones in the arms and legs. Short bones are shaped like blocks. Many of the bones in the wrists and ankles are short bones. Flat bones are large. They have smooth, broad surfaces. The ribs and skull are examples of flat bones. Some bones do not fit into these shape categories. They are irregular bones. Bones that make up the spine have an irregular shape. They are rounded with several structures that stick out. They each have a hole through the middle where the spinal cord runs through.

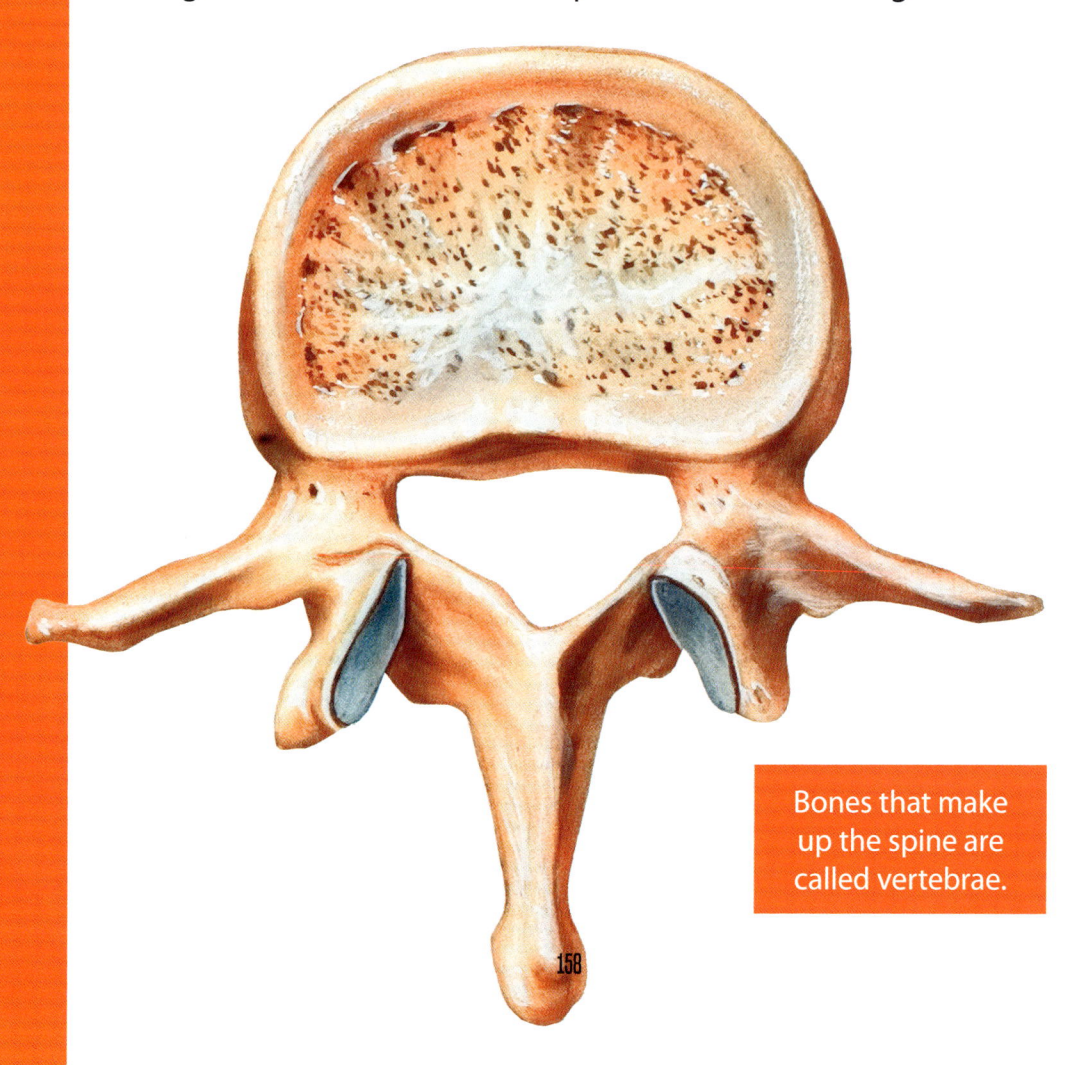

Bones that make up the spine are called vertebrae.

Milk is a good source of calcium. Other foods like spinach are rich in calcium too.

WHAT ARE BONES MADE OF?

Bones are made of a strong protein called collagen. One ounce (28 g) of collagen is stronger than steel of equal weight. Collagen is the most common protein in the human body. It is also found in the skin and connective tissues. About one-third of all proteins in the body are collagen.

Bones are also made of calcium. This mineral helps strengthen bone. More than 99 percent of the body's calcium supply is found in the bones. The bones release calcium into the bloodstream to help with muscle movement and other processes. Milk and foods that are rich in calcium help maintain the calcium supply in bones.

Bones are tough but lightweight. This is because bones have different layers of tissue. The outer layer is made of collagen. The inner layer has tiny holes. It has a spongy appearance. These holes are arranged like honeycombs. This structure is very stable. It helps keep bones strong. In some bones, the inner region of bone is filled with bone marrow. This is the fluid that produces blood cells. Bone marrow creates the body's supply of red and white blood cells, as well as platelets.

Even though bones are very strong, they can still break. This is called a fracture. Bones may fracture when they experience an extreme amount of force. They may break as a result of a car crash

Muscles are able to move bones because bones are lightweight and hollow.

or a collision while playing sports. Certain medical conditions may also cause bones to become weak. People with these conditions are at greater risk of bone fractures.

Casts prevent bones from moving. They make sure that a broken bone heals in the correct position.

The fingers have many joints that help with the fine movement needed to play the piano.

JOINTS

Bones connect together at the joints. Some joints do not allow for movement. This includes joints in the skull. Other joints only allow for a little bit of flexibility. Joints in the ribcage bend slightly as a person breathes. But other joints are used for a wide range of movement. These are called moveable joints. They include many joints in the arms and legs.

There are many types of moveable joints. The type of joint depends on how the bones fit together and the type of movement they allow. Ball-and-socket joints allow for the greatest range of movement. The rounded end of one bone fits in the pocket of another. The hips and shoulders are examples of ball-and-socket joints. Movement in all directions is possible. The hips and shoulders can move side to side, as well as back and forth. They can also rotate.

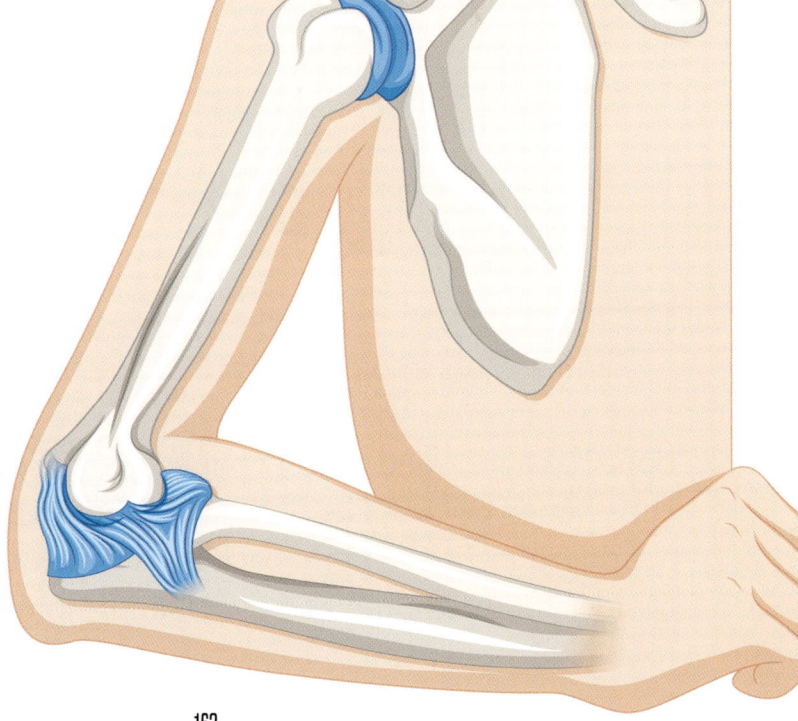

The shoulder joint can rotate. The elbow joint can only bend back and forth.

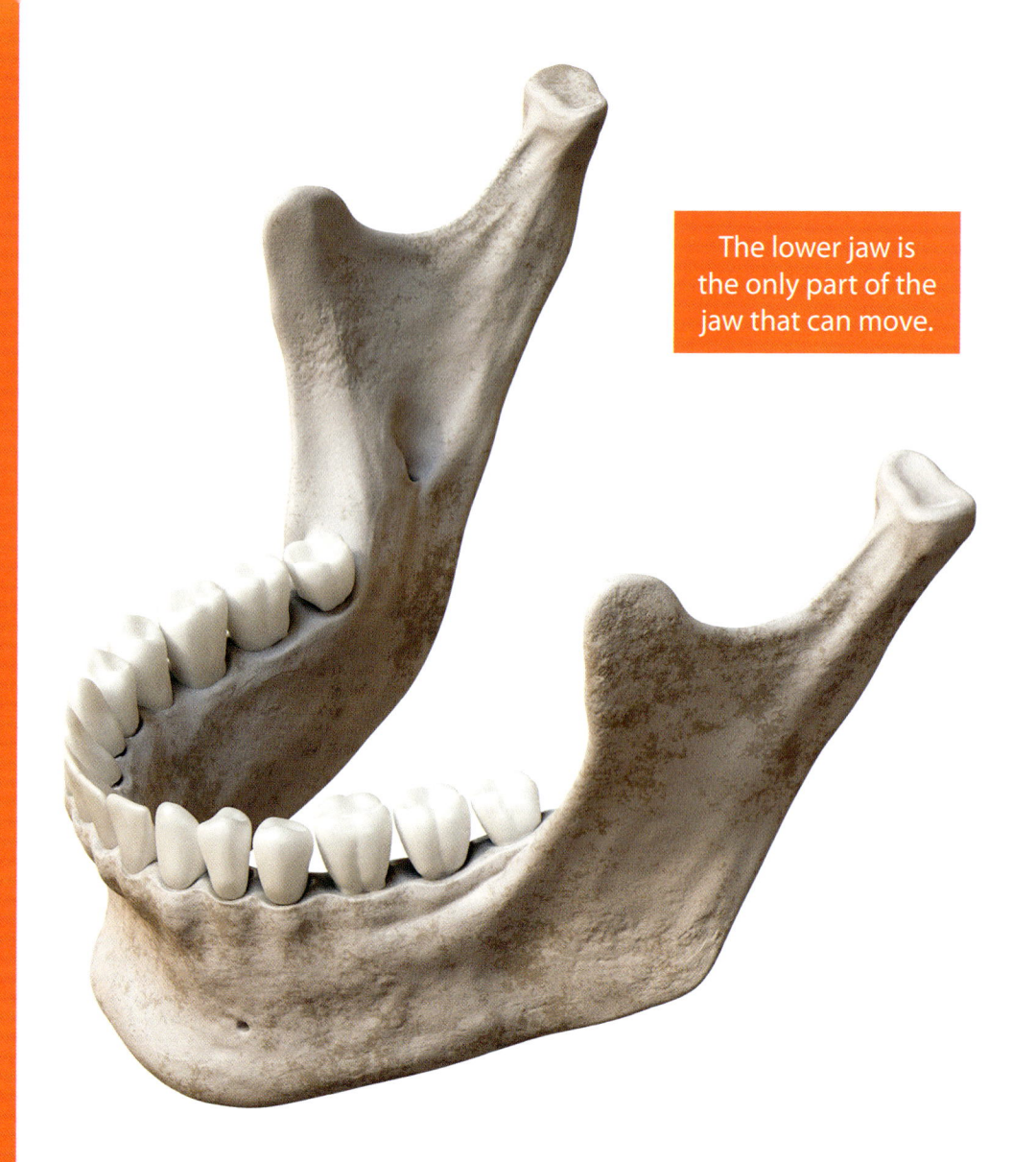

The lower jaw is the only part of the jaw that can move.

Saddle joints also offer a wide range of movement too. They are a similar shape to ball-and-socket joints. One bone has a rounded end. It connects to the other bone in a cup-shaped pocket. The base of the thumb is an example of a saddle joint. It can bend back and forth. It can move side to side. But the thumb and other saddle joints do not allow rotational movement.

Condyloid joints offer similar movement to saddle joints. They can move in all directions, but they cannot rotate. They differ from saddle joints in shape. They are made when the ends of both bones are oval-shaped. The jaw is an example of a condyloid joint.

Joints in the neck allow the head to lean backward and forward.

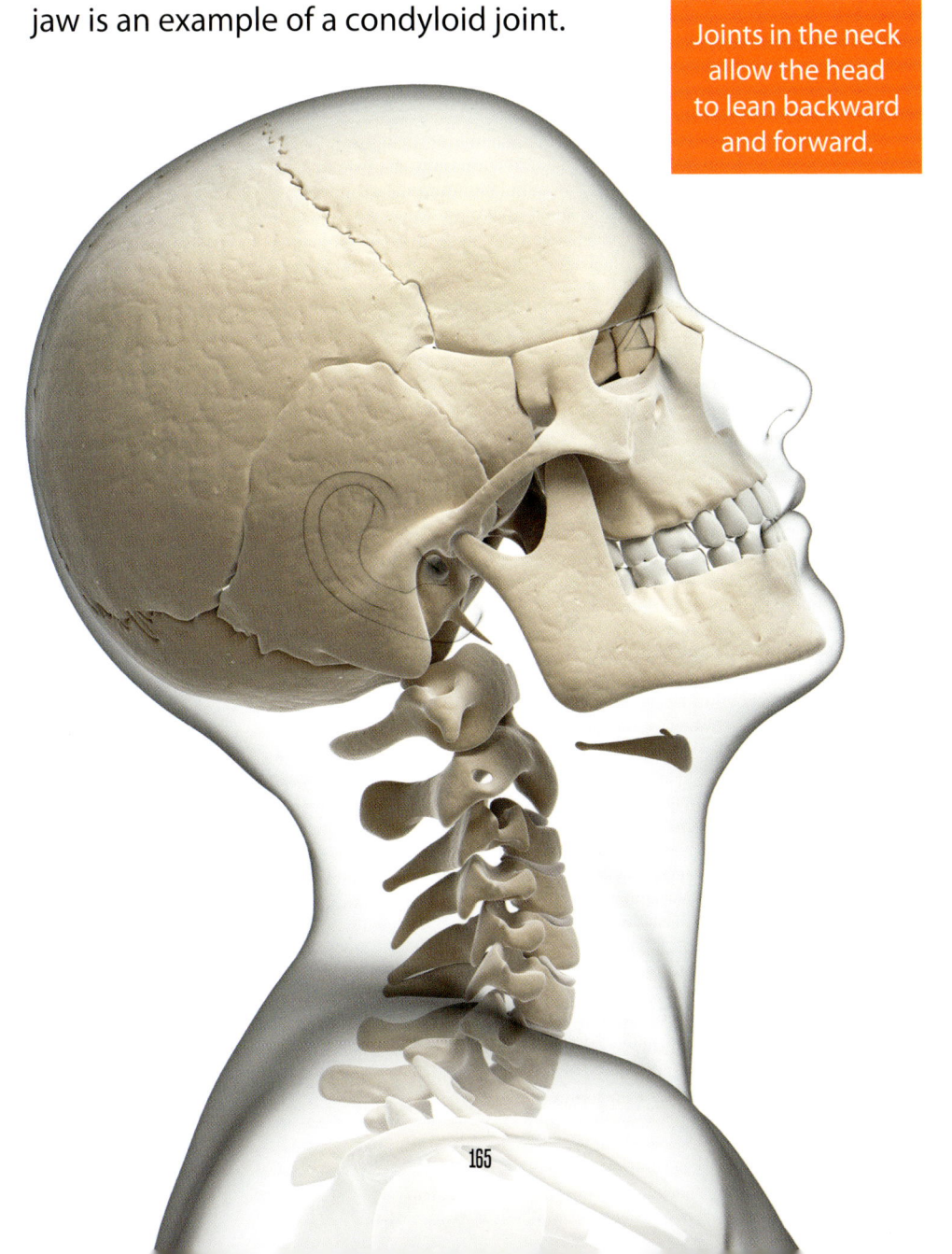

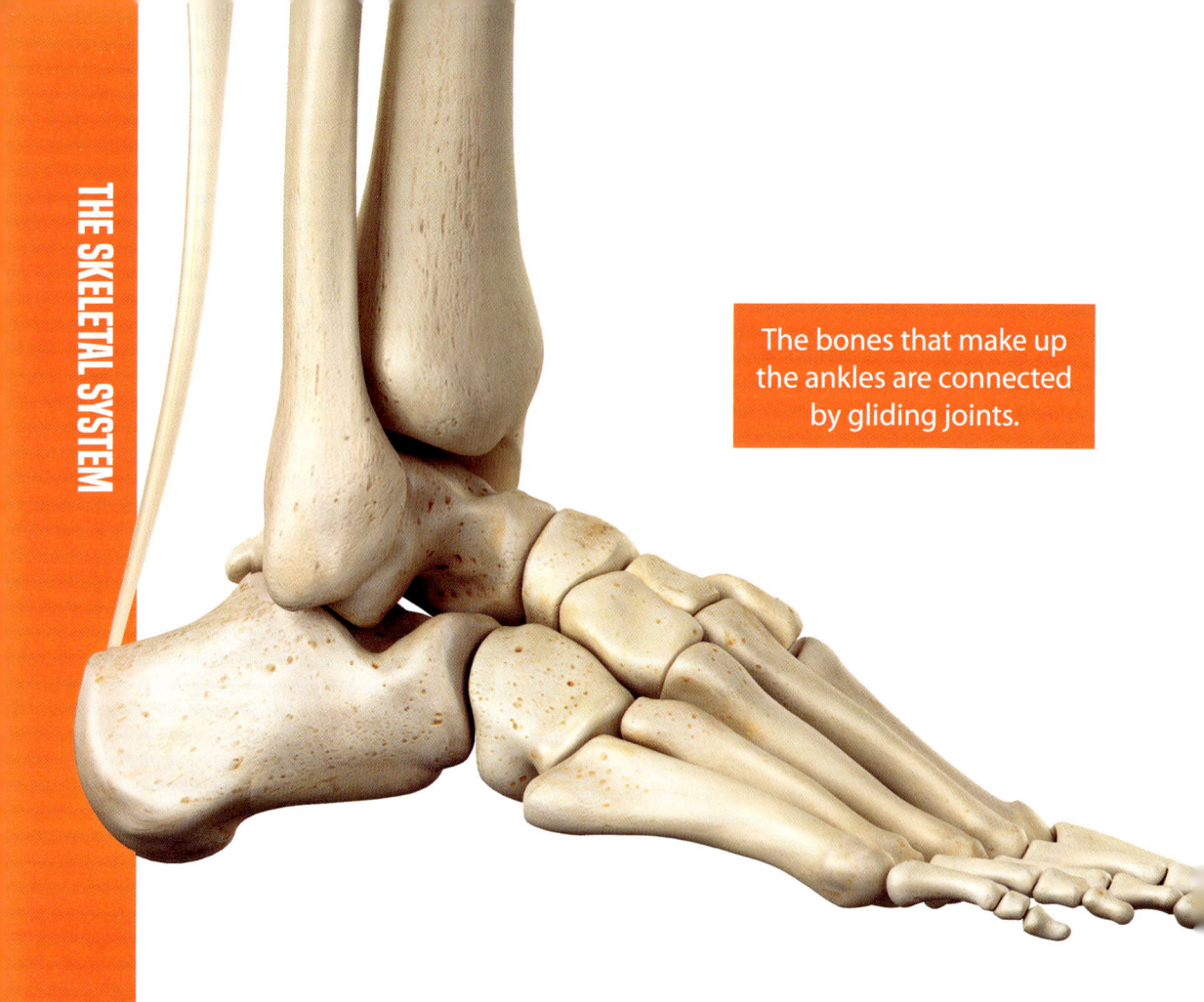

The bones that make up the ankles are connected by gliding joints.

Hinge joints work like hinges on a door. They swing forward and backward. The knees and elbows are hinge joints. They have limited movement. They can bend in only one direction.

Pivot joints are formed when one bone forms a ring around another bone. The bone on the inside is able to swivel. The neck has a pivot joint that allows a person to turn his or her head.

The last type of moveable joint is the gliding joint. These joints are made when bones with flat surfaces connect with each other. The bones can slide over each other. The bones in the wrist are connected by gliding joints.

CARTILAGE, LIGAMENTS, AND TENDONS

In addition to bones, the skeletal system includes other tissues that create structure and help with movement. These tissues include cartilage, ligaments, and tendons. Cartilage is a type of connective tissue. It is mostly made of collagen. It is more flexible than bone. Cartilage is found in the nose and earlobes. It gives these body parts structure. Cartilage is also located at the tips of bones. It prevents bones from rubbing against each other, which can be painful.

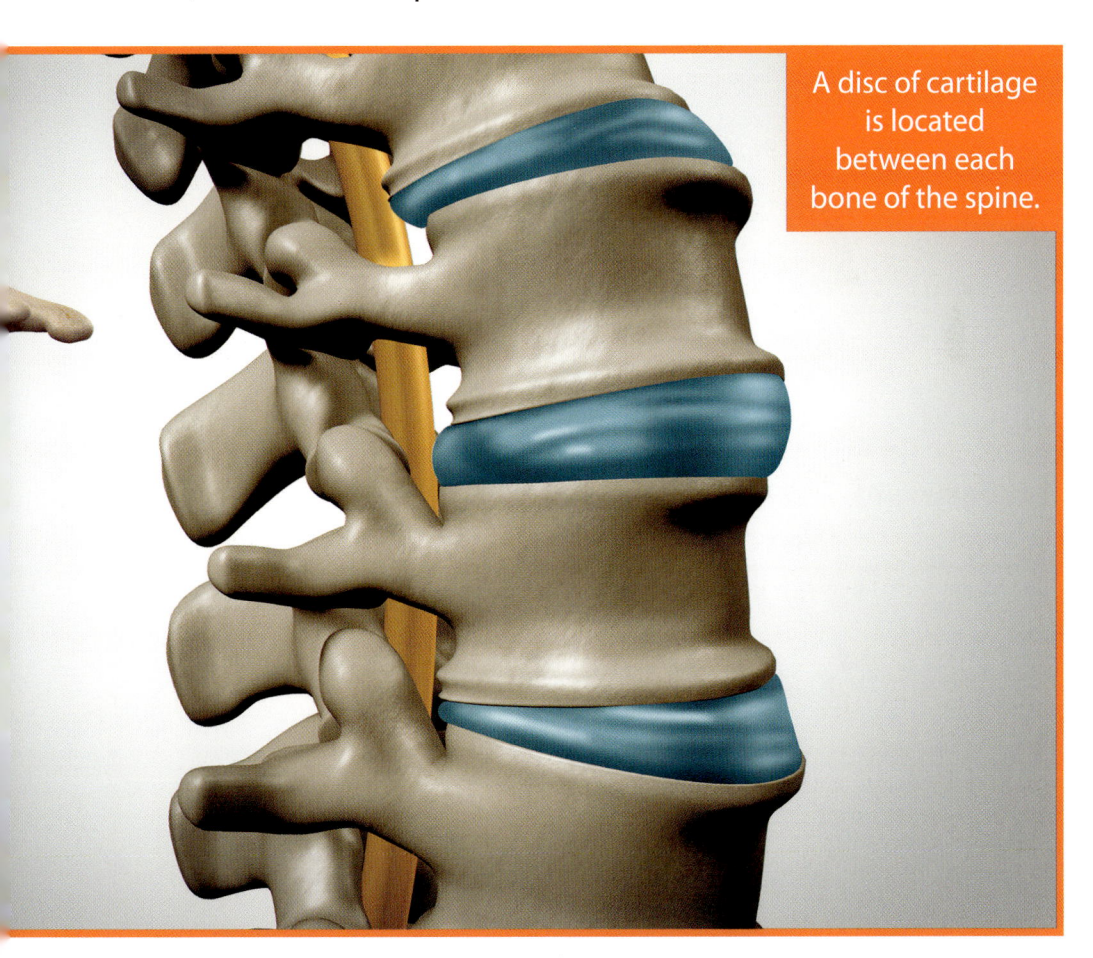

A disc of cartilage is located between each bone of the spine.

Cartilage acts like padding. It provides cushion to bones as they move. Certain activities put a lot of stress on bones. Running is an example. When a person runs, his or her feet make a hard impact with the ground. The impact travels through bones in the feet, legs, and spine. Cartilage absorbs some of the shock.

As a person gets older, cartilage can wear away. This creates a condition called arthritis. Bones rub against each other. Someone with arthritis may find it difficult to move without pain.

Arthritis typically affects older adults, but young people can develop arthritis too.

Ligaments and tendons are made of strong connective tissue. They play different roles in the skeletal system. Ligaments attach bones to other bones. They provide stability at the joints and make sure bones stay in place. Tendons attach bones to muscles. They help with movement.

There are more than 900 ligaments in the body. Most of them provide support in the arms and legs. The anterior cruciate ligament (ACL) is a major ligament in the center of the knee. The ACL connects the femur to the shinbone. It keeps the shinbone from sliding forward. Tearing or spraining the ACL is a common sports injury. It can cause extreme pain and weakness in the knee.

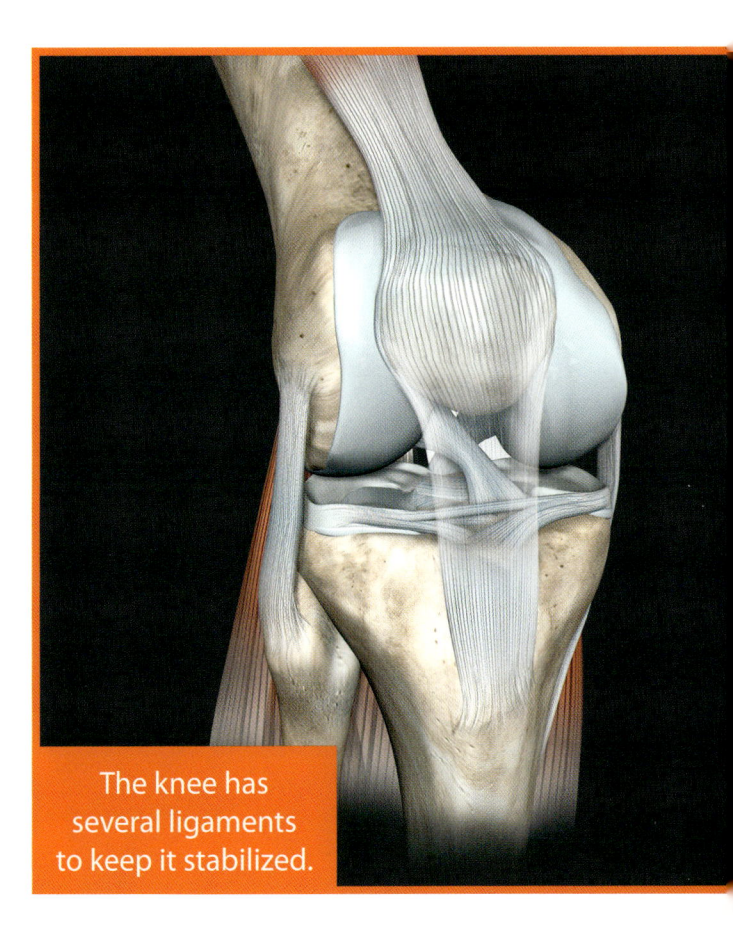

The knee has several ligaments to keep it stabilized.

Tendons make sure that bones and muscles move together. When a muscle contracts, tendons pull the bone so that it moves as well. There are approximately 4,000 tendons in the body. A tendon injury is known as a strain. Like injuries to ligaments, strains can cause pain and affect movement.

COMMON DISEASES

People can suffer from many types of diseases. Each disease has different symptoms. It is important to understand how diseases affect the different body systems. Knowing the symptoms of diseases helps doctors make diagnoses. Doctors can treat the disease or its symptoms and make sure the body is functioning properly.

Doctors listen to a patient's symptoms to know how to best treat a disease.

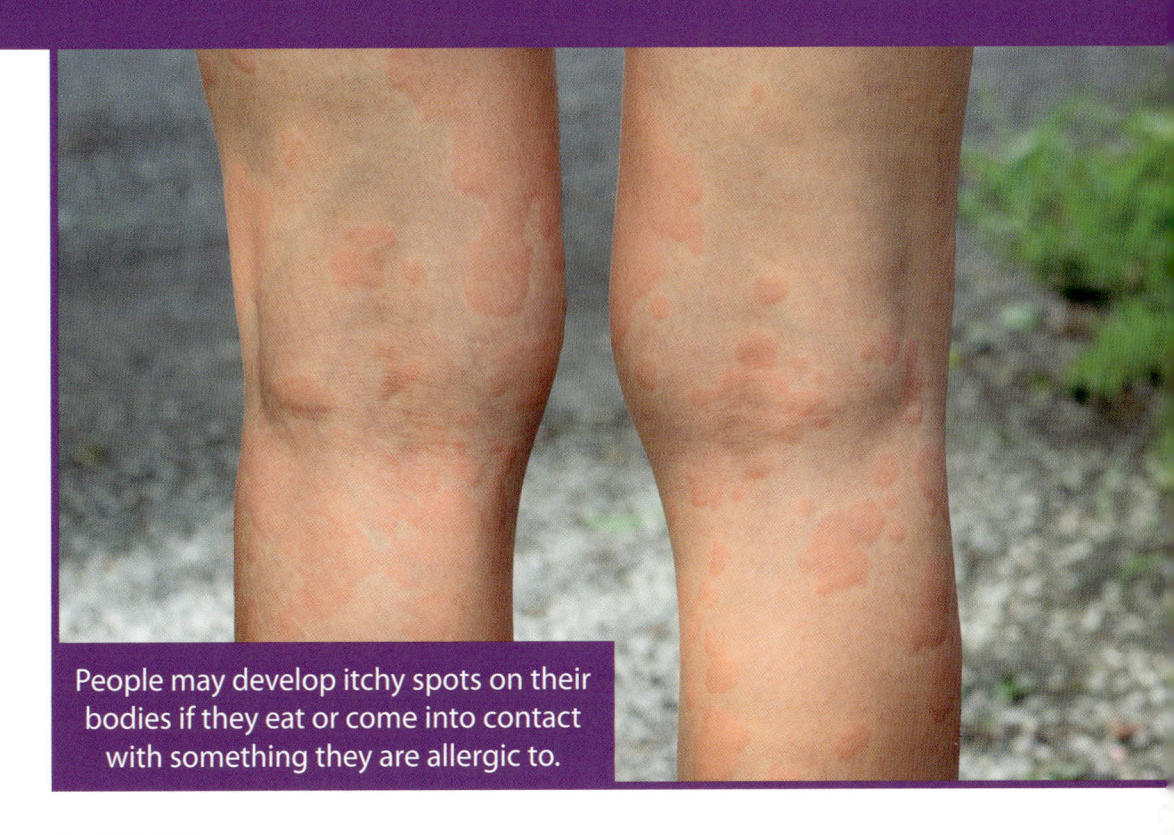

People may develop itchy spots on their bodies if they eat or come into contact with something they are allergic to.

ALLERGIES

Allergies occur when the immune system reacts strongly to a foreign substance. This substance is harmless and would not otherwise cause an illness. Pollen and dust can trigger allergies. Foods and medicines can also cause allergic reactions. Things that trigger an allergic reaction are called allergens. During an allergic reaction, white blood cells attack the allergen. Some white blood cells produce a substance known as histamine. Histamine causes many allergy symptoms, including a rash or a runny nose. In severe cases, histamine can affect the airways of the respiratory system. It may cause the airways to swell shut.

ASTHMA

Asthma is a condition that affects the respiratory system. It is often diagnosed in childhood. Asthma causes airways to narrow. This makes it difficult for the body to receive enough oxygen, which

An inhaler helps relax the airways, making it easier for someone with asthma to breathe.

it needs to function. Asthma symptoms include chest pain, wheezing, and shortness of breath. Cold and dry air can trigger asthma symptoms. It is easier for the lungs to handle air that is warm and moist.

COMMON COLD

More than 200 types of viruses can cause the common cold. Symptoms of this disease are a runny nose, a sore throat, and sneezing. The virus enters the body through openings such as the eyes, nose, and throat. Then it infects cells in the upper respiratory system. The upper respiratory

Many cold viruses belong to a family of viruses known as rhinoviruses.

system includes the nose, throat, and windpipe. If the virus infects cells in the lower respiratory system, it causes a chest cold.

COVID-19

COVID-19 is caused by the virus SARS-CoV-2. The virus mainly affects the airways and lungs. Symptoms of COVID-19 include coughing and shortness of breath. However, the disease can affect other organ systems as well. Some people experience digestive problems such as nausea and diarrhea. It can also affect sensory neurons in the nose. Some people with COVID-19 lose the sense of smell.

In severe cases of COVID-19, a patient may need a ventilator to get enough oxygen.

An insulin pump can provide a constant supply of insulin for someone with diabetes.

DIABETES

Diabetes is a condition that causes problems with regulating blood sugar. It is a problem of the endocrine system. When food is digested, it is broken down into a sugar called glucose. The pancreas typically produces a hormone called insulin. This hormone helps remove glucose from the bloodstream. It stores the glucose in cells so that it can later be used for energy. There are two types of diabetes. Someone with type 1 diabetes does not produce insulin. Someone with type 2 diabetes does not respond to the insulin the pancreas produces. In both types, high amounts of glucose build up in the bloodstream. This can cause health complications including kidney damage and heart disease.

HEART DISEASE

Heart disease refers to a group of diseases that affect the heart. It is the leading cause of death in the United States. The most common type is coronary artery disease (CAD). In CAD, major arteries to the heart become narrowed or blocked. This is caused by a buildup of plaque on the artery walls. Blood is not able to circulate through the body as easily. The heart is unable supply the oxygen and other nutrients that the body needs. Symptoms of CAD include shortness of breath and chest pain. A person has a heart attack when an artery to the heart is completely blocked.

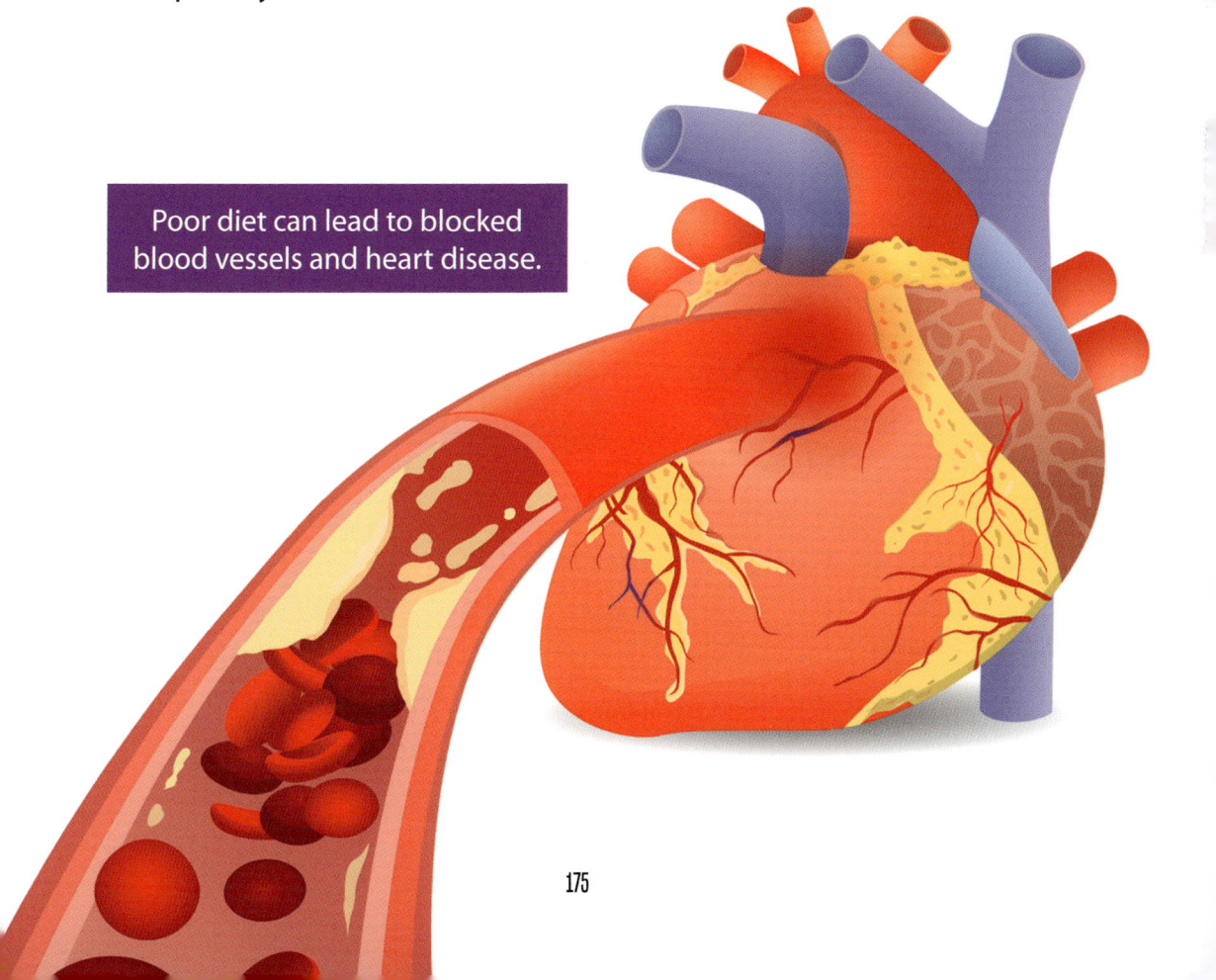

Poor diet can lead to blocked blood vessels and heart disease.

OSTEOSARCOMA

Osteosarcoma is a type of bone cancer. It is a rare disease. It typically occurs in people between the ages of ten and 30. Like all cancers, osteosarcoma happens when cells begin to grow out of control. They form masses called tumors. The bone cells in an osteosarcoma tumor are unhealthy. They form weak bone tissue. The tumor cells can spread to other regions of the body.

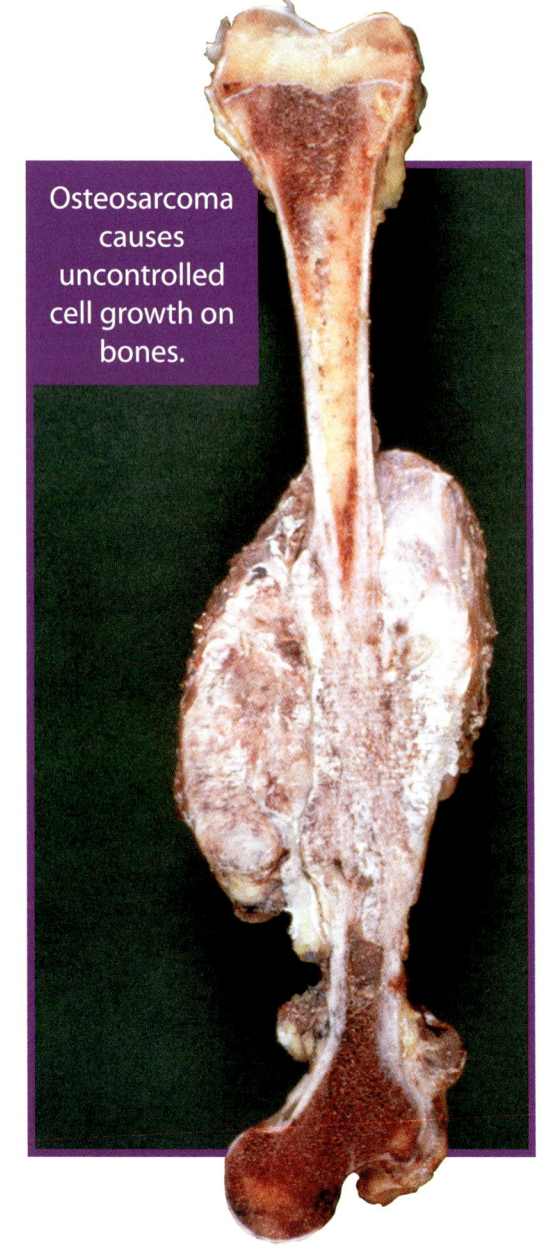

Osteosarcoma causes uncontrolled cell growth on bones.

PNEUMONIA

Pneumonia is an infection of the alveoli in the lungs. This infection is usually caused by bacteria, but viruses and fungi can also cause pneumonia. Pneumonia causes the alveoli to become swollen. They fill with fluid. The alveoli are the site where gas exchange occurs. When a person has pneumonia, the body may not get enough oxygen. Oxygen does not easily pass from the lungs into the bloodstream.

A person may experience shortness of breath and coughing. In severe cases, the lips and fingers may turn blue from lack of oxygen.

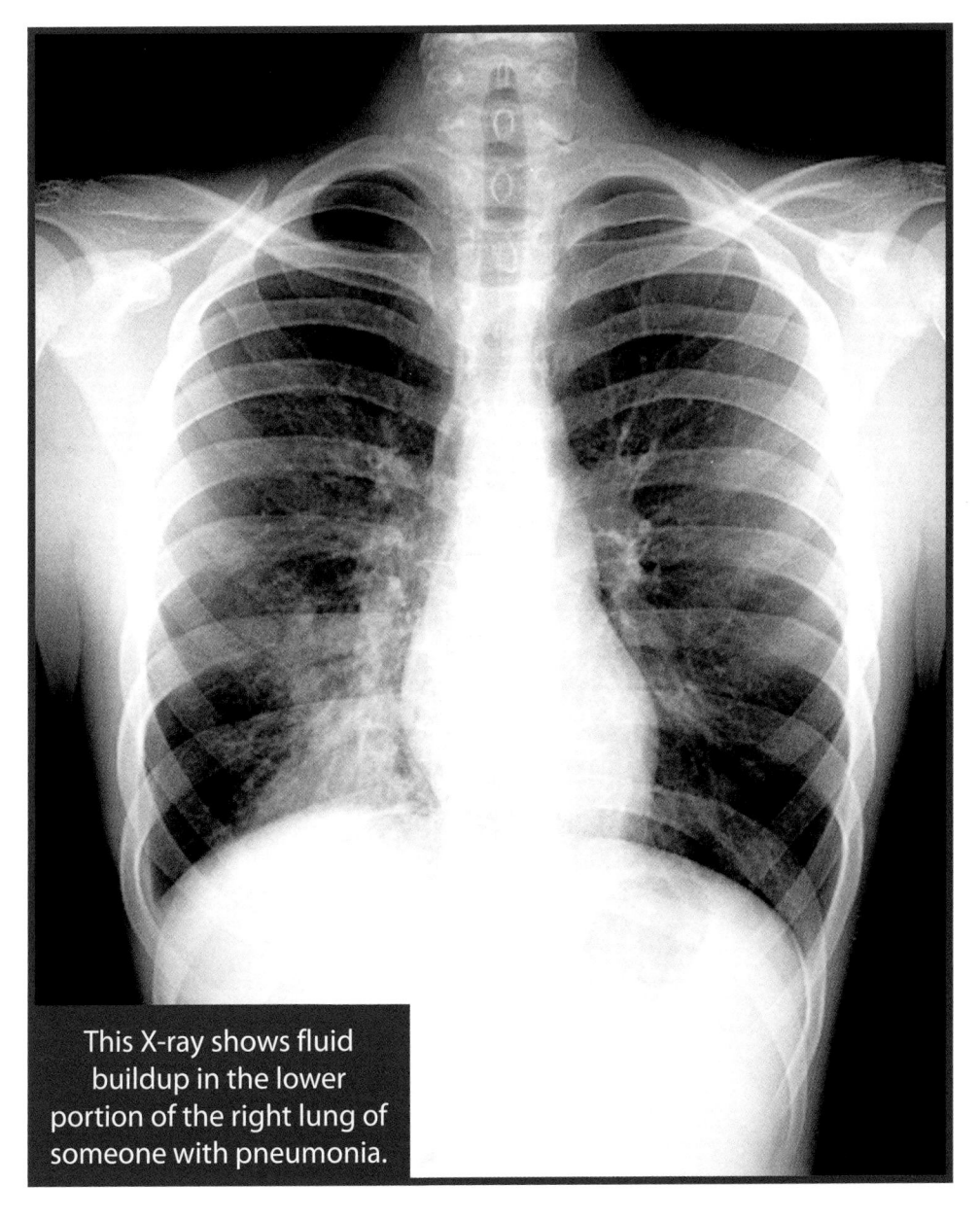

This X-ray shows fluid buildup in the lower portion of the right lung of someone with pneumonia.

STAYING HEALTHY

Eating a balanced diet is an important part of staying healthy. Different foods have different nutrients. The body needs a mix of nutrients to function properly. Nutrients include carbohydrates, proteins, and fats. They also include vitamins and minerals.

These nutrients give the body energy. They are necessary for many bodily functions. They are used to build muscles and produce hormones. They improve bone health. Proper nutrition also protects the body from diseases such as heart disease and cancer. It boosts the immune system. People who do not eat a balanced diet may get sick easily. They may feel tired often and have low energy.

In order to get all the nutrients the body needs to survive, a person should eat from a variety of food groups. Healthy eating means eating foods with whole grains such as wheat. Wheat is high in carbohydrates. Other foods like rice, corn, and potatoes also have high amounts of carbohydrates. Fruits and vegetables have important vitamins. Beans, nuts, and meats are rich in protein.

Bananas are a good source of an important mineral called potassium. This mineral helps with digestion and other functions.

A poor diet can cause someone to have low energy.

People should avoid eating unhealthy foods. These are foods that are high in fat and sugar but contain little nutrition. Eating too much fat can lead to unhealthy weight gain. It can cause problems with circulation and lead to heart disease. Eating too much sugar can cause similar health problems. Having too much sugar in the blood can be a sign of diabetes.

Exercise improves lung health and boosts energy levels.

EXERCISE

Regular exercise has many health benefits. Muscles play a major role in movement. During exercise, a person uses many muscles. As these muscles are used, they get bigger and stronger. They can handle more intense tasks without getting tired. Strong muscles help protect joints and bones.

Exercise benefits physical and mental health.

Exercise also promotes bone health. Like muscles, bones get stronger with exercise. They become thicker, which makes them less likely to break. As people get older, their bones typically become weaker. They may break bones easily. Regular exercise throughout one's lifetime can protect against these effects.

Muscles grow bigger and stronger with regular exercise.

184

Exercise may allow people to spend time outdoors.

Muscles require a lot of oxygen during exercise. The heart and the circulatory system deliver oxygen throughout the body. The heart pumps blood more rapidly during exercise. This is to make sure that muscles have a constant supply of oxygen. Exercise improves how well the heart is able to circulate blood. With regular exercise, the heart is able to deliver oxygen more effectively. A person becomes able to exercise for longer periods of time without feeling tired.

Exercise also improves a person's well-being in other ways. It can help people feel more energetic and focused. They may sleep better at night. Exercise improves mental health. It boosts mood and can reduce symptoms of anxiety and depression.

Regular exercise can protect the body from certain diseases, such as heart disease and cancer. It can help control blood pressure and reduce the risk of strokes. Exercise can also help a person lose weight. Being overweight can lead to long-lasting health conditions.

Joining a sports team is a good way to stay active and make new friends.

Children and teens between the ages of six and 17 should get about 60 minutes of exercise each day. Most of this exercise should be aerobic exercise. The heart is able to supply oxygen to the body for long periods of time during aerobic exercise. Aerobic exercise improves heart health. It includes activities such as walking and jogging. In addition to aerobic exercise, children and teens should do exercises that improve muscle and bone health. This includes things like push-ups and running. They should do these activities three times a week.

GLOSSARY

antibody
A protein produced by white blood cells that recognizes a specific germ.

cartilage
A type of connective tissue that provides structure and support.

cilia
Tiny hair-like structures that help move particles or cells.

enzyme
A protein that speeds up a chemical reaction, such as digestion.

fetus
A child developing in the uterus, from two months after fertilization until birth.

gland
A cell, tissue, or organ that secretes substances that affect bodily processes.

hormone
A chemical messenger that helps regulate bodily processes.

metabolism
The way the body converts food into energy.

nutrient
A substance that the body uses for energy, growth, and development, such as a carbohydrate or protein.

organ
A group of tissues that work together to perform a specific set of functions.

paralysis
A partial or total loss of sensory or motor function in part of the body.

pathogen
A bacterium, virus, or fungus that causes disease.

puberty
A developmental stage caused by changing hormone levels that results in sexual maturation; puberty typically occurs in the teen years.

reproduction
The process of producing children.

stroke
A serious health condition that occurs when the brain does not receive oxygen or nutrients due to a blocked blood vessel.

TO LEARN MORE

FURTHER READINGS

1,000 Amazing Human Body Facts. DK Publishing, 2021.

Reilly, Kathleen M. *The Human Body: Get Under the Skin with Science Activities for Kids*. Nomad Press, 2019.

Shoals, James. *Cells, Tissues, and Organs*. Smartbook Media, 2021.

ONLINE RESOURCES

To learn more about the human body, please visit **abdobooklinks.com** or scan this QR code. These links are routinely monitored and updated to provide the most current information available.

INDEX

PHOTO CREDITS

Cover Photos: Shutterstock, front (brain), front (gallbladder), front (spine), front (heart), front (stomach), front (thyroid), back (antibodies), back (tendon); Deep A Designs/Shutterstock, front (intestines); Liya Graphics/Shutterstock, front (lungs); Matt L. Photography/Shutterstock, front (neurons); Phonlamai Photo/Shutterstock, front (red blood cells); Alex LMX/Shutterstock, back (pancreas)

Interior Photos: Shutterstock, 3, 4, 6 (bottom), 7, 8, 9, 10 (bottom), 15, 16, 19, 24, 25, 26, 30, 31 (bottom), 36, 37, 38, 42 (bottom), 44, 46–47, 47, 48, 49, 51, 55, 57 (bottom), 58, 62, 64, 66, 67 (bottom), 68, 70–71, 73, 80, 81, 83 (top), 83 (bottom), 84 (bottom), 88 (top), 89, 91, 92, 95, 97, 98, 100, 102, 105, 107 (bottom), 108 (bottom), 109, 110, 114, 117 (top), 119 (top), 121, 122 (top), 129, 132–133, 136, 138, 139 (top), 140, 142, 143 (top), 143 (bottom), 144, 145, 152, 153, 154 (right), 155 (bottom), 156, 156–157, 160, 163, 165, 166–167, 167, 172 (top), 174, 175, 178–179, 180–181, 182; Matt L. Photography/Shutterstock, 5, 101, 164; Jose Luis Calvo/Shutterstock, 6 (top); Yoko Design/Shutterstock, 10 (top); Andrey Popov/Shutterstock, 11; Gritsalak Karalak/Shutterstock, 12, 13; Yakobchuk Viacheslav/Shutterstock, 14 (top); Living Art Enterprises LLC/Science Source, 14 (bottom), 177; QA International/Science Source, 17 (top), 155 (top); Bio Photo Associates/Science Source, 17 (bottom), 67 (top), 107 (top); Design Cells/Shutterstock, 18; Sofiko S./Shutterstock, 20–21; AJ Photo/Science Source, 22; Katalin Macevics/Shutterstock, 23; Ekaterina Kondratova/Shutterstock, 27; Alex Mit/Shutterstock, 28; Monica Schroeder/Science Source, 29, 137; Artorn Thongtukit/Shutterstock, 31 (top); Teguh Mujiono/Shutterstock, 32; Elise Walmsley-MacWha/Stocktrek Images/Science Source, 33 (top); Kraken Images/Shutterstock, 33 (bottom); Alila Medical Media/Shutterstock, 34, 71, 72 (top), 72 (bottom), 134; Jukov Studio/Shutterstock, 35; BNP Design Studio/Shutterstock, 39; Andrea Danti/Shutterstock, 40; Tatjana Baibakova/Shutterstock, 41; Alex LMX/Shutterstock, 42 (top); Southern Illinois University/Science Source, 43; Gunilla Elam/Science Source, 45; Nolte Lourens/Shutterstock, 50; Medic Image/Science Source, 52; Kateryna Kon/Shutterstock, 53, 75, 113, 128, 172 (bottom); Amorn Suriyan/Shutterstock, 54; BSIP/Science Source, 56, 141; Candice Brophy/Shutterstock, 57 (top); Monkey Business Images/Shutterstock, 59, 130–131, 186–187; Nick Starichenko/Shutterstock, 60; Syda Productions/Shutterstock, 61, 104–105, 168; Larisa Stefanjuk/Shutterstock, 63; Ann Rodchua/Shutterstock, 65; Double W Science Images/Science Source, 69; Christoph Burgstedt/Shutterstock, 74; Singjai Stocker/Shutterstock, 76; Hrecheniuk Oleksii/Shutterstock, 77; Keith Chambers/Science Source, 78–79; Juan Gaertner/Shutterstock, 79; Veronica Falconieri Hays/Science Source, 82; Aldona Griskeviciene/Shutterstock, 84 (top), 85, 86, 87, 146; SPL/Science Source, 88 (bottom); Africa Studio/Shutterstock, 90–91; Dragon Images/Shutterstock, 93; Suzanne Tucker/Shutterstock, 94–95; Martin Novak/Shutterstock, 96; Hank Grebe/Shutterstock, 99; Kate Studio/Shutterstock, 103; JPC Prod./Shutterstock, 106; Substance T Productions/Shutterstock, 108 (top); Sophie Jacopin/Science Source, 111; Prostock Studio/Shutterstock, 112, 124–125; Harvinder Singh/Science Source, 115; Blue Ring Media/Shutterstock, 116, 117 (bottom), 120, 122 (bottom); Tatiana Shepeleva/Shutterstock, 118; DK Images/Science Source, 119 (bottom); John Bavosi/Science Source, 123; Betty Ray/Shutterstock, 125; Yurchanka Siarhei/Shutterstock, 126–127; Natalia Deriabina/Shutterstock, 133; Chu Kyung Min/Shutterstock, 135; Bill O'Leary/The Washington Post/Getty Images, 139 (bottom); Maurizio De Angelis/Science Source, 147; Giuseppe Lombardo/Shutterstock, 148–149; Arthur Glauberman/Science Source, 150; Tim Gray/Shutterstock, 151; Medical RF/Science Source, 154 (left); Medical Art Inc./Shutterstock, 158; VP Photo Studio/Shutterstock, 159; J. Amphon/Shutterstock, 161; Kulinenko G./Shutterstock, 162–163; Axel Kock/Shutterstock, 169; Bear Fotos/Shutterstock, 170, 181; Kang Ho Photo/Shutterstock, 171; Czarek Sokolowski/AP Images, 173; St Bartholomew's Hospital/Science Source, 176; Jacek Chabraszewski/Shutterstock, 182–183; Cherednychenko Ihor/Shutterstock, 184–185; Allen Sima/Shutterstock, 185

ABDOBOOKS.COM

Published by Abdo Publishing, a division of ABDO, PO Box 398166, Minneapolis, Minnesota 55439. Copyright © 2023 by Abdo Consulting Group, Inc. International copyrights reserved in all countries. No part of this book may be reproduced in any form without written permission from the publisher. Abdo Reference™ is a trademark and logo of Abdo Publishing.

Printed in the United States of America, North Mankato, Minnesota.
052022
092022

THIS BOOK CONTAINS RECYCLED MATERIALS

Editor: Angela Lim
Series Designer: Colleen McLaren

LIBRARY OF CONGRESS CONTROL NUMBER: 2021952319

PUBLISHER'S CATALOGING-IN-PUBLICATION DATA

Names: Cernak, Linda, author.
Title: The human body encyclopedia / by Linda Cernak
Description: Minneapolis, Minnesota: Abdo Publishing, 2023 | Series: Science encyclopedias | Includes online resources and index.
Identifiers: ISBN 9781532198755 (lib. bdg.) | ISBN 9781098272401 (ebook)
Subjects: LCSH: Human body--Juvenile literature. | Human anatomy--Juvenile literature. | Human physiology--Juvenile literature. | Biology--Juvenile literature. | Encyclopedias and dictionaries--Juvenile literature.
Classification: DDC 612--dc23